A Thousand Pounds

Download your
FREE JOURNAL

SCAN ME

I am primarily inviting you into my story as a means to discover yours. I want to walk hand-in-hand with you in your own journey to authentic integration, peace, and hope. As a way to facilitate this, I have created companion journals entitled *Finding the Strength to Carry a Thousand Pounds*. My hope is that these journals will invite you to explore the depths of your own grief so we can wrestle together through the hard parts of being bereaved.

www.aThousandPoundsBook.com

"Bri Edwards speaks honestly and gracefully about living with a weight that will not go away, sharing the painfully personal while also reflecting on the universal. This book is a gift to those coping with the sudden unexpected death of a young child and anyone wanting to stand by their side. It is filled with sound guidance about the difficulties a bereaved parent faces, while being a testament to self-discovery, love, and faith. You will be moved by the beauties of its truth and its hope."

DR. RICHARD GOLDSTEIN, M.D.
Director of Robert's Program on Sudden Unexpected Death in Pediatrics,
Boston Children's Hospital, Harvard Medical School

"There are times in life when someone's story leaves you changed after reading their words. This is one of those times. It is written with stunning grace and wisdom. This is a voice the world needs. Amidst the rubble, it brings hope and light. Amidst the heartache, it teaches gratitude and humility. This is as much a story of love as it is a story of loss."

LISA LESHAW, M.S.
Clinical Mental Health Counselor

"In this book, Bri Edwards beautifully wrestles with the hardest questions a grieving parent faces as she shares her own journey after the loss of her son, Lachlan. Combining research and story, Bri isn't afraid to go deep, and her authenticity is felt in every word. Her ability to grieve out loud holds space for the big emotions of anyone who is in the trenches of grief."

JESSY PAULSON
Founder of Gritty Faith Magazine

"This is a wrenching journey from raw pain to mental, emotional, and spiritual survival. The book is an academic/anecdotal treasure and a lifeline to those suffering loss. With personal experience, salient quotes and solid research, the author courageously leads the reader through the labyrinth of tragedy to health and healing. Crafting a powerful message from a brutal experience is an amazing tribute to the son she lost, and a gift to others who suffer any kind of traumatic loss. The courage Bri displays inspires, gives hope and, in many ways, gives grievers permission to be human. Peruse with sticky notes handy."

ELAINE DOLL-DUNN, PSY.D.
Counselor

"Brianne Edwards is a gifted storyteller. Stylistically weaving the details of her grief journey with poignantly-chosen truths on grief and loss from well-known secular and non-secular resources, *A Thousand Pounds* ministers to grieving families and those looking to support them. With each turn of the page, Brianne becomes a trusted friend and mentor who also walks the lifelong journey of child loss. In her wisdom and experience, Edwards speaks validation and encouragement into the hearts of her readers."

JESSIKA SANDERS
Founder of Praying Through Ministries, a nonprofit serving NICU, PICU and Child Loss Families

"*A Thousand Pounds* is beautifully written with such heartfelt intention. Bri shares the real struggles one experiences in loss and how she and others on the journey have learned to lean in and face these challenges with grace. She offers much perspective along with tangible ways to cope, in order to move toward hope and healing. As a fellow bereaved parent, this book gives voice to so many of the thoughts and feelings deep within my heart."

KARRI ALLEN
Bereaved mother, Founder of Healing Hope Ministries

"Brianne takes her audience through the throes of bereavement in losing a young child unexpectedly in a candid and raw fashion. She allows her reader to experience the depths of grief with her in partnership to her journey. She ties in the self-development and growth that is necessary in the journey of loss. It's candid and visceral, a must-read."

HALEY HALLOCK, PSYCH-K, CCH

"As a freelance editor, I work on all kinds of projects... I have worked on memoirs and personal stories before, but this book is on a different level. I have experienced the death of loved ones, but I have never lost a child. I felt Bri's story and words in my core. This story is going to reach so many people—not only those who have experienced a similar loss, but even those who have experienced different losses or want to help someone who has lost a child."

AMY WELDE
Dragonfly Editorial

A THOUSAND POUNDS

Finding the Strength to Live and Love under the Weight of Unbearable Loss

BRIANNE EDWARDS

CATHOLICPSYCH
PRESS

This book may bring up very difficult feelings, especially if you are grieving a life-changing loss. If you feel like you need someone to talk to or if you have thoughts of hurting or killing yourself, please reach out for help. The National Suicide Hotline connect callers to trained counselors in moments of concern or crisis. Call or text 988 to contact the U.S. National Suicide Prevention Lifeline.

Library of Congress Control Number: 2022910608

E-book: ISBN-13 978-1-7327635-1-7
Hardcover: ISBN-13 978-1-7327635-2-4
Softcover: ISBN-13 978-1-7327635-3-1

CatholicPsych Press
1177 High Ridge Road
Stamford, Connecticut 06905
www.catholicpsych.com
www.aThousandPoundsBook.com

Then rise again from ashes,
let healing come to pain;
Though spring has turned to winter,
and sunshine turned to rain.
The rain we'll use for growing,
and create the world anew,
From an offering of ashes,
an offering to You.

This book is
an offering of my ashes,
an offering to You

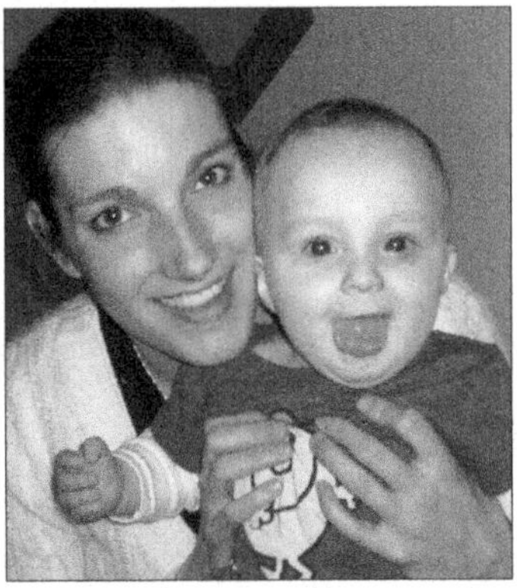
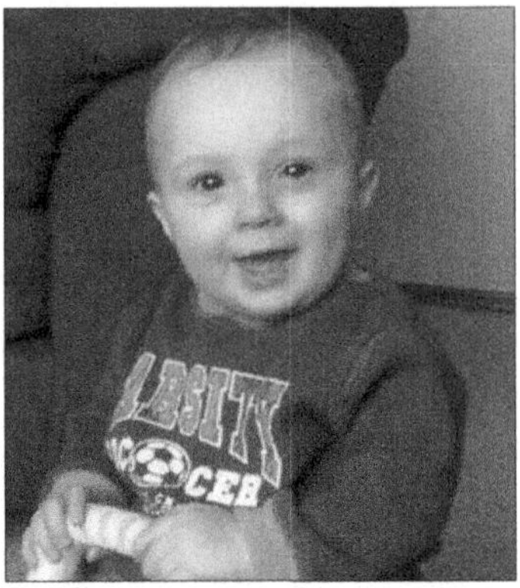

for my

LACHLAN

Your legacy is not what you left *for* people.

It's what you leave *in* people.

Contents

FOREWORD

Relationship is the basis for everything important in life. We are created out of relationship and made to return to relationship, for eternity. Anything important that has ever been said, or will ever be said, pertains to relationship.

In an ideal situation, we most naturally learn this crucial truth from our parents and the family relationships we grow up with. When the situation is not ideal, we end up needing a lot of healing, and in fact a lot of the work that is done in therapy is to reconfigure what has been mislearned in childhood. And yet at the same time, most of the greatest character traits and virtues are learned from our parents and other elders.

The most important relationship we can learn about is the one with our Creator, if it is possible to know a Creator and develop a relationship with Him. When parents have faith, they can answer questions from their children about the deepest yearning of the human heart for something infinite and unquenchable. Something in us desires to never end, and for relationships with others to never end, and therefore for there to be some kind of "life after death."

Sometimes, in a strange, disordered, and painfully ironic twist of pedagogy, our children teach us parents. The young teach the old in ways they aren't supposed to. The innocent and inexperienced teach the wise.

Brianne had one of these experiences. She's been taught about time and eternity from her ten-month-old son. Her relationship with Lachlan was a School of Love that she is still learning from, but she's in an advanced class compared to those of us who have not been through what she's been through. The book you hold in your hands is a work of love, from a big sister who has learned about life from something we hope and pray never happens to us. And yet if it does, we can follow her lead and let it teach us the most important truths about life. She wants to share the fruit of her excruciating experience so that we can know something more about time and eternity also, and something really important about love.

That it doesn't end with death.

This is the fundamental truth of our lives we spend a lifetime learning. And even that only points to a more fundamental truth—that we are made for eternity. We slowly grow into awareness of the temporality of time itself the way we slowly grow into our parents' shoes. Most of us are children waddling around in Dad's giant shoes until life experiences stretch us to fill them out.

I pray that you can learn these hard-won life lessons without having to go through what Brianne did. I also pray that if you have, or anything else that touches the human heart's capacity for suffering in like manner, you can find consolation in these pages knowing there is a context of love that fills all the holes and voids we suffer. The separation of death is temporary, the bonds of love are eternal.

Dr. Gregory Bottaro
Director of The CatholicPsych Institute

Before We Begin

The first part of this book is hard. Sacred, and painful, and beautiful, and hard. I open by telling you the story of my son's death, and I tell that story without sparing you from the torment of my soul. In big, hard stories like these, many tend to dance over the details, to delicately brush over the most brutally painful parts (and in many settings it is rightfully so), but that is not what you'll find here. I give you my story in all its rawness.

The story is told this way with heartfelt intention and purpose for the reader. When I was new in my grief, I longed for the people who wouldn't dance around the hardest stuff. I deeply desired the stories and the people who allowed me to encounter what felt unspeakable. I needed people who could meet me where I was, and I needed the light of others in those darkest places. For those who are grieving, I am offering you something that I needed in my own grief but was often hard to find—a companion in my dark night of the soul.

For those who are here to peer through a window into the heart of a bereaved parent to support someone you love, or simply for your own personal growth, this story is for you, too. One of the most powerful gifts that others gave me in my grief was a heart open to hearing my story and eyes that didn't avert their gaze from my pain. That ability often doesn't come naturally. Yet, by practicing the skill, we can grow in our ability to accompany someone who is grieving with a sacred and open presence to their experience.

I am inviting you to step into my story about the death of my little Lachlan (Lock-lan) and to lean into what is hard. Sometimes the stretching of a heart is painful, but it is always worth it in the end. While I invite and encourage you to stick with the story and avoid the temptation to avert your gaze, this is also an invitation for you to be attentive to your own needs. If it is too triggering, then be kind to yourself and honor your current needs by skipping ahead to Part 2. There you'll find many of my thoughts and ways of growing through my grief without the more emotionally difficult details of the story. You can always come back to Part 1 on another day.

It always takes courage to step into what we know will be hard, but amazing things happen when we learn to get comfortable being uncomfortable. Welcome to my story.

Bri Edwards

www.LachsLegacy.org
www.aThousandPoundsBook.com

JOURNALING

I am primarily inviting you into my story as a means to discover yours. I want to walk hand-in-hand with you in your own journey to authentic integration, peace, and hope. As a way to facilitate this, I have created companion journals entitled *Finding the Strength to Carry a Thousand Pounds*. My hope is that these journals will invite you to explore the depths of your own grief so we can wrestle together through the hard parts of being bereaved.

There is powerful healing that happens in the simple act of telling our stories—whether we tell them to another person or write them down simply for our own benefit. There is value in being intentional about putting words to our experience and in giving an outlet to the thoughts and feelings that are taking up space within us.

When we connect the experience and emotions that are primarily stored in the nonverbal right brain with the language and logic held primarily in the left hemisphere of the brain, we lay the foundation for the integration and healing of our experiences.[1] We can dramatically reduce our stress and the intrusion of hard emotions by recognizing, organizing, and giving language to our thoughts, feelings, and experiences. We may have to tell and retell the story hundreds of times to really find the version that is most reflective of the lived experience and all it contains.

Expressive writing about traumatic experiences reliably improves both mental and physical health. Journaling has been shown to decrease the symptoms of asthma, arthritis, and other health conditions; improve cognitive functioning; strengthen the immune system; and counteract many of the negative effects of stress.[2] After a traumatic loss, so much feels out of our control, and journaling provides a space where we can influence our own path to stress management, gentle integration, improved health, and discovery of a life that still feels worth living.

The phrase "the work of grieving" is one that is often used because healing in grief doesn't come without effort. The "work" is a call to step to the edges of our comfort zone. It means doing things we've never done before and allowing ourselves to bare what is vulnerable. It will require courage to start and it often leaves us feeling exhausted in the moment, but we will be stronger in the end.

Whether you have experienced the loss of a child, the loss of a baby during pregnancy, or a loved one, there is a journal option for you. Visit *www.aThousandPoundsBook.com.*

Let my story be a path that leads you through your own wilderness of grief.

INTRODUCTION

You think your pain and your heartbreak are unprecedented in the history of the world, but then you read. It was [books] that taught me that the things that tormented me most were the very things that connected me with all the people who were alive, or who had ever been alive.

JAMES BALDWIN

G. K. Chesterton opened his book *Orthodoxy* with a story he fantasized of writing about an English yachtsman who, getting off track at sea, discovered England under the impression that it was a new island in the South Seas. He elaborates with the thought of this yachtsman landing, ready to plant his British flag on this land of his discovery, to find that the barbaric temple he expected was rather the Pavilion at Brighton. And he would rightly feel rather a fool.

My words in reflection to finding solace in my grief can closely echo those of Chesterton in his quest for orthodoxy, "For if this book is a joke, it is a joke against me. I am the man who with the utmost daring discovered what had been discovered before . . . for this book explains how I fancied I was the first to set foot in Brighton and then found I was the last . . . When I fancied that I stood alone I was really in the ridiculous position of being backed up by all of Christendom."[1]

A voyage through grief is much the same. It is an intensely personal journey of peril and despair, of discovery and enlightenments. And when we've finally found our way to land, certain it must be a new island in the South Seas, we find rather, that it is a place already well known and inhabited. It is a place that has been inhabited for all of human existence and is really not a unique discovery at all.

As such, the journey through my grief is not unparalleled. While it is uniquely my own, it is also a path that has been discovered and rediscovered by the bereaved for all of human existence. This is more than an individual story. It is a story of being human. Nonetheless, others have given me the gift of hope and perspective by telling their own stories, and so I make the efforts to tell mine too. Those personal stories were a lifeline for me as I grappled to simply survive. They gave me the gift of words when I couldn't find any of my own. They were instrumental in helping me process my experience. And there were never enough of them. Every story brought a new combination of viewpoints, some I didn't really connect with, and others that brought life-changing perspective. Each story brought with it something to hold onto while I was groping in that deep darkness, searching for anything to restore some equilibrium.

And so, I tell my story. An experience of deep grief is so big. It is a kaleidoscope of a million tiny, moving parts. I could tell this same story in a hundred different ways, each version highlighting different elements of the experience. There is no one way to think about grief, not even within ourselves. I simply offer this version of my story as one of a million possible perspectives on learning to bear the unbearable. My hope is that you might find even a fragment of new perspective that brings comfort as you grieve. I pray it offers something to your experience of discovering land on the other side of this ocean of grief—a land of rest, and peace, and hope, and love; a land that makes life feel worth living, even after a shattering loss.

PART 1

Download a free version of the accompaniment journal at
www.aThousandPoundsBook.com

1

The Weight Drops

Whosoever survives the test must tell his story.
That is his duty.

ELIE WIESEL

It happened on an ordinary Monday, the day after Mother's Day. I was up early to be at work before seven o'clock and our household was in the morning bustle to start our week. I breastfed the baby in a hurry, annoyed by how easily he was being distracted by his big brother. I needed him to finish nursing so I could get to work, but he kept stopping to look around at every noise that was made. I stroked that wild wisp of hair on the top of his head, trying to keep his attention on his task. Westin, the big brother, ran by and the baby pulled away again. Done or not, we had to call it quits. I stood Lachlan up at the windowsill so he could look outside, and I hurried out the door. My only goodbye was a wave through the car window at my two boys and their daddy watching me drive away.

I was working as a physician assistant in a demanding general and bariatric surgery practice. My workday started out with typical Monday busyness, but then had an unusual gap in the afternoon schedule. We worked with a constant attention to efficiency, still aiming to do the work with care and consideration, giving each patient their due time, but always striving to find ways to be more efficient. This gap in the ever-running to-do list was a rarity.

In this downtime, I considered going to pick up the baby from the new daycare for a while. The previous week had been my children's first week at this daycare, and we were all still adjusting to the new arrangement. Westin, as a two-year-old, was still having difficulty with the drop-off, and I didn't want to put him through that twice in the same day, but I thought about picking up Lachlan to spend a little bit of one-on-one time with him. I seriously considered that option, but I ended up deciding to use that time to show the new medical student around and to review the technique for the big surgery scheduled that afternoon.

At 2:30, I was just grabbing my blue bouffant hat to be appropriately garbed for the sterile space of the operating room when my phone rang with a call from the daycare. I answered a bit hesitantly, wondering what it could be, expecting something entirely routine. It was the voice of the owner on the other end, not one of the young women who actually took care of the kids. He was someone I'd barely met, and I could tell in an instant that he was shaken.

His voice quivered, "I need you to come to the daycare. Lachlan is not breathing. The paramedics are here."

With those words, it was as if I entered an alternate universe. Time warped (and it still does even now as I simultaneously recall and relive the story).

My head spins. Logic and reason escape me. Social graces are nonexistent. We had just learned that Lachlan had several food allergies, so my first thought is that this is the problem. "Is it an allergic reaction to something he ate?" I stammer.

"No," the owner replies. "All he had this morning was the cup of pears you brought for him."

"I'll be right there," I reply and hang up my smartphone. Without a word to the student at my side, I dart through the nearest door and down the stairwell. I run clumsily in my clogs to get the keys from my locker and then to the parking garage where my little red Cavalier is waiting. The shoes that continue their threat to fall off of my feet are slowing me down, making me feel as if I am running through quicksand.

As I run, it is as if I am seeing the first glimpse of an imaginary man, huge and ominous, carrying a weight that is much too heavy for any human to bear and he is walking in my direction. There is panic and pleading in my head that this weight is not for me, yet a fear and a knowing that it is.

I frantically call my husband while I drive. "The daycare called and Lach is not breathing!" David barely understands what I am saying and asks me to repeat it. I then call my office to tell them I left the hospital due to an emergency, and I won't be there to help with the surgery that is starting any minute.

I am driving in the turning lane to pass all the traffic that dares to drive the speed limit during my emergency. Despite every effort to keep moving, running stop lights, and creating my own lane, I am stopped at an intersection with no way around as a funeral procession crosses in front of me. I am forced to sit still and watch it go by in some cruel cosmic form of foreshadowing. The man with the unbearable weight meets my gaze. Time freezes. I plead with God, wailing out loud to not let this happen.

As I near the daycare, I come over the crest to see it surrounded by the flashing lights of a multitude of emergency vehicles. The entrances to the parking lot are blocked by them. I stop my car right in the road and fly from the driver's seat, not even closing the door behind me. Running toward the daycare door, I am stopped by a police officer standing guard. He puts his hands on my shoulders and restrains me from entering. "I'm his mom!" I plead.

"You can't go in," the officer insists.

I make several futile attempts to go around him. He is just as persistent as I am and reaches to physically restrain my efforts to get around his guard. He tells me he doesn't know what is happening inside, but he will see if he can find out.

My husband shows up at my side. We stand outside in the patch of spring-green grass on this windy May day, heads spinning . . . no one seems to know for sure. Time stands still. We pace and plead.

My husband and I both have seen and participated in resuscitations. We both know, without knowing: it has been too long. The EMTs are still here and not rushing him to the ER. Yet, I still plead with the heavens that I'm wrong, as I pace frantically, trying to figure out how to get that guard to let me through the door. I need to know.

That invisible ominous man with the unbearable weight is now standing over me.

Then they emerge—the crew of flight paramedics, in their blue jumpsuits with the red stripe down the side. Monte, a familiar face from my work in the hospital, leads and is flanked by his team. Monte's head is hung and shaking gently as they step out of the building. With that, I know. My world spins furiously. Monte speaks through ragged breaths, fighting to keep his composure. I hear the words as though they're background noise: "I'm sorry, there is nothing we could do."

The weight drops. It's like a thousand pounds have landed on my shoulders.

I crumble to my knees under that invisible weight. I find my body violently dry heaving. It's as if my own soul has separated from my body. I am surprised by my own physical reaction. The thought fleets across my mind of worry that I may vomit on someone's shoes.

It's as if I were alone in the eye of a tornado. My husband exchanges a few words with the team, and even though they are right next to me, I cannot see nor hear them. The world is spinning in massive chaos around me, yet it is somehow simultaneously still and surreal. From this moment, my memory becomes a whirlwind, unable to recall even some of the big events or basic timelines, dotted with moments that are crystal clear and perfectly preserved. It resembles the childhood experience of being on a fast-moving merry-go-round. The world spins too fast for you to see much of anything, but then you lock your gaze on something and can see it clearly for just a moment before the world starts to spin again.

I am frozen, paralyzed by this unbearable weight that has dropped. I can't think, can't see, can't breathe. I clutch the grass. I wail to the heavens in protest. I am nauseous and spinning.

David and I decide we need to call our parents. So we find a spot near the building where the phone call could be sheltered from the wind. My mom works as a teacher in our hometown which is 400 miles away. I know the office woman who answers the phone. "It's Brianne. I need to talk to my mom," I say. It must be something in my voice. I give her no preface and no explanation, but without question or hesitation, my mom's voice is there a few minutes later. I sense the concern in her voice as she says hello. I quaver. How do you even tell someone something like this? I choke on the words and can't bring myself to say it out loud.

"Can you come?" is all I can muster. Of course, that isn't quite enough for her to walk out the door in the middle of the school day to take a 400-mile drive with no notice.

"Why? What happened?" she asks.

There it is. I'm backed into a corner, and there's no way out. The words must be said.

"Lach died."

And so, I say it out loud for the first time. It's like bile in my mouth—so very bitter. My world goes fuzzy again. Those two words cannot possibly belong side by side. It is entirely unfathomable. Every parent's very worst nightmare is now my living terror.

The following moments all spin wildly without a timeline in my memory. My thoughts are everywhere and nowhere. They pause momentarily here and there, and the mental image is seared into my memory before it all goes fuzzy again.

I have a vague notion of news crews standing outside the daycare. The cruelty of being recorded in those moments for other people's viewing does not go unnoticed, but I am too distraught to care. I feel sorry for the parents of other children at the daycare who are in a panic at seeing the emergency vehicles. They don't know what's happening inside and are not allowed to go in. How horrible.

I need to see Lachlan. I need to be with my baby. When I beg to see him, we are told that he was taken through the back door of the building and is already en route to the hospital. I'm horrified. How can they take him away without my consent? They've taken my baby away without even a discussion. I'm told an investigation needs to be completed before we can see him, and we will be notified when the autopsy is complete.

Westin was still napping inside the daycare. He is carried to us, coming out of the building wearing his red and black firetruck shirt and jeans, barefoot, and squinting as his sleepy eyes adjust to the daylight. He is fascinated by the trucks and the flashing lights that have just introduced the nightmare we are now living. He is ignorant of the events of the afternoon. We, and the firefighters present, pretend for a moment, for Westin's sake, that the world is right. They invite him into the firetruck to see it. How do you tell a two-year-old that his baby brother is dead? It's too much. Not yet.

Someone has called our local parish and a priest joins us. We are sent to drive the few blocks home. David climbs into the car that I had abandoned in the street, and the priest, Westin, and I load into our second vehicle with Lachlan's empty car seat in the back—its emptiness is like a black hole sucking my soul into its vacancy. The priest sits in my passenger seat. He is young, newly ordained, shy, and *way* out of his comfort zone. He says little. I feel terrible for him having to be there with us in those moments. I feel pressure to make conversation, to ease the tension, but I can't. We sit in awkward silence.

The uneasy silence continued after arriving home. We sit in the living room, the petrified priest and I, not knowing what to say to each other. My husband, David, is the one who navigates social situations comfortably. He makes small talk without effort. He can sense the mood of the person he's with and diffuse negative emotions with ease. I, on the other hand, more introverted by nature, am tortured by such settings. I rely too much on him when breaking the ice with people I don't know, but now David has disappeared into the back of the house and doesn't seem to be coming back. When I go to look for him, I find him standing helplessly in the boys' room with the last thing Lach wore pressed to his face while he inhales deeply. He's searching for Lachlan, for his scent.

Westin clearly senses the shift of energy but carries on as two-year-olds do. He needs this, he wants that, he wants to talk and play. I can't give my attention to the needs of a toddler; I need to hand off that responsibility for the time being. Our dear friend and neighbor is across the street mowing his yard. As I cross the street with Westin in my arms, I could tell by the look on my neighbor's face that he could see the terror in mine. I asked if he could take Westin for me for a while. He said he would and followed with, "What's going on?" There it was again. Pressed to say the unthinkable out loud.

In the chaos of my storm, I remember a vivid moment while sitting on the red couch in my living room. I was in the same spot where just a couple of months earlier we had recorded a video of Lachlan sitting on my lap, batting at my face. As he made contact with my cheek, I would turn my head in a dramatic fashion, and he would laugh with delight from the depths of his belly. Over and over, we played this game, his amusement never fading.

Now, I sit here, with an empty lap, head held in my hands. I realize with piercing clarity that *everything* in my world had just changed. I knew I would never be the same. I knew this was far too big for me to understand what my life was going to look like and what this would mean for me. I felt as if a giant earthquake had hit, and I now stood on the other side of an uncrossable chasm. Everything I had previously known and the world as I knew it were suddenly unreachable. This was huge and deep in what it would mean for the rest of my life, and there was going to be a lot of uncharted and brutal territory for me to cover.

While sitting in that spot, the first of the stream of company arrived. I remember a car pulling up and watching to see who it was. The wife of my boss came around the vehicle with her dark curls tucked behind her ears, and a look of gentle determination on her face. We were little more than acquaintances at the time. She had gotten word of Lach's death, and she dropped everything to come. It was as if she were personally delivered by the hands of God. She was amazing. I can't quite put my finger on why her presence was so comforting to me, especially considering that I didn't know her well, but she had such a way about her that things seemed better when she was there. She was a pressure valve release. She seemed to find a quiet place in the background and gently stepped in to fill the roles that I was not capable of filling. The nagging feeling to tend to the priest faded with her presence. She greeted the visitors who started to trickle in, she answered the phone, and she made coffee and offered it to those who showed up.

The next arrival was the senior priest from our parish. He met me with a deep and sympathetic hug. He led us in a prayer. His warmth was palpable. He, too, was an enormous comfort, helping me sense in some way that I was not completely alone in this.

The next hours were filled with aimless wandering around my house. Family began to arrive, including an aunt and uncle who lived nearby, and both sets of our parents. Mealtime came and went. I remember people pressuring us to eat. "You need to eat something," they told us. I was nauseous and the thought of food was repulsive. The care and concern of our loved ones, manifesting in a push to eat, was abrasive. The people who simply handed us a bottle of water, giving us permission to not have an appetite, were so much easier to receive.

Oh, how I needed to see my boy! This was something I had no say in, no control over. The authorities were calling the shots. They didn't seem to care that I was his mother. It didn't matter that in every other moment of his life, I made the decisions for him. It was my call to decide what he ate and when, where and how he slept, into whose care he was entrusted, and what medical care we wished to pursue. Now, I felt as if Lachlan had been unjustly removed from my care by authorities who were overstepping their bounds. He is *my* child! Yet I was helpless in getting him back into my care.

God's hands were made visible once more in the coordination of events to see my baby. My boss was a leading surgeon in the hospital that Lach had been taken to. When my boss was a little boy, three of his siblings were walking home from the pool and were struck by a vehicle, killing all three of them. As the child of a bereaved parent, he had a sensitivity and an acute awareness of what it means to experience the death of a child. He used his rank in the hospital in coordination with the nurse who was at the ER control desk that night. She had recently experienced the death of her infant grandchild. The powers within the system that night were fiercely advocating for us and our need to be with Lachlan. I'm not sure how the conversations and bargaining went down. All I know is that minds were changed and arrangements were made for us to be able to go up to the hospital to see Lachlan that evening. I was both relieved and scared.

We debated long and hard about whether we should bring Westin with us to see his brother. Would bringing him along help him start to see and understand that Lachlan died? Would it help him understand that his brother's body stopped working? Although so young, he too would need to say goodbye. Does it need to happen now? We were paralyzed by the decision, feeling the weight of what we were choosing. Our families were as unsure as we were and offered no real guidance. Then there were the questions of how we would get to the hospital. Were we okay to drive? Who would come along?

My boss and the curly-haired angel-in-disguise, who were now our grief guides, gently decided for us. We would leave Westin at home this time. This moment was for us. They would drive us to the hospital and escort us in to help navigate. Together their presence lightened that ominous weight that was crushing me, relieving just a hint of the unbearable pressure.

We left our house full of family and drove in silence to the hospital. The shadows were long now, half a day after receiving the news that sent my world spinning. I had been in the ER hundreds of times, but always to help as a provider in someone else's crisis. This time, the crisis was mine. I walked through the hall as if with tunnel vision, unable to see or look at anything around me, afraid I might meet the gaze of someone I knew. We were led to a room in the back of the ER. It was the same room where I had repaired the lacerations of others and took care of the man whose hand was broken in a fit of rage when he delivered a punch to a brick wall.

We stepped inside the room, and there he was. Lachlan looked so tiny, laying on that adult-sized cot. He was covered to his chin with the blue blanket that we had sent with our bouncing baby boy to daycare that morning. A small stuffed puppy rested on his chest. His eyelids were slightly parted, as they often were when he slept—a trait he got from his mama and his grandpa Lloyd. My baby's skin was blotchy and mottled, ears appeared bruised, froth was visible in his nostrils, and his lips a deep purple.

I reached to touch and to stroke him. He was so cold. Mothers are hardwired to keep their babies warm. That cool skin tore at my instincts. I moved to uncover him, knowing that this would be the last time I would be able to see, to touch, or to hold him. This was the little body that I had grown within my own, that I had held, rocked, bathed, fed, comforted, and admired. The existence of my mind, body, and soul had been intimately intertwined with his in every moment through the nine months of my pregnancy and the ten and a half months since his birth. Now this little body was being ripped away from me, leaving the fibers of my whole being in shreds.

When I reached to uncover him, the investigator stopped me. Though everything suggested his death was consistent with Sudden

Infant Death Syndrome (and the autopsy would later confirm this), I was told that an investigation still needed to take place, and I was not allowed to uncover or to hold him. While answering the slew of questions from the investigator, we sat next to Lachlan, gaze locked on what remained, trying to memorize every piece of him. There was some feel of interrogation, but I had a deeper sense that it was part of the routine proceedings. The questioner seemed somewhat apologetic as he ran through his list of questions. Even as he went through his checklist, my attention was barely on him. He was part of the whirling storm, with Lachlan and me alone in the eye of that emotional hurricane.

My desperation to be able to study the body of my own child mounted. I longed for him now just as I longed to inspect every inch of him in the moments after his birth—those long fingers, tiny fingernails, precious feet, and fuzzy back. When they are born, we soak them in by stroking their baby-soft skin, feeling the puppy-like looseness of it over their frame. We admire every hair, the eye color that seems to shift daily, every facial expression and grunting noise, and breathe in deeply that scent of a newborn. And now as my baby lay lifeless, I knew this was my last chance. The enormity of this last opportunity weighed on me. I knew that after his autopsy, he would look and feel less like the boy I held lovingly on my lap that morning. There were whispers and movement in the back of the room, and again, the right people were on my side. The investigator, who had just stopped me from uncovering my little boy, told me I could go ahead.

What I remember more than studying that little body one more time, is scooping him up to hold him. It felt familiar, yet all wrong. He seemed heavier. He didn't wriggle in my arms, nor collapse into my body like he did when he slept. Nonetheless, I sat in the rocking chair with him in my arms and wrapped him in that blue blanket in a futile attempt to keep him warm. I kissed his forehead, the feeling of that cool skin on my lips searing deeply into my memory. Our grief-guide companions had gently suggested that we take a few photos. Photos that we could tuck away and never revisit, but photos that mark the last moments of our time together that someday we might be glad to have. We agreed. The first of these last photographs was taken while I rocked him in that chair. I could have stayed right there all night, and would have preferred to, but I began to feel the unspoken pressure of those around me. None of them had all night. I handed Lachlan's little frame off to my husband, giving him that same uneasy opportunity to rock him one more time, to start the unbearable process of saying goodbye.

As we left, we were given a slew of details that were difficult to absorb about what was next for Lachlan. They had drawn some blood, sending it for a large panel of tests including toxicology, which would take weeks to get the results back. The pathologist who does these autopsies was out of town, so Lachlan had to be sent 400 miles across the state for the autopsy. In no way had I begun to separate myself from this baby of mine, and it felt so unnatural being forced to put 400 miles of distance between us. He's never been that far away from me, and now these authorities seem to have forgotten that his little body is my own flesh and blood. Questions started to race through my mind: *Who would be taking him? How would they be transporting him? How would I know they were going to take good care of him . . .?*

I was tormented by not being asked for consent in the decisions that were made for my child. Yet, in the end, the practical nature of the details worked out. David and I were high school sweethearts, and we grew up in a little town about an hour's drive from where the autopsy would take place. With our roots and our family on the west side of the state, we decided to hold Lachlan's funeral service and burial in the place we'd call "home" no matter where we lived. That meant Lachlan's body would need to be transported across the state anyway.

We left the hospital with a box of mementos, including handprints, footprints, little clay imprints of his thumb tied around the neck of a stuffed angel bear, and various pamphlets on the death of a child. I could barely focus on what was in the box, but I sensed the importance of having these last tangible items as proof that my child lived.

On the long and silent drive home, my husband and I were each reeling in our own heads. Our drivers participated in that silence. When we arrived home, we put Westin in the bathtub to start his pre-bedtime routine, aiming to preserve a hint of normalcy for him. The evening routine was part of the day we always did as a family, both boys in the tub together. That night, as Westin sat in the water alone, he asked, "Where's Lach?" pronouncing his L with a Y sound. And so the process began of explaining something to a two-year-old that is unfathomable and incomprehensible to even our adult brains.

I made the first feeble attempt to explain death to my toddler: "Lachlan died, honey. His body stopped working."

This apparently meant little to Westin because he continued to ask in intervals, "Where's Lach?" as if looking for an answer that made sense. When we tucked him into bed that night, the empty crib on the other side of the room seemed to fill every remaining inch of space.

Lachlan had not been a good sleeper. This was partly due to parents who never let him learn to fall asleep himself, and were always rushing in to rock and quiet him before his noise would wake up his brother. We had a lengthy bedtime routine of rocking, bouncing, and swaying him until he would finally lay his head on a shoulder, with his sweet baby breath on our necks. Once he was good and relaxed, on the verge of falling asleep, we'd switch to holding him in a cradle position, preparing to lay him in the crib. We'd continue to rock and sway, and when he'd finally drift off, we'd delicately, with breath held in hopes that he'd stay asleep, set him in the crib. The moment he touched the mattress, he would pop awake, fussing and protesting at the change. We'd scoop him up and start the whole cycle again, repeating over and over until a successful transfer to the crib was finally made. Now, without Lachlan there, the emptiness of the bedtime space was unbearable.

At some point that evening, we sifted through the box given to us at the hospital. In its contents we found a little children's story titled *Water Bugs and Dragonflies*.[1] This simple little story struck a chord with us right away and planted a seed of comfort.

The story tells of a community of water bugs at the bottom of a pond. Now and then, one of them climbs the stalk of a reed and never returns. The bugs held a meeting and agreed that the next one who climbs the stalk will come back to tell everyone where he's gone. The next day, the very bug that called the meeting finds himself climbing the stalk. As he emerges to the surface of the water, having transformed into a dragonfly, he finds a huge, new, beautiful world and a set of wings that he's never had before. He lies in the sun to let them dry, and once they are ready, he begins whizzing around exploring this beautiful new world in a new and glorious form. Suddenly he remembers the promise he made. He makes an attempt to get to his friends below the surface, but he cannot get under the water in his new form. He also realizes that even if he could, they wouldn't recognize his new body. They would just have to wait until they made the climb themselves to understand.

With that story, the dragonfly became a symbol of comfort and hope. Lachlan was still alive, still present, but in a new form and just above the surface.

Usually I am a good sleeper, quick to fall into deep and dreamless sleep. We went to bed that night later than usual, knowing it was likely to be a useless attempt at sleep. That night was the first of many, many nights that I laid in bed for hours, staring at the tiny green light on the smoke detector, while my thoughts reeled in a million different directions.

2

One Moment at a Time

And on through the hours the quiet words ring,
like a low inspiration: "Do the next thing."
AUTHOR UNKNOWN

The next several days after Lachlan's death became a complete haze. Compared to the spinning chaos of the previous day, the feeling now resembled a thick and heavy blanket that separated me from the rest of the world. It was like being overtaken by a deep and disorienting darkness, where you can see nothing around you. Even when you're not alone, your means of perceiving the presence of others is almost absent.

Grief is a journey that you take alone. David was at my side through every step of this, but he too was trapped in his own solitary world of grief. From time to time, we reached out in that disorienting darkness and made contact, reassuring one another that we were in this together, yet neither of us really knew what to do or where to even begin.

My worldview had no room for things of this sort. I was a 26-year-old whose life had gone pretty much how I planned it. I grew up as a relatively successful student-athlete. I would set a goal, work toward that, and it would predictably become my reality. I decided in high school that I wanted to be a physician assistant. I applied to the competitive PA program early, as a junior in college, and was accepted. I was allowed to defer my acceptance while I finished my undergraduate degree and collegiate track and field eligibility. As a teenager, I set my sights on David and married him after our junior year of college. We both had dreams of building a family, and Westin was born while I was in graduate school. When I finished the PA program, I landed the job that I wanted, and we bought a little starter house. Lachlan was born a few months later. My life was just as I had planned it. Safe. Predictable. Controlled.

My experience of death was limited too. My dad's mom, whom we visited once a year, died when I was a fourth-grader. I remember watching my dad's tearless demeanor through the funeral service, and I remember seeing my grandma's body in the casket. It was a curious thing for me to see for the first time a body that resembles the person you know, but with a look that communicates clearly that they are no longer there. During that childhood experience, I felt a bit more like an observing bystander than a grieving participant.

My mom's mom lived in the same town we did and was a more regular part of our lives. She died during my freshman year of college, a few months after she was diagnosed with pancreatic cancer. I definitely experienced more grief with her passing, but the death of a grandparent still fit within the order of life as I expected it and knew it to be.

The only experience that I recollect of a child dying happened when I was still in elementary school. I didn't know the family personally, but I remember studying those bereaved parents carefully every Sunday as they came into church. I was haunted by the look of vacancy and pain in their eyes that I was certain I could see in them for many years after their daughter died. As they showed up for Mass week after week I would examine to see if they still looked sad. For as long as I watched, I was sure I detected the sadness in their eyes. I understood, even as a little girl, that the depth of their grief must be something entirely different from what I'd witnessed in other grievers.

Now, as a young adult, I was thrust into this completely foreign world where *my* child died, and others were studying my eyes to see if the sadness remained. When my child was torn from my life, all sense of predictability and control was ripped away with him. The death of a child is supposed to be something that only happens to *other* people. I had no room for this in my life plan. This was a sword that pierced through my shield of control and landed its tip into the depths of my heart. It knocked the wind out of me and stole my breath in an enormous way. This was *not* part of my plan!

I was drowning in the fact that I would have to live the rest of my existence without my child here. Every minute without him was unbearable. How could I possibly endure another 60+ years like this? I pleaded with the universe, "I can't do this!" I didn't personally know of anyone who had lost a young child, and I had no one to show me that it was even possible to survive a loss like this.

The day after Lachlan's death, friends started to stop by. I wondered how they even knew. One of these friends was the only person I knew who might be able to relate to a grief and a pain this big. The year before she had lost a daughter in her seventh month of pregnancy. Although we had never really talked about her loss before, I remember standing in my living room and leaning into her hug, begging for her help.

"I can't do this. How am I going to live like this? I can't do this!"

She whispered her response as she held me in her hug, so simple and yet so profound, "Just get through one moment at a time, one step at a time."

She may never know how profound and lifesaving that advice was for me. Her words gave me a place to be grounded. I didn't have to do the next 60 years right now. That was *way* too much to bear. But could I get through this very next moment? Could I make the one next decision? Yes. Barely, but yes. I could do the one thing that was next. Every time I found myself drowning and overwhelmed with the enormity of what was in front of me, I came back to this truth. *I didn't have to live all of that yet, I just had to get through this one moment.*

I wandered aimlessly in my darkness for the next several days. I didn't know what to do, and I didn't feel like I was being given much guidance. Are we supposed to choose and call a funeral home? I'd never been involved with planning a funeral before. I suppose people were afraid to tell us what the next steps were because they were steps that communicate the finality of a death we couldn't bear to accept.

I knew many people put together slide shows for funerals, so we scoured through photos to find all of our favorites. There was the photo of our perfect, happy little family on the day Lachlan was born. The one of him dressed like a pumpkin, sitting in a pumpkin patch at Halloween. The well-timed Christmas photo that captured him spitting up on his fancy suit. The one of us playing peek-a-boo in the mirror, or the picture with his tongue way out as he was getting teeth and figuring out what his mouth could do. There was my favorite of him when he was eight months old, lying on his belly, big brown eyes gazing into the camera, wearing the same green and orange striped polo that he died in, with his faint little dimple just visible. The pictures of him at ten months, showing how long he had lived, and that last photo we took of him lying in a laundry basket of warm clothes fresh from the dryer, happy as can be. David had teased me about taking too many photos. "What are we even going to do with all of those?" he had asked. Now all of those hundreds of photos were not nearly enough.

We collected his favorite things to bring across the state with us as a display of his life at the funeral. We chose a few of his favorite toys, like the stacking cups that we used in a game we dubbed "Skyscraper Baby." The object of the game was for Westin to stack the cups into a complete tower before Lachlan could make it across the room to knock it down.

We chose stuffed animals that were part of our daily games. The boys' room was jungle-themed, and near the doorway was a shelf holding a lion, an elephant, and a gorilla with her baby. We would often pause to make the noises of each of those animals as we went in and out of the room.

We pulled some of the photos of Lachlan off the wall to add to the display. My dad expressed concern that we were already pulling the photos of him off the wall. He was relieved to know it was just so we could bring the photos with us.

The ache of the emptiness of time and space without Lachlan's presence was overpowering, crushing me in every second. It was as if he was everywhere, but nowhere. The remnants of his last bottle on the counter. The backup container of soy formula and the fruit cups that were just for him in the cupboard. His empty high chair with smudges from his sticky fingers still present. There was the walker toy that he was so close to actually being able to push around. The window ledge that was just low enough for him to peer outside, and the baby board books still scattered on the floor by him. His laundry was in the hamper. His crib waiting for his return.

The emptiness of time was equally painful. I wasn't supposed to be able to help Westin to the bathroom without, at the same time, wrestling Lach to keep him out of the toilet. Offering food to one child, without portioning tiny pieces for Lach at the same time, left too much downtime during meals. I was supposed to have to get out of bed several times during the night to tend to his cry. His absence was felt in every minute, day and night.

Eventually, we loaded all of our things and the items we had selected to bring to his funeral service and headed across the state. This was the first time venturing outside of our protected bunker at home, surrounded only by people who knew the hell we had entered. I felt painfully vulnerable.

As we were leaving town, we stopped for gas. I went inside the store with my mom for a bottle of water. At check out, the unsuspecting clerk asked with a chipper smile, "How's your day? Where are you headed?"

I panicked and froze, leaving a long and terrible silence. My mom panicked and blurted something about my baby dying and us driving across the state for his funeral. It was awful and awkward for all of us.

This was the first time of many that people would unknowingly and casually ask, "How's it going?" or "How are you today?" Society trains us that the only appropriate response is "good," or maybe if it wasn't such a great day, you could say "fine, thanks for asking." How do you respond when your day is beyond the most horrendous you could imagine? Do you lie and reply as trained, say "good" and just keep walking? Do you say nothing? Do you give them the real answer?

The 400-mile drive was a continuation of the whir of thought and emotion. Our first stop as we arrived at our destination was at the funeral home. We had to deliver the clothes we had chosen so they could get Lachlan ready for us to see. We had chosen the only dress-up outfit he had that would fit. It was his little Christmas suit—the one he was spitting up on in that photo. In all the other funerals I'd attended, the deceased was dressed in their finest. Does that still apply to a baby? None of the funeral customs that we learn for an adult seemed quite fitting for a baby. They all seem too formal, too stuffy.

When we delivered the suit to the funeral home, the staff recommended that we find a hat for him. Lachlan rarely wore a hat, and if we tried to put one on, he just pulled it right back off. Would we even be able to find a hat his size to coordinate with the outfit we had chosen? When we pushed back, the funeral home team told us, as gently as such things could be said to newly-bereaved parents, that the hat was needed to cover an incision line across the top of his head from the autopsy. I still hated the idea of a hat. He didn't wear one, so it wouldn't look right on him, and it would cover that curly wisp of hair that I was always trying to get to lay down while he was nursing. Nonetheless, we sent some family members on a mission to find a hat.

In the days before the funeral, we stayed at my mom's house. I sat alone in my grief while the household buzzed around me. Visitors drifted in and out, dropping off casseroles and cards. The idle chitchat and stifled laughter were like a Brillo pad on my raw nerves.

I remember opening the first card from a long-time friend of our family and finding a generous gift of money. It hadn't even occurred to me that people might give us money, and I was surprised to see it there. Shocked, horrified, offended, and angry is more like it. *My child died and you give me money as if it will somehow make up for my loss?!*

However, as I opened more cards, most containing gifts of money, I started to understand. They all knew that I was experiencing every parent's worst nightmare. There was nothing that they could actually do to make it better or to bring him back; a gift of money was a gesture of love, given so that we could do something special in his memory. My heart and emotion on the matter quickly shifted. Instead of offense at the monetary gifts, I felt humbled by the generosity of so many people and deeply appreciated their gifts that were given to express their love and sympathy.

The knots in my stomach never let up. I was nauseous and uncomfortable. Our loved ones worried to see us barely eating. I felt like people were constantly pushing and offering food that I had absolutely no interest in. I remember one of these moments in particular. Despite having no interest in eating, I accepted a plate of food simply so that other people could stop worrying about me. I sat at my mom's kitchen table, in a folding chair brought out to accommodate the extra flow of people. My elbow was on the table, my head resting on my hand. I took a few bites. The food felt dry, tasteless, and made my belly hurt worse.

Forcing myself to eat just to please other people was adding to my pain, and I couldn't do it. I pushed the food aside and cried. I knew others' concern came from love, but they didn't understand that they were adding to my struggle. I was too lost to be able to communicate that.

This was a first glimpse in understanding that I was going to have to stand up for my needs in a way that I never before had needed to. My nature has always been to go with the flow, working to meet the expectations of the people around me, whether that was a great fit for me or not. I was going to have to learn a different way of being.

We made our way to the funeral home to visit Lachlan, this time with Westin along. It was time for him to see what we meant by "Lachlan's body stopped working." We stepped inside the building to the unwelcome smell of a funeral home. Our apprehension was softened by the warm and compassionate greetings of the funeral home staff. Lachlan was ready for us in a quiet room off the lobby. We stepped into the gently-lit room, where the tiny white casket sat on one side, with two chairs placed with care in front of it. We approached that little casket, Westin in my arms.

This casket was not a miniature version of a beautiful metal or wooden one crafted for an adult. It was the only one the funeral home had available for a child his size. It reminded us of an Igloo cooler with a bumpy plastic shell, then padded and draped to create a comfortable resting space. This casket was designed for infants, but Lachlan, just five and a half weeks shy of his first birthday, was almost too big for it. However, the next size casket was far too big for him.

The ill-fitting and unimpressive casket wasn't something that bothered me as much as it bothered David. I suppose it was because I had no expectations for what a baby's casket should look like. I'd never imagined anything different because I'd never considered any part of this at all. Children are not supposed to die—especially not *my* children.

Nonetheless, we stood there in that room with one child wriggling in my arms, the other lying lifeless in front of me. We approached, and Westin looked at Lachlan's body for a few moments, and then with a gentle prompt to do so, he kissed his forehead quickly before insisting on getting down to run around. He seemed to sense the strange energy, but outwardly it was difficult to tell what he was processing. Did he understand? We didn't really know. Someone took over the care for Westin so David and I could have a few quiet minutes of our own with Lachlan.

The funeral home had done a nice job preparing him, his mottled skin and purple lips were now covered with that standard thick post-mortem makeup. His eyes were gently closed all the way, without the classic part to his sleeping eyelids. He was wearing the suit we had selected, topped by the hat that had been dropped off by David's brother and his wife. Although the funeral home had done a nice job and clearly invested a lot of care and love in their preparations for us, there was nothing they could do to mask the fact that our little boy was no longer present in that tiny body.

We were told we could hold him if we wanted. This again was a thing that felt so strange and abnormal in comparison to the funeral customs we knew. We followed our instincts and picked him up to hold him. This time, he felt even further from the bouncy boy we knew than he did on the night of his death. I had thought this would be a good opportunity for me to hold him for as long as I wanted, without feeling the pressure to be done like I did in the ER. However, this time, I found much less comfort and satisfaction in having him in my arms than what I had hoped for. It was so easy to see that he wasn't there. He was more rigid and seemed unusually heavy. He just didn't feel quite right. While I was still appreciative to have that opportunity, it didn't take long before I felt ready to put him back down. The thing I was longing for wasn't there.

Perhaps due to our medical background, David and I were not intimidated at the thought of seeing the wound across the crown of his head. It was more important to me to see it for myself than to just accept the necessity of a hat that didn't belong. We found the incision covered neatly with strips of Telfa gauze. It was back far enough that by simply cradling his head a little with the blanket he was lying on, we could easily cover the evidence of the autopsy. We removed the hat to reveal that beloved, wild patch of hair. This looked so much better to me.

Our parents joined us as we met with the funeral home staff in their big conference room. Wheeled office chairs surrounded the giant, glossy, cherry wood table. We started running through the checklist of decisions to be made. I was surprised at how much instinct bubbled up in making those choices. I had never considered any part of this, and yet, together, David and I answered most of these questions with confident decisions as if we had it all planned out.

There was some weight to these decisions, though. Every single one felt like part of the last things I would ever get to do for Lachlan. Part of me would have loved to think, study, and search for ideas that would lace this last event for him with all the greatest ideas, perfectly personalized. Yet, neither the time nor the energy were available for that kind of planning. I was grateful for these strong instincts that surfaced to guide us through the process.

One of the items on the checklist was deciding who would unfold the pall cloth to cover the casket at the beginning of the funeral Mass. Up to this point, David and I had made all of the decisions without much involvement from anyone else in the room. We thought this piece of the ceremony might be a nice place to involve his grandparents, and we asked them if they'd like to do that part. They balked. Freezing up, not having much to say, they instinctually expressed uncertainty about whether they could do it. I see the response now as an expression of the depth of their grief. To participate in any way was no easy task, and for them, too, this was one of the hardest things of their lives.

In the moment, however, I was annoyed, frustrated, and a bit angry. Every single piece of this, and every single decision made, was the hardest thing I had ever had to do. Each impossible task was something I couldn't run from and had to face with courage that I didn't think I had. I was frustrated that "it's too hard" was even an option for them. Yes, everything about this is impossibly hard and the burden is more enormous than I ever could have imagined, but it still had to be done. It's fine, we decided reflexively. David and I would do the pall too.

We were sent home with the tasks of writing an obituary and choosing readings and music for the funeral Mass. We were given a booklet containing some common funeral readings and songs as a guide in making those decisions. I would have loved to spend weeks preparing and choosing. There was so much scripture and music from which to choose, and I wanted it to be perfect. Yet, even the few options in the guide were overwhelming to sift through. Even if I had all the time I wanted, my thoughts did not seem cohesive enough to have the capacity for a more in-depth scripture hunt. My head was still spinning, thoughts continued to be everywhere and nowhere. I felt unsteady, unfocused, and disoriented, like being terribly seasick on a violently rocking boat.

Although my memory is hazy in recalling the choices we made for readings and songs, there are still pieces and lines that are meaningful. From the Book of Wisdom, we chose:

> But the righteous one, though he die early, shall be at rest. For the age that is honorable comes not with the passing of time, nor can it be measured in terms of years . . . an unsullied life is the attainment of old age. The one who pleased God was loved, living among sinners, was transported—snatched away, lest wickedness pervert his mind or deceit beguile his soul. . . Having become perfect in a short while, he reached the fullness of a long career; for his soul was pleasing to the Lord, therefore he sped him out of the midst of wickedness. But the people saw and did not understand, nor did they take that consideration into account. *(Wisdom 4:7-11, 13-14)*

I had to grasp at any tiny thread of comfort I could. In this reading, I was reminded to be comforted by all the suffering that Lachlan did not have to endure—no skinned knees, no broken bones or broken hearts. If I were given the task of choosing the cause of death for my children, without question I would choose that they die peacefully in their sleep. Lachlan was pleasing to the Lord. His early death spared him from the suffering and corruption that life brings. His innocent perfection was preserved.

My own feelings, though, are like those of the people, and I didn't understand. On one hand, I knew I should aim to direct some level of trust in God's good will, but at the same time, my thoughts were screaming: *Why did You do this to me, to us, to him? I thought I could trust You to take care of us and* this *is what You gave us?!*

The psalm was an easy choice. In our Confirmation class in high school, David and I learned and memorized Psalm 23. We continued to pray it together for many years after that. And now the line, "*Even though*

I walk through the valley of the shadow of death, I will fear no evil, for you are with me" was speaking, reminding us that even in this dark valley, God promises to be present. He's there, though we can't always tell.

I'm still afraid of this dark. This valley is too big, too dark, too scary. I feel like the child who panics in the moment the lights are turned off. *It's too dark! I can't see!* It's disorienting. I feel alone even if I'm surrounded by people who love me. I can't see them in this darkness. The line from this psalm is like a voice coming from the dark. A voice from someone I can't see and can't feel, but a whisper heard . . . *I am with you.*

The reading that I remember most clearly was the gospel reading of the story of Jesus raising Lazarus from the dead. This is the story from John 11:1-44, where Jesus' friend Lazarus dies. When Lazarus became ill, his sisters sent for Jesus, hoping that He would heal Lazarus and prevent his death. Jesus waited three days before He went to them. When Mary came to where Jesus was and saw Him, she fell at His feet and said to Him, "Lord, if You had been here, my brother would not have died."

I heard my own voice echoed in Mary's. *Lord, I thought You protected people and healed people. Where were You?! If You had been here, Lachlan would not have died!*

The story in the Gospel of John continues. Jesus wept with them. He then raised Lazarus from the dead after he had been dead for four days. I longed, unrealistically, for Lachlan to be raised from the dead too. I wanted nothing more than for this whole terrible nightmare to be over. I had no idea what a priest would do with a reading about a man being raised from the dead at the funeral for a boy who was going to stay dead. Nonetheless, that's what I wanted, and it's the reading we chose.

One moment at a time. One painful and ugly task at a time.

An obituary also needed to be written. David and I were the only ones who intimately knew Lachlan, leaving us as the only ones that could write an intimate summary of his life. Obituaries are traditionally a list of how people invested their lives—education, accomplishments, work, hobbies, and the people they loved. How do you write an obituary that is fitting for a ten-month-old? It was another task that I despised doing, but it was too important to me to hand it off to someone else. I couldn't bear the idea of something generic that wouldn't honor the unique life that was his, but was it silly to write about the things that a baby did and loved? I painfully plucked away at the keyboard. I asked for thoughts from our family, but it was too delicate a job for them to offer much feedback. In the end, this is what we wrote as his obituary:

LACHLAN JON EDWARDS was born June 21, 2007 in Sioux Falls, to parents David and Brianne Edwards. He died peacefully in his sleep on May 12, 2008.

In his short time with us he was loved deeply by many. He was a happy baby with an infectious smile. He loved to play ball, make animal sounds, dance, listen to loved-ones on the phone, play peek-a-boo with his daddy, snuggle with his mommy, and share belly laughs with his brother. He will be held closely in our hearts forever.

We added a "survived-by" and "proceeded-in-death-by" list of his family members out of custom, but that's it. The essence of a whole lifetime, a whole soul, a tiny person with infinite and eternal value, all summed up in six little sentences. How unbearably inadequate.

Lastly, we chose the photo for the obituary, the icon photo of his lifetime. We sifted together through all the pictures again, narrowing down the choices a little at a time, to choose the one that was a nice face shot, with a sweet little grin, and his tiny dimple just visible.

One more task had been accomplished. There was one last big step in the funeral preparations to go: the painful job of choosing the burial spot. This step left a mark on my soul too.

We met with the woman who worked in the parks department for the city and she took us up to the cemetery. She unrolled her oversized map that was difficult to hold in the wind. We first looked near the place where some of my extended family was buried. There was no space available there. She looked at the map for available space and led us here and there, only to backpedal after looking at her map again and realize that those spaces were not actually open. There was the "baby-land" area reserved just for infants. While a good fit for many, I couldn't stand the thought of him being buried away from loved ones. It was enormously frustrating trying to pick out a location when the woman showing us what was available didn't seem to understand her map or know what our options were. All the while we were there, every ounce of my being protested the cosmic injustice of having to be there at all. I was a 26-year-old kid myself, and I should have no business picking out a place to bury my child!

Ultimately, we wandered to a place at the back of the property. This spot was easily the most beautiful place in the cemetery. Upon being there, I remembered that I had made a mental note of this spot once before. I had a high school classmate whose father died just after we graduated. In attending his burial, I remember standing in that very spot, wondering at the time how it was possible that plots were still available in that location. It seemed like that beautiful place should have been the first area of the cemetery to fill up. It stands on the edge of a plateau overlooking the mouth of a breathtaking canyon and a golf course with its water fountain and greens.

Now, here I stood in that same spot, and there were several plots still available . . . she thought. She would have to verify when she got back to the office and let us know for sure. It turned out that a block of four plots was available there, and we purchased all four of them. As healthy and heartbroken young adults, my husband and I chose our own burial locations with that of our child. We went ahead and purchased the fourth spot in the block for the potential unpredictable tragedies that we could no longer pretend just happened to other people.

Now that the necessary steps of funeral planning were complete, it was back to the stream of people coming to bring their condolences, my own soul being swept away and nearly drowning in the white waters of grief.

3

Saying Goodbye

Grief is love turned into an eternal missing. . .
It can't be contained in hours or days or minutes.

ROSAMUND LUPTON[1]

On the morning of Lachlan's funeral, I awoke in my childhood bedroom. I pulled back the same tribal-print comforter I had slept under as a teenager and my feet moved to land on the muted blue carpet. The moment is etched in my memory as I surfaced to awareness. I found myself feeling paralyzed by my grief, unable to start this dreaded day. It was like the utter opposite of the exciting days of a wedding or other big event when you feel eager to start the day. Maybe if I didn't do anything and didn't move from that spot on the edge of the bed I could stop this day from coming. Unlike the day he died when I started the day oblivious to the tragedy that would be mine, today I knew before I even began, that this would be one of the most difficult days in my life.

I sat in that same spot for a long time. How do you get ready for your own child's funeral? How do you choose something to wear for that occasion? Does what I choose to wear somehow reflect what I feel? I knew I would never again wear the clothes I chose because they would forever be what I wore to my son's funeral.

David came into the room, and I lamented to him about not even knowing where to begin. He leaned back on the advice from a few days before, "One thing at a time, Love. Just do what's next. Right now, the next thing is for you to get in the shower."

I guess I can do that. It's a curious thing about deep grief that even the most mundane things become insurmountable challenges. It was so bizarre to be in a place where you need help to know that getting in the shower is the next thing to do. Showering was a simple thing that I did day after day without even thinking about it. And yet, there I was, with the weight of every moment so crushing that even the most ordinary and simple tasks felt overwhelming.

With the water of the shower, I was pulled back under the violent current of grief. Time lapsed. In the car on our way to church, my consciousness surfaced again capturing another still-shot moment for my memory. It was a beautiful, sunny, but breezy Saturday morning. We were headed through the edges of our little hometown, down the narrow, paved road without a shoulder, curb, or gutter when I spotted a man out mowing his lawn

I was violently struck by the sight of someone carrying out a regular household chore as if he had no care in the world and as if this Saturday was like any other. When your whole universe has shifted and crumbled, it is surreal, shocking, and hardly believable to see other people moving through their day, unknowing and unaffected by the tragedy that has struck yours.

In attending other funerals, I always had the sense that the funeral was for the family to say their goodbyes. My attendance was a way to support them in their final goodbye to their loved one. Now that I was burying my child, I understood that this funeral was not going to be where I found closure. For me, a funeral was only the beginning. It was a place to begin my grieving, not end it. This loss was too big for me to be able to say a neat and tidy goodbye and then pick up and move on with my life. This funeral was for everyone *else* to say goodbye. It was a place for them to come to pay their respects to us, to express their condolences, their sympathy, their concern, and then go back to mowing their yards like they did every other sunny Saturday afternoon.

We arrived at the church and started walking through the motions of the funeral proceedings. I had a strange sense of playing a character on stage. I felt distant from myself, with every move, every gesture watched and analyzed by an audience looking for clues to answer their most burning question: *How is she holding up?* There was a steady stream of people making their way through the door. Some people I knew, some I didn't, some I hadn't seen in many years, and some had traveled a surprising distance to be there. I was astonished and comforted by the number of people who made an appearance. The vast majority of them had never met Lachlan. I knew they weren't there for him as much as they were there to show their love and support for us.

It's interesting that, while there was something comforting about the crowd, the individuals were a complete blur. Without the guestbook, I could only name a small handful of people who were amongst that crowd. There was a sense of the multitude being God's hands coming down to comfort us. The comfort was of the collective, too big for any individual in attendance to take credit, but all participating together to show us extraordinary love and support.

The time neared to begin the service and to close the casket for the last time. This was an enormous dread. There was such a heaviness to knowing that these moments were the last that I would lay eyes on my sweet little boy. We were taken into a side chapel, and I walked feeling every ounce of that weight. Westin was tended to by family while David and I said our final goodbye.

Lachlan looked nice all dressed up in his little suit, but it seemed stuffy and uncomfortable. Even when he wore it while still alive, it was cute to have him dressed up, but with the collar, sweater vest, and jacket, it was an awful lot for such a little person to wear. When he wore it, there was relief in getting him back into comfortable clothes. I had the same feeling about the darling suit now. It didn't feel right to be tucking him in forever wearing that fancy suit.

I felt a longing to take him out of that suit and to make him comfortable before we tucked him in for his eternal rest. As two working parents, the most consistent time we got to spend with Lachlan was in the evening, and we enjoyed the time with our baby through the supper and bedtime routines. So much of our time with him revolved around tucking him in for the night. There was something reminiscent of that now. We just wanted to tuck him in one more time with his fuzzy footy pajamas and a good swaddle.

In the day prior, we had made our request to change him into his pajamas ourselves. Though by this point, we had no idea what was normal and what wasn't, the response of those around us suggested that this request must have been unusual. I know there was some discussion about whether that would be too much for us to bear and whether we should be allowed to do so. Ultimately, with a little hesitation, the funeral team helped us arrange to do that.

Now, that time was here. We stepped through the doorway of the little side chapel, delicately prepared with window blinds drawn. The lullaby music that was part of our bedtime routine for the boys played quietly in the background. David and I began the process of preparing our baby to be tucked in that one final time. We removed the little three-piece suit, leaving the onesie underneath in place. Undressing and dressing him was a bit challenging with his stiffened body not cooperating in the process. Though all wrong in the way it was difficult, there was something right in having to work a little at getting him into his pajamas. It was somehow reminiscent of the lively boy who, in being laid on the floor after his bath, would immediately roll over and crawl away as quickly as he could, giggling with glee while we chased him down trying to get lotion, diaper, and pajamas on him. It was never easy to get his pajamas on him, why should it be now?

Although he had grown too long to fold the bottom of the blanket up over his feet, Lachlan had still liked to be swaddled up with his arms wrapped tightly against his body. My husband and I together swaddled him snugly one last time, going through the same motions with him that we had done hundreds of times before. We held him and rocked him to the lullabies and then laid him in his little casket.

We tucked him in with a few of his favorite stuffed animals: the squeaky teddy bear named Peef, and the baby gorilla from the mother-baby pair that sat on the shelf in his room. The mother and baby gorilla were now torn apart and separated—just like Lach and me. We tucked in the edges of the cloth lining, everything now snuggled in around him. He looked cozy and comfortable, so much better than in the suit. We watched painfully as the lid, prepped for its final seal, was laid on top.

Those may have been the most excruciating moments of my life.

There are no words for how painful it was to participate in those final preparations, yet at the same time, there was something healing and helpful for my soul. I was (and still am) grateful that we were allowed to do it.

His little casket was wheeled to the doorway of the main chapel, and the service began. We lined up in the back: David, Westin, and I, trailed by our families. All eyes were on us. This was the beginning of the end. These were the last few moments of having something to do to care for this little body that was created in and from my own flesh and blood.

The last time I prepared to walk down that aisle, I was dressed in my wedding gown, holding the arm of my daddy. On that day, I was beaming with the pride and excitement of getting to marry my best friend, my high school sweetheart, the man who was everything to me. On that day, when we promised "for better or for worse," we had no idea what "for worse" really meant. I had imagined maybe one of us being ill for a long stretch, or the difficult parts of marriage when it seems impossible to get along. I had never imagined this. It was unimaginable that "for worse" could mean burying your child together. Yet, here we were.

At the prompting of the priest, David and I unfolded the pall and laid it over the tiny white casket. I couldn't bring myself to make eye contact with anyone, but I couldn't avoid hearing the sniffles from the pews. As we started down the aisle to the front of the church, Westin, who loved all things with wheels, moved to the front and insisted on helping push the roller cart that held the casket. He didn't understand what was happening in those moments; he just wanted to help push the thing with wheels. There was something so sweet and heartbreaking in having the pure innocence of a toddler and the bitterness of death all wrapped up into one heart-wrenching scene. The sobs crescendoed.

During the funeral service, I sat in the front, clutching David. Thoughts whirred into a blur, and I hardly saw or heard any of what was happening. I felt all of the eyes watching our every move.

Then the priest momentarily captured my attention when, in his homily, he suggested that we think of each day from here on out, not as a day further away from Lachlan, but as another day closer to seeing him again. I couldn't stand the idea of living through another day without him, getting further and further from my existence with him here. When the perspective was flipped, hope was introduced in a tiny mustard seed form. I could get to the end of one excruciating moment and say to myself, *I'm now one moment closer to seeing him again.* Every day was one day closer. *Today* was one day closer . . . and that gave me something to hold onto.

As the funeral was concluded, we streamed outside to go to the cemetery. Westin watched as the little white casket was loaded into the back of the shiny black hearse, and we were led the short distance up the hill to the cemetery, with a long line following behind. Traffic was stopped as we drove by and my memory flashed back to a few days before when my drive was halted by someone else's funeral procession.

We sat in the chairs placed in front of that casket, hair blowing in the wind. I sat with whirring thoughts of disbelief that this was it. This would be the final resting place of my child. I remember nothing of what was spoken at the graveside. Only the song played holds a space in my memory. My sister-in-law was uncertain that she could keep enough composure, but she honored our request for her to sing by pre-recording "Amazing Grace." Each family member had been given a tiny, red, embroidered heart sticker by the funeral home. The song played while they streamed forward to place that little heart on the casket as a final gesture of love. All the while, I was unaware that the song was being knit into the fiber of my being and from then on would be tied to a very visceral memory of those final moments.

After the service, we lingered behind until the crowd had left. This was our moment to sit and say goodbye without feeling like we had an audience. The infant-sized coffin was too little for the typical burial vault into which the casket would be lowered, and too small for the lowering device. We asked how they would put the casket into the ground and were told it would be lowered by hand. This was the very final thing to be done for his body on earth, and it was completely unceremonious. I stood watching as David, on one end, and the funeral director on the other, picked up the casket from the graveside table, and then knelt, to lower it into the shallow grave. The team from the cemetery would bring the dirt to cover it after we left. We returned to our vehicle and silently drove back to the church where the reception was waiting for us.

I felt the room's energy shift as soon as we joined the reception. With each group of people we approached, the conversation hushed, expressions changed, and people stammered to search for something to say. Several people commented on how nice the homily was, and that Father Tim did such an excellent job. I wondered what the homily was about. Although I was physically present during the funeral, my head was a million miles away. I couldn't recall any of it except for the "one day closer" part. We tried to take time to greet each group in attendance, but we quickly ran out of things to say. Small talk was too petty and dead babies were too difficult to talk about, so we just thanked them for their sympathy, thanked them for coming, and then walked away. There was an awkward silence from the group and then the conversation would swiftly move away from babies dying back to the comfortable everyday discussion of things like weather, sports teams, and happy life updates.

As I looked around the room, I remember being surprised at how many of these people had even known that my baby had died. They had all cared enough to be informed of the funeral arrangements and clear their schedules to come. I had nothing to do with communicating any of it, but there they were, and I was grateful. There was nothing any of them could do to actually make it better, but their presence showed me that I had a community of people who cared. Although the comfort was small in comparison to the burden I was holding, it was something. Exchanged words were entirely inadequate, but their simple presence spoke volumes.

The crowd dissipated and that was it. The funeral proceedings were over. The physical goodbye was done. Everyone else went back to life as they knew it. It was a heavy day for everyone present, but for most, they were able to set that weight to the side, push the thoughts away, and carry on with their regularly-scheduled activities.

What was *I* supposed to do now? The rituals of mourning were completed, and I had not even begun to process this. My crushing weight was still just as present as it was the moment it was dropped. In fact, maybe it was even more burdensome because now I was exhausted too, and I was just beginning to see how heavy this weight really was. This was my new life, and as much as I didn't want to, I was going to have to figure out how to live it.

4

The Weight Stays Put

When you come out of the storm, you won't be the same person who walked in. That's what the storm's all about.

HARUKI MURAKAMI[1]

I wandered through my motions, in what seemed like a thick fog. I felt trapped under a heavy blanket and in the deep darkness. I was hardly able to breathe. I was unable to concentrate on anything. I remember feeling particularly frustrated about being asked repeatedly by a variety of people if, or when, I was going back to work. I wasn't sure if I would eat or even breathe that day. I didn't care about ordinary everyday tasks of living. A decision about work was way beyond my capacity. I knew I couldn't, or wouldn't, go back to work in the same way as before. I was not even close, however, to being ready to figure out what a change would look like.

As we made the 400-mile drive back home a few days after the funeral, we stopped midway across the state for gas and a bathroom break. I entered the gas station with my wheel-obsessed toddler and saw a little antique-looking tricycle on the floor, front and center. Like a moth to a flame, Westin went straight toward it. I suggested he leave it alone but wasn't up for the fight. Instead, I kept an eye on him to ensure he wasn't getting rough with the trike. The gas station attendant was displeased. First she told him that it could break, and then made a sharp comment to me that if he broke it, I would have to buy it. I quickly and rudely snapped back at her that if she didn't want little kids to touch it, placing it on the floor directly in the entryway wasn't a smart move.

My response caught me by surprise. *This is not who I am.* The old me would have dutifully pried the toddler from the bike, returned it to its spot, apologized to the attendant, and carried the wailing toddler to the car. *Who was this stranger in my skin?!* Standing up for myself didn't seem all bad, but to snap in response to a comment from a complete stranger seemed uncalled for. I wondered if this was the beginning of a slide into being some bitter and horrible woman who grew cold and nasty in response to the death of her child. Would I forever be angry and resentful, a nasty old hag who would make life miserable for everyone else, too? I had hours to ponder what was going to become of me as we finished the drive home.

I was petrified of going back home. Somehow it signified the beginning of this new life that I didn't want to live. We had taken a brief time-out from life, but it was now time to go back to reality. There would be mundane chores of meal prep, cleaning, laundry, and lawn mowing. I would again be the primary caregiver for Westin, without a safety net of family to help when I couldn't do it. All this, while feeling my heart torn from my chest every time I tripped over using the verb *was,* instead of *is,* when referring to my baby boy.

While we were away for the funeral, my curly-haired angel in disguise had called me to ask if she and a friend could clean for us while we were gone. I had agreed. As we stepped through the threshold of our doorway—into this new life that I didn't want to be living—we were welcomed by their gentle gesture of love. We found more than just clean sheets and less dust. We were met with the scent of lilacs from a handmade bouquet of fresh-cut flowers on the table. There was a new gallon of milk and some fresh fruit in the refrigerator, little things that were a huge relief because that meant I didn't have to race to the grocery store for those necessary toddler items. I was also relieved to find Lachlan's space was untouched. His laundry was right where we left it, and his fingerprint still on the mirror. I was humbled and grateful. The welcome home by those simple gestures was warm and gentle.

The next days and weeks were all lost in the heavy fog of grief.

So many people had offered, "If you need anything, just let me know," which was appreciated, but useless. I didn't know what I needed. There was nothing wrong with me physically, so in no way was I truly *unable* to do the ordinary work of living. Emotionally, though, I was so wrecked that I didn't care to. I would let laundry pile up and chores go undone long before I would call anyone to say, "Hey, my heart hurts too much today, can you come to do a few loads of laundry for me?"

There were a few precious human-gems around us who, rather than the generic "call if you need anything" statement, would be direct and specific. They would say, "If it's okay with you, I'd like to mow your yard for you." Oh, the relief. They made it easier to say yes than no. They lightened my load and made it comfortable for me to accept their gift despite my pride and my desire to always *be* the helper, not the one who needed help.

I didn't know how to be in the role as the one *being* helped. I didn't want to be a burden. I didn't want to appear weak, or helpless, or broken. I didn't want people to judge me for what I could or couldn't do. So when those few precious people came in, asking only for permission to help with what they had in mind, they gave me a gift. They taught me how to be the receiver of those acts of kindness and generosity, and also how to be a more humble and generous giver.

Acts of love and generosity can be big or small, yet when they are experienced as one gift from a community, they become increasingly meaningful. I was reminded of the times that I had witnessed other moments of tragedy within a community and people responded by banding together to create a powerful movement of generosity and support. We were recipients of that kind of love, too. My job required that I encounter people in a variety of departments throughout the hospital system, making my name and face relatively known. David was also known by many at the same hospital because he had worked in the ICU for several years before he went back to school. I'm told that it became a movement, a bandwagon of sorts, among hospital employees to donate vacation hours to me. In the end, I was gifted with nearly three months of vacation time, allowing me to have time and space to grieve with no pressure to decide what I would do about work.

I was enormously humbled and grateful for this response. There was no way for me to thank the individual donors, or to even know who they were. It felt very much like the hands of God again, at work through the community around us, scooping us up to hold and support us as we navigated through this life-changing pain—an anguish that encompassed not only an emotional agony, but also a social, spiritual, and even a very physical one.

In graduate school, I remember being taught briefly that grief could also bring very physical reactions, but I was surprised at how physical it actually was. My chest felt crushed, my heart physically hurt, and I felt like I was barely able to breathe. If I had not been a medically educated, perfectly healthy 26-year-old female who had just experienced the death of her son, I would have thought I might be having a heart attack. I had another bereaved mom recall to me that in those earliest days of grief, her only goal for the day was to breathe because even that felt impossible to do.

My empty arms ached constantly. I missed the feeling of Lachlan's weight in my arms, his warm body against my chest, his head on my shoulder, and his soft breath on my neck. My head ached relentlessly. My eyes felt puffy, and my nose was raw from the constant need of a tissue. It seems a silly little thing, but I was so grateful for the softer, gentler Puffs Plus tissues when they found their way into my hands. Sleep was erratic and often restless. Other times it was deep and still, the only escape from the torment of living. I could still barely bring myself to eat.

I thought most of the physical symptoms were just in my head, psychosomatic kinds of things. Nothing had happened to me physically, so I assumed all of it must be somehow made up. I thought they were pseudo-symptoms of someone on the brink of a breakdown, imagining the physical symptoms for which there was no real cause.

I wish I had known how normal the physical pain of grief is and that there are real physiological changes that happen to our bodies in times of such stress. I wasn't crazy for feeling these things. I was human.

I learned many years later that the physical response of grief is a very real one. There is even something called "broken heart syndrome" where newly-bereaved people feel crushing chest pain. Cardiac enzymes and EKGs can measure changes in these achy, grieving hearts that mimic a heart attack. There are also studies suggesting that acute and intense grief can actually increase the risk of having a heart attack. There are studies that show changes in immune function, and even genetic changes at the cellular level in response to grief. When I learned of this scientific information, there was a relief and reassurance for me to know that I was not crazy. Feeling all of that intrusive physical pain was a very real and organic part of such intense grief.

As distressing as the physical response was, it was just a shadow of the much bigger and deeper emotional pain and distress.

I felt as if I had lost myself somewhere in this mess. I couldn't think clearly about anything. I couldn't read even a short paragraph and retain the information—a relatively foreign thing for someone who had recently completed her master's degree. My thoughts, behaviors, and emotions were all over the place. I couldn't follow a train of thought from beginning to end without being derailed by an intrusive grief-related thought. I would erratically alternate between wanting to busy myself in an attempt to distract myself from the pain—going through the motions of activities that felt somewhat normal—and on the flip side, being almost catatonic and unable to force myself to do even basic things.

This erraticism of thought and emotion was so far from my usual self, the focused and attentive type-A planner, scheduler, and organizer who loved to learn and read. My way of living had always been planned and thoughtful. My emotions tended to be pretty even-keeled. Now, I felt as organized as a game of "52-card pickup."

There was a real sense of dissociation, I felt detached from the reality of my surroundings and disconnected from my physical and emotional experiences. Schizophrenia is a mental disorder that involves the breakdown in the relation between thought, emotion, and behavior, and a sense of mental fragmentation. My thoughts and feelings were now all a tangled contradictory mess. I wondered if this is what schizophrenia feels like.

I wanted my deceased son to be raised from the dead. I longed to die, myself. I daydreamed about how my life could end. The suicidal thoughts scared me, even though I never felt like I would actually act on them. I also knew that I had important things to live for. I felt the most extreme feelings of sadness, anger, and denial all mixed up with moments of gratitude for so many of the little things that brought a light or comfort to the days. I didn't know it was even possible to experience so many enormous and contradictory emotions all at one time.

This interior craziness and chaos of thought and emotion are some of the hardest feelings to acknowledge and relay as being part of the experience. They are not understood or accepted by society. For those who have not had the experience of such intense grief firsthand, it is hard to understand these feelings of interior craziness and chaos. When others hear about these thoughts and feelings, it will often elicit concern for our mental well-being. Just the existence of those crazy and chaotic thoughts created feelings of shame within me. That shame just added to the difficulty in being able to admit to those feelings that seemed unacceptable. I was sure that if I shared those thoughts out loud to anyone but David, I would be sent for inpatient psychiatric care.

This stranger in my skin was exhausting to live with.

Everyday activities tormented me. If I made it to the store, shopping without having to tend to a wriggly and impatient baby was too easy. I was reminded in every step that Lachlan wasn't there with me. Walking by a rack of clothes with "12 mo" on the tag made my head spin, and I had to fight furiously not to break down in tears. At mealtimes, I sometimes pulled out four plates from the cupboard and then broke down in tears as I put one back. I would think I heard his cry and turn to get him, only to remember again that he died. At times I would wake up with a start during the night, instinctively surprised that he hadn't woken me up yet—and then lie awake for the remainder of the night with my gaze locked on that tiny green smoke detector light, lamenting that he would never cry out for me again. I got myself ready for the day too easily without having him strapped to my chest in the baby carrier to appease his demand to be held. I got out of the car and stood with soul-sucking emptiness while David unbuckled Westin from the driver's side, not having Lachlan to pull out of the car from behind the passenger seat.

Everything was fog, fight, disorientation, and emptiness—all assaulting me over and over again. Violent and unexpected waves of grief would hit without warning. One day or one moment, I would start to think I was feeling a little better, only to be blindsided by another blow and knocked lower than I had been before.

I still felt some joy and happiness, especially in Westin's presence, but every fleck of joy also made my cup of sorrow even deeper. I could see and appreciate Westin doing something new, funny, or adorable; learning something new; or admiring the wonder of our world. But in the same moment, I was also caught by a deep pang in knowing that I would never see Lachlan do those things.

It was an entirely new experience to feel intensely happy and grateful while simultaneously feeling immense sadness and pain—with all of these feelings prompted by the same moment or event. I thought happy and sad were on opposite ends of a spectrum. I thought we could be *either* happy *or* sad, or maybe fall on the grey scale somewhere in between. I had never before really perceived that it was possible to be happy *and* sad at the same time.

For many months, any time we crossed paths with one of my husband's little cousins, I would catch her watching me, studying me thoughtfully. She would ask me, "Are you still sad?" I would nod, and tell her that I was. My answer stemmed partly out of fear that saying anything different would somehow mean that I was "over it" or no longer missed Lachlan. I didn't yet have the understanding or the words to be able to tell her that, while I was still heartbroken and sad, I had many things to be happy about too. I was happy to have all the other people in my life whom I loved dearly, and I was happy to be there with her.

I wandered through my days in that fog, in that storm. I was hunkered down, waiting for the fog to lift and the storm to pass. I waited for the physical pain to ease up. In every other negative experience of life, it was just a matter of waiting it out a bit. Until now, time was always enough for the heartache to eventually lighten and the negative emotions or the anxious thoughts to fade so I could carry on as I did before.

I thought to myself over and over, *How long until this gets better?! I can't live like this!*

I had gotten the impression that this pain would never really go away, but I didn't really understand what that meant, or how that would look. I just needed this unbearable crushing weight to be lifted so I could move, and breathe, and think again. I didn't want to be dysfunctional and broken anymore.

The shift came the day my boss invited us over to his house, and I was introduced to his mother. I knew the story of her loss, the tragedy of having three of her eight children killed when they were struck by a vehicle walking home from the pool. In meeting her for the first time, she exuded such genuine warmth, sincerity, and love. If I had to be a bereaved mother, I wanted to be a bereaved mother like her.

Some people respond to tragedy by becoming closed off to the world around them, bitter and ugly. Some, on the other hand, become better, warmer, and more loving. At the time, it seemed impossible to be softer, warmer, and more loving because of this experience. The woman who stood in front of me was the first visible proof that it was indeed a possibility.

We ended up outside in a long conversation, just the two of us. She was not shy about describing the depths of pain after the deaths of her children. She spoke clearly about a long, deep, and very dark depression. She, too, had been frozen and lost in her grief. She didn't like to leave the house and couldn't stand the interactions with other people if she did. She sat in that hole of grief for a long time, just like I was still sitting in mine.

The turning point for her was when her little five-year-old boy said to her, "Mom, I wish I died so you would think of me." Ugh. Knife to the heart. But it happened to be what she needed to decide she had something to live for, and to remember that she wanted to give herself to her living children too. She started the climb that day. Her present state of warmth and love, in combination with her ability to be vulnerable as she meaningfully shared the most painful and dark moments of her life, spoke very powerfully to me.

At one point in the conversation, I asked her how long it might take before I started feeling better. While I don't remember her response verbatim, I know I walked away from that conversation with a heart that understood that this weight was staying put. It would never go away, and it was something that I was going to have to learn to live with. This shift in perspective was subtle, invisible to anyone else, and was barely perceptible even for me, but it was the starting point of being able to move toward a life that I could live.

I left that day with a tiny yet life-changing shift in my survival tactics. This shift didn't change anything about the pain and heartache, or the very physical longing for the child who wasn't there. It didn't erase the burden that my thoughts felt crazy. Nor did it change that I didn't really know what to do with myself to get through a day in this world that my child no longer lived in.

Now, however, I was able to see that waiting for all of those things to pass was futile. They weren't going anywhere. I had to figure out a way to make peace with this soul-crushing weight and learn to live my life while carrying this burden. I now knew that it was *possible* to live beautifully under that weight, even when it was like mine multiplied times three.

There is a quote by Vivian Greene that has become one of my very favorites and speaks to the heart of this shift. "*Life,*" Greene says, "*isn't about waiting for the storm to pass, but about learning to dance in the rain.*"

I could sit inside, hunkered in the basement to take shelter, or just sit alone staring out the window at the gloom while I feel sorry for myself. *Or*, although in my deepest being I wished this storm wasn't here, I could find a way to dance in this rain.

PART 2

Download a free version of the accompaniment journal at
www.aThousandPoundsBook.com

5

Intention to Heal

Man is not fully conditioned and determined but rather determines himself whether he gives into conditions or stands up to them. In other words, man is ultimately self-determining. Man does not simply exist but always decides what his existence will be, what he will become in the next moment.

VIKTOR FRANKL[1]

In a single moment my husband and I were thrown into the depths of the ocean of grief and we didn't know how to swim. All we could do is thrash in disbelief that this had happened to us and to our healthy baby boy. We were drowning in the pain that comes with such an enormous and unfathomable loss.

It is only natural to protest this new and horrific experience with every ounce of our being. A loss this big infiltrates every single moment of our lives, with tentacles reaching into every thought, every breath, awake or asleep, into every mundane task and every meaningful moment. Grief is often all-consuming. It is dirty and messy. It is excruciatingly painful. This grief is an unwelcome invasion, and by all outward appearances, seems to be an enemy—the thief that came in the night and stole our joy and our purpose.

It's normal to feel the need to fight this enemy of pain, flee from it, or lie down, limp in defeat. For a long time, that's what I did. I hurt like I had never hurt before. It was as if my fists and jaw were clenched like a scrappy cage fighter desperately trying to get the upper hand that I could never seem to find. Over and over I screamed within: *It shouldn't be this way! It's not fair! I can't—and won't—live like this!* When I was too exhausted to fight, then I would try to turn and flee from the pain, looking for ways to pretend this wasn't the life I had to live. As humans we will work to do whatever it takes to avoid uncomfortable moments, and to dodge painful feelings and memories. When running from those feelings doesn't work, we are tempted to give up hope for a meaningful life and ever finding joy again. We are tempted to surrender to the thought that we'll be forever broken and ruined.

By talking to other bereaved parents, I understood that these are natural and very normal responses. Our bodies and our brains are designed to react in "fight or flight" response to threatening situations to help us avoid physical harm. But grief is a threat of a different nature. Grief doesn't have to mean living in a constant fight or flight mode—at least not forever. But how do we go about learning to live in a different way?

I wanted to live a life of warmth and generosity, truly loving the people around me, and feeling joy and purpose—however, only if I could also live in a way that honored healthy boundaries and if it was deeply sincere and authentic. I didn't want to forget my loss or my pain. I didn't want to paint a happy smile and pretend I was fine. That would be like living in a superficial world with a hidden underground crawling with the agony I refused to address. I wanted to make peace with the grief and pain and to learn to live comfortably in their presence. I wanted to rebuild my life from the ground up, not hide the ugliness that was there. Even though I had some vision of who I wanted to be, I was nowhere near experiencing that version of myself.

I knew I would never be able to be that desired version of myself if I was constantly fighting my own state of existence. So, little by little, I turned toward that pain and hoped to learn to be less miserable sitting in the dark. I hoped that giving this wound the attention that was necessary would keep it from being angry and festering forever.

In my work in surgery, I deal with a lot of physical wounds. Some are superficial, clean and simple cuts that heal by just giving them a little time. We don't need to put much thought or effort into the healing process, and the next time we think about the wound, it is nearly gone.

There are other wounds, though, that don't simply heal with the passage of time. Some wounds require intentional effort and must heal from the inside out for true restoration to occur. We have to turn into the wounds, rather than away from them, to allow for healing. If we let the skin seal over without having the inside cleaned up and healed first, the wound will continue to be problematic, and we end up with a chronic abscess that never really goes away. In order to allow a wound like that to heal, we have to be very intentional, packing and debriding the wound, letting it slowly heal from the inside out. Wounds of the soul can be the same.

In the infant loss group we attended, the counselor told us a story of a 90-year-old woman who had come to him for counseling after the death of her husband. As they started their work together, she confessed that the healing work she needed to do wasn't really in regard to the death of her husband. Instead, her grief was more about the death of her child that had happened some 60 years earlier. She had never intentionally faced and mourned that loss and that pain had waited for her all those years, remaining present although hidden. Her grief was like a chronic abscess that needed to be reopened in order to heal properly.

Over the years, I've seen bereaved parents who, like the elderly woman, swept their pain under the rug, hoping it would eventually go away, instead of *turning into their pain* to process the loss. There are a million reasons why people are inclined to run from their grief, or just turn away from their pain, rather than getting to know it. But grief is a mess that does not go away. The pain will stay, a steady thorn in our side, always nagging and waiting to be addressed until we are ready to push our sleeves up and start the work of grieving.

The death of a child is one of those deep and messy wounds that needs a lot of attention. I seemed to understand early on, whether by grace or instinct, that this wound meant I would never go back to living the same life that I had before. In many ways after the death of my sweet baby, Lachlan, I wished for some physical sign or representation of the emotional pain I was working through. I wished that people could see, just by looking at me, that I was hurting and that I was in a process of doing the really hard work of healing.

I imagined the grief of losing a child as the emotional equivalent of losing a limb in a traumatic accident. With Lachlan's death, part of me was gone. When a life-changing event is of a physical nature, we expect people to need extraordinary patience and support as they are adjusting to the changes. We understand the extreme amount of pain, suffering, adjustment, persistence, and resilience that occurs as they work to create a new normal for their lives. We expect an intense period of pain and suffering. Life as they know it has changed and they have to find new ways of doing the most basic tasks of everyday living, and that takes time. There is something of themselves that is missing. Though invisible, that same time for adjustment can be needed for emotional pain too.

I felt so torn apart without my son and I longed for people to somehow be able to see the gravity of my wound. C. S. Lewis gave me clarity in what I was feeling:

> To say the patient is getting over it after an operation for appendicitis is one thing; after he's had his leg off it is quite another. After that operation either the wounded stump heals or the man dies. If it heals, the fierce, continuous pain will stop. Presently he'll get back his strength and be able to stump about on his wooden leg. He has "got over it." But he will probably have recurrent pains in the stump all his life, and perhaps pretty bad ones; and he will always be a one-legged man. There will be hardly any moment when he forgets it. Bathing, dressing, sitting down and getting up again, even lying in bed, will all be different. His whole way of life will be changed.[2]

Though these amputees don't have a choice in the hand life has dealt them, they do have a choice in how they will respond. Will they count themselves as crushed and then live the rest of their lives focused on their new limitations, feeling bitter that the life they had hoped for is no longer available to them? Or will they choose to rise above, finding the ways in which they *can* live the life they've been given to its fullest?

If we look up the word "heal" in the dictionary, we'll find that it is defined in several ways. It can be the idea of correcting a wound, injury, or person, but it can also mean simply to *alleviate the distress or anguish*. "Healing" from a grief this big isn't like healing a skinned knee, or a broken bone, or an appendicitis that, once healed, allows you to carry on with life as you once knew it. There's no "all better" with this one. We are not restored to our previous state of being. Our grief becomes more like healing after a limb amputation, in which the loss is assimilated into our life in a way that allows us to re-engage in the world around us, though in a way that is permanently altered.

Another great word for referring to the healing of grief is "integration." *To integrate* is to combine one thing with another so that they become a whole. I love this word because it doesn't ask us to move on, to forget, or to pretend our loss didn't happen—but neither does it demand that we live forever drowning in our grief and pain. We don't have to pick sides; we can have both. It is not escaping the unbearable; it is growing in our capacity to bear the unbearable. We can remember, honor, and grieve, *and* live in love, joy, and celebration of all the good things life still has to offer. In fact, the word *integration* shows us that the way to wholeness is to hold space for all of the things life has to offer—the amazing, the terrible, and the ordinary.

In the wake of my loss, there was a piece of me that wanted to give up on life, that didn't want to live this new existence, that wanted to curl up in a hole and disengage from the world around me. But there was another piece of me that wanted something different. If my life had to continue, then I wanted it to mean something. I wanted to make life better for other people. I wanted to find purpose, peace, and joy.

I sensed that I had to be willing to loosen my grip on the life that I *had* in order to open myself to the possibility of embracing the life that I now *have*. In no way does this mean that I had to let go of my love for Lachlan, my memories of him, or what he brought to me and my life. What it does mean is that I had to let go of the idea that the only way I can love him is through our *physical existence*. I had to dare to let go of the part of him that was gone so that my eyes could be opened to what I still had: an eternal love that transcends all of time and space.

There are a lot of meaningful analogies that help us see the value of being open to our pain. The right visuals can help us to be curious about our experience, and courageous enough to look into the darkness to find hope. They can inspire us to look for the healing that comes when we allow our loss to be integrated into the threads of our being. Let me introduce you to a few of these comparisons, perspectives, and theories that have resonated for me. These ideas have inspired my perspective on how to think about working through my grief and they continue to stick with me.

The first idea is that of applying the mindset of an athlete to my grief. As an athlete, we learn very quickly that the fastest way to improvement is to push to the edge of discomfort and then take one more step. If we try to bite off more than we're ready for, we'll end up wounded and spend the next weeks or months recovering from our injury. The most efficient way to move forward is to always be ready and willing to *lean into what is uncomfortable* but without forgetting that regular recovery days are also essential to the process. It is absolutely necessary to have days with a lighter workload to recover and regroup in order to avoid injury.

These same principles are applicable to developing the strength to carry this thousand-pound emotional burden as well. Lean into the discomfort. Take recovery breaks.

The second visual, and one of my favorites, speaks to the idea of *turning toward the pain*. Author Jerry Sittser experienced the deaths of his mother, wife, and daughter all in one horrific car accident. After the incident, he was thrust into the feeling of terrible darkness and described a dream that gave him clarity about the direction he needed to take:

> I dreamed of a setting sun. I was frantically running west, trying desperately to catch it and remain in its fiery warmth and light. But I was losing the race. The sun was beating me to the horizon and was soon gone. I suddenly found myself in the twilight. Exhausted, I stopped running and glanced with foreboding over my shoulder to the east. I saw vast darkness. I wanted to keep running after the sun, though I knew that it was futile, for it had already proven itself faster than I was. So I lost all hope, collapsed to the ground, and fell into despair. I thought at that moment that I would live in darkness forever. I felt absolute terror in my soul. . .
>
> The quickest way for anyone to reach the sun and the light of day is not to run west, chasing after the setting sun, but to head east, plunging into the darkness until one comes to the sunrise.[3]

When I first read Sittser's story, his words reverberated through my soul. I connected deeply with the feelings of desperately chasing to hold onto the impossible, and the terror that set in with the realization that there was no way to avoid what was next. This story does not try to deny the darkness or suggest that there is any way around it. Chasing what is already gone will only serve to extend the time we spend in the darkness. This visual inspires hope that by courageously turning to face that darkness, albeit with knees shaking, we can move through it with intention, purpose, and efficiency. Lastly, it plants seeds of hope that, indeed, the sun will rise again. Winston Churchill said all of that in much simpler words: "If you're going through hell, keep going."

Viktor Frankl, a psychotherapist and concentration camp survivor, wrote about a useful method for overcoming many fears and anxieties. This method of paradoxical intention involves counterintuitively turning toward the thing that is distressing. Frankl notes: "As soon as the patient stops fighting his obsessions and instead tries to ridicule them by dealing with them in an ironical way—*by applying paradoxical intention*—the vicious circle is cut, the symptom diminishes and finally atrophies."[4] We are applying this method to our grief when we turn toward our distressing thoughts, emotions, and bodily reactions. It is necessary to be aware of the possibility of giving our grief excessive attention (which can create problems of its own), however, paradoxical intention is finding freedom from the burden of grief, not by outrunning it, but by getting comfortable in its presence.

The next inspiration that helped me approach my grief with more curiosity than judgment was from CarlyMarie Dudley. After the loss of her baby, she described that healing began when she shifted her thoughts by "turning the WHY into 'What Heals You?'" She used the insight to create a social media project called "Capture Your Grief" which gave photo and journaling prompts to encourage grievers to be intentional in their own healing. This project reminded me that by being intentional in seeking the little lights that bring healing, I can begin the process of building a new life to love.

I often found myself trapped in the abyss of asking "why?" in a ruminating way. *Why me? Why us? Why him? Why now? Why... why... why?!* No matter how many times I lamented with these questions there were never any answers. Spinning my wheels in this cycle of unanswerable questions never made me feel better in any way. Instead, I usually felt singled out, alone, uniquely unfortunate, and worse than before. When I was feeling particularly bitter, lost, or despairing, it was just so easy to focus my attention on all the negative things.

When I shifted my attention to look for the things that made me feel a little less restless, angry, and resentful, it gave me a place to focus my thoughts that was actually helpful. There was no one thing that was a magic cure-all, but by being intentional to call to mind the little things that seemed to help, refocusing my attention on those things, and seeking out more of them over and over again, I followed my own intention to heal. What we allow ourselves to meditate on ultimately becomes part of our character and our future.

I began to gently coax my thoughts from unhelpful rumination to helpful intention. *What brings comfort? What helps? What heals? What creates peace? What inspires hope?* The answers to those questions revealed themselves a little at a time. They came by curiously exploring many different things and through a lot of trial and error.

Sitting under this crushing grief is a place to get to know ourselves and our needs in a whole new way. It is a marathon journey of self-discovery and rebuilding from the bottom up. As I began to try different things and spent time reflecting on them, I noticed it was like having my eyes adjust to the dark. What initially seemed to be completely pitch black, became dotted with tiny lights of hope.

Some of the lights that I began to see in the darkness were easy little things, bringing a shallow and immediate comfort. A hot bath, a frilly coffee, a good cry, a hard run, a tight hug. Something deep inside me would relax and soften with these kinds of things, even if just for a few minutes.

The things that seemed to have subtler and longer-lasting effects were those that felt a bit like cleaning out the dead tissue of a wound or maybe like a deep-tissue massage. They started out hard, painful, and uncomfortable in many ways, but days later I could see that something good came from the experience. I would leave a meaningful conversation utterly exhausted with my whole body aching. It was painful to have conversations that exposed those wounds. However, I would find in the days afterward that the burden felt a little lighter, and there was some sense of relief that had come through that hard and uncomfortable work.

The last illustration that I have found especially helpful is to think of *grief as a teacher*. Whether I wanted to or not, I was learning lessons on the hardest things of life. I was learning intimate lessons about pain and suffering. I was learning about myself and my God. I found, little by little, that if I tried to view my grief as a teacher, rather than an enemy, something softened inside of me, and it allowed a place for hope to take root. C. S. Lewis expressed the same sentiment, saying, "If you think of this world as a place intended simply for our happiness, you find it quite intolerable; think of it as a place of training and correction and it's not so bad."[5]

The constant ache of missing a child is so much to bear on its own. Are we really helping ourselves by fighting the invisible enemy of pain, or are we just adding a tremendous struggle to our already-heavy burden? What if we unclenched our fists and laid the boxing gloves aside? What if we softened our eyes and our hearts and saw this pain as a teacher bringing growth to our lives?

Some of the greatest teachers are the ones who demand the most of us. They present challenges that seem impossible and push us way outside our comfort zones. The lessons are painful, yes, but if we give them space to take root, something beautiful just might grow.

This particular teacher, though, has too many deep lessons to think we can tackle them all at once. Grief is not a neat and tidy lesson plan. This is a subject that will take a lifetime to learn. If there's a task that's too big in the moment, that's okay; maybe it's a lesson to be tabled for now and approached again at another time. If we are open to it, bit by bit, we can learn from our pain and let grief be our ally to grow in love and wisdom.

Grief is not a neat and tidy lesson plan. This is a subject that will take a lifetime to learn.

When I stopped to consider this pain of loss as my teacher, rather than an enemy to evade at all costs, everything inside of me softened a bit. I am reminded of the experience of labor and childbirth. It is an all-encompassing physical pain. I can fight that, tightening every muscle of my body, dreading with anxiety every contraction that's coming, and in doing so, add exhaustion, tension, and emotional distress to my pain—or I can know that while this is a painful experience, it is a natural one. I can know that I have a good support team, that I will be okay, and that something beautiful and life-changing will come from this experience. C. S. Lewis wrote: "It doesn't really matter whether you grip the arms of the dentist's chair or let your hands lie in your lap. The drill drills on."[6]

In being open to the pain of labor or the dentist chair, rather than fighting it, we change the experience entirely. It is much the same in the pain of loss. When we stop fighting the experience, the sadness remains, but so much tension, bitterness, and anger fade away. And with that, our eyes are opened to the opportunities for growth, and we can start to see the beauty that can emerge from the dirty, the messy, and the ugly.

However, even with a deep desire to find a sense of equilibrium again and a perfect intention to heal, it was painfully slow to start feeling like there was any real progress forward. Early in my grief I heard it said that a bereaved parent should be considered *newly* bereaved for five years. *Five.* I was both horrified and relieved to hear such a thing. Horrified that I should expect to feel the life-altering depths of this grief for such a long time. Every single moment was unbearable, and the thought of having to live that way for so long was suffocating. Yet, simultaneously, there was also a feeling of relief. I was relieved that I wasn't *supposed* to feel any better than I did. It gave me permission to have really bad days for a really long time without the self-criticisms that I should be "over this by now." Three years into my grief I could find myself in a puddle, and when the thoughts that were accusing me of being weak tried to make their way in, I could combat them with the reminder that it was okay that I was a mess because, after all, I was still *newly* bereaved.

It did, however, set me up to think there would be some magic lifting of that weight when I hit that five-year mark. It didn't come. What I did recognize though, is that by the time I'd been carrying this weight for that long, I'd found a softer space to carry the profound and unpredictable nature of grief. It didn't go away, but I had learned to be okay with its presence.

So, without knowing what it would look like, I knew I wanted to move my life in a direction that would allow it to become something beautiful. It will never be okay that my baby died, and I will never be glad that it happened, even when taking into account all of the good things in my life now that would never have become a reality without his death. However, I *can* be grateful for the lessons, the perspective, the personal growth, and the new relationships that have come through living that experience. With an open heart, an intention to seek what heals, and a desire to learn to carry this burden peacefully, we can find a life that feels worth living, even while carrying that thousand pounds.

6

Stepping into the Arena

The friend who can be silent with us in a moment of despair or confusion, who can stay with us in an hour of grief and bereavement, who can tolerate not knowing . . . not healing, not curing . . . that is a friend who cares.

HENRI NOUWEN

In an instant, death puts life into crystal-clear perspective. In a heartbeat—or in the cessation of one—it becomes immediately obvious that our relationships with other people and the love we exchange are the only things that *really* matter. I would give everything to have Lachlan back in my life. I would live jobless, homeless, car-less, hungry, and in sickness if it meant I could spend the fullness of my life with the physical presence of my little boy.

Without hesitation, I would even exchange my own life (as most parents would) to give my boy the opportunity to live more of his. There is only one swap I wouldn't make in order to have him back— that of another life, another Love, another person with their own set of meaningful relationships.

It's interesting though, that when we're not staring death in the eye, we have a tendency to live our lives striving for all kinds of things that just don't matter in the grand scheme. We work long hours to have a bigger house, a nicer car, more clothes, shoes, and vacations. We nitpick people and hold grudges when others offend us. When someone we love has died, all of these superficial things that we put effort into become immediately peripheral and unimportant. No one will care too much what we did in our nine-to-five grind, what kind of house we lived in, about the shape of our bodies, and how we dressed ourselves. What *will* be remembered is how we made people feel. They'll remember if they felt seen and loved in our presence. Everything else in this world is temporary. Love, however, transcends time and space and even death. It is the only thing worth striving for because it is the only thing in our existence that is permanent. We grieve because we love and our grief is persistent because our love is permanent.

This clearer perspective, and the new and deeper appreciation regarding the value of the people and the relationships in our lives, were things that I wanted to hold onto. I wanted to live intentionally and love others by learning to be more warm, genuine, empathetic, and forgiving. I longed to live those virtues as a way to honor the impact that Lachlan has had in my life. But love is risky and vulnerable. I was petrified to allow myself to love people because I knew it put my heart at risk of being wounded again.

Love is risky and vulnerable. I was petrified to allow myself to love people because I knew it put my heart at risk of being wounded again.

I was slowly able to come to the conclusion that love is worth the risk. Here's the thing that tipped the scale for me. If I were given the choice, knowing what I know now—both of the love and joy that Lachlan brought to my life *and* of the pain and agony that came with his death—I would still choose to have him as part of my life. I wouldn't even consider giving up the opportunity to be his mom in order to avoid the pain of losing him. He was worth the heartache. I would wholeheartedly choose it all again, even if I knew I would only have him for ten months, and then have to live the rest of my life longing for his presence.

Setting an intention for where I wanted to go personally and emotionally was easy. I knew both what I did and did not want to become because of this experience of life-changing loss. The problem was getting there. I felt much more like the person I didn't want to be than the person I did.

I realized it was going to be impossible to follow my intention and desire to reengage in the world around me without actually finding the courage to step out into the arena of life. When we decide that we are ready to step back into the arena, we become like gladiators facing death with courage and tenacity. We know there will be social, emotional, and spiritual battles that will leave us feeling bruised. We know we will fall. We expect there will be pain, but we do it anyway because there is something deep inside us that tells us it will be worth it. In choosing to fight for who we want to become, we may never reach the full potential of our intention, but if nothing else, we can enter the arena with a gladiator's resolve to fight our battles with courage, humility, and fortitude.

If I was ever going to feel like I could live again, I was going to have to start addressing and battling all of the things that scared me about reengaging in the life around me. The world is a big and frightening place when we're feeling so vulnerable and broken. Everything has the potential to be a trigger for an unexpected and overwhelming wave of grief. Interacting with people in any way, especially those who were not in my innermost circle, was so unpredictable. There was no way to tiptoe back into the world without encountering some really hard things.

Brené Brown is a researcher who has spent her life's work interviewing thousands of people to understand the workings of courage, vulnerability, shame, and empathy. The ideas she presents are very fitting to my experience of learning to live and engage with the world again after Lach's death. Her work gave me clear affirmation that my feelings of uncertainty, risk, and emotional exposure were not just an individual experience within my particular circumstance, but rather, a very *human* experience. Feelings of vulnerability are huge, and deep, and ripe in a world that is overflowing with the anguish of losing a child. This resistance to vulnerability was one of the barriers that made it hard to want to reengage in the world around me. Brené Brown's words about vulnerability affirmed what I had learned in finding the courage to step back into the world. She wrote:

> Vulnerability is the core, the heart, the center of meaningful human experience. . . Vulnerability is not weakness, and the uncertainty, risk, and emotional exposure we face every day are

> not optional. Our only choice is a question of engagement. Our willingness to own and engage with our vulnerability determines the depth of our courage and the clarity of our purpose; the level to which we protect ourselves from being vulnerable is a measure of our fear and disconnection.

The kicker is that vulnerability, though uncomfortable, has extraordinary value. Brown goes on to say:

> Vulnerability is the birthplace of love, belonging, joy, courage, empathy, and creativity. It is the source of hope, empathy, accountability, and authenticity. If we want greater clarity in our purpose or deeper and more meaningful spiritual lives, vulnerability is the path.[1]

Uncertainty. Risk. Emotional exposure. Those three words could almost sum up the experience of child loss. Yet, it is in our willingness to accept our vulnerabilities and engage in the world despite them, that we find the path to courage, hope, empathy, love—and yes, even joy.

Let's consider some of what makes the loss of a child an epitome of vulnerable experiences and how that creates new tender spots for us to tend to. First of all, just becoming a parent puts us in an extremely vulnerable position. When we are handed that wriggly newborn, we are also given a duty to care for them to the best of our capability.

As much as we want good things for them, parenting brings inescapable uncertainty and risk. We have no idea if our parenting methods are actually helping achieve the goals we have in mind for our children. They will act against our wishes and make choices that are ultimately harmful for them. We don't know if our children will love us back, and we can't guarantee they will want to maintain relationships with us as they grow. There is no promise that they will remain part of our lives, and separation—whether by choice or by tragedy—is always a possibility. Parenting is full of uncertainty and risk.

In many parent-child relationships, the risks remain largely theoretical. Other times, however, they become a very deep and brutal reality. Vulnerability—that uncertainty, risk, and emotional exposure that become present in a powerful way when we become parents—increases exponentially when a child dies. It is a very natural response to feel like we have somehow failed our children when their lives have been cut short. That feeling of failing at the job that means the most to us exaggerates our feelings of vulnerability, and can plant additional seeds of shame to contend with as we step back into the arena of life.

I found that the more I tried to fight, ignore, and run from the negative emotions, the more I felt like I was becoming the person I didn't want to be. Trying to box up the hurt and trying harder to be loving weren't working. It took so much energy to control those emotions that I had nothing left to give to the people around me.

Eventually I was too exhausted to keep fighting and striving to avoid the experience of pain. I couldn't keep up the façade and something interesting happened when I stopped fighting it. Counterintuitively, I began to feel small movements toward peace and authenticity—and that seemed like a step in the right direction.

I realized we can't really get anywhere without beginning from where we are. We have to master basic math before we can learn calculus. We might have a destination in mind, but if we don't start by figuring out how to navigate the roadblocks that are immediately in front of us, we'll never get very far.

We don't remove the suffering from our lives, but we integrate it into our existence. And when we do, suffering no longer carries the power to hold us back from living the life our hearts desire.

By taking the time to get comfortable sitting with our hard things, we become less afraid of them. The roadblocks become more manageable when we take the time to understand them. When we dare to step into the arena with our vulnerabilities and fears, we don't remove the suffering from our lives, but we integrate it into our existence. And when we do, suffering no longer carries the power to hold us back from living the life our hearts desire.

So it seems that the good fruits of the soul are not things that we can directly grasp and take as we please. Instead, they are gifts that are given to open hands for those who are courageous enough to face and wrestle valiantly with the dark and ugly giants that keep us from living with virtue and love.

Embracing the ugly emotions means that grief and mourning are not a pretty process. It is often two-steps-forward and one-step-back. First we turn inward, maybe to protect ourselves, or maybe to start exploring the workings of our own hearts. At some point we feel a teensy bit better and we are ready to turn outward, maybe in hopes of finding support from the community around us, or maybe to create purpose by giving something back to our communities. And then another hard day comes and we retreat inward again.

In her book, *Bearing the Unbearable*, Dr. Joanne Cacciatore compares grief to a model of contraction and expansion that is common throughout the natural sciences, from the death of a star to the process of childbirth. She writes:

> Contraction is necessary for expansion—and thus, contraction is itself part of expansion. A contraction of grief occurs when our attention and energy are pulled inward, our surroundings made smaller perhaps because, in this particular moment, we feel overwhelmed. Feeling overwhelmed, we contract and tighten emotionally; we conserve our energy and attention, focusing intently on grief—and on self. In a moment of contraction, it feels as if our very survival may be in question. We may feel unsteady, unsafe, unheld; we may feel tenuous, desperate, fearful, and vulnerable. In such moments, we may curl up and hold our breath. In such moments, we feel the call to self-protect. We sense on some level, that contraction will save us.
>
> Expansion may come with the deep in-and-out breath, in a period of small, even minuscule, growth post-contraction. Allowing contraction to just be, in time we see it naturally ebbs, and the tightness loosens, we grow larger, and we become more willing to venture out and explore, to take risks, to open and unfold. And we find ourselves in a moment of trust, safety, curiosity, willingness, connectedness, belonging—and maybe even hope.[2]

The important shift in my grief journey was learning to embrace wherever I was in the moment and trying to live that with honesty and authenticity. We are so well-trained by society and social media to paint the picture of what we think others want to see from us, rather than just letting our hearts, thoughts, and emotions be seen. If we strive to create harmony within our mind, body, and spirit by letting our expressions speak our truth, we start down a path of peace and healing. This is hard because it reveals to others where we are wounded and tender. Our unique loss and our grief mean that we have been wounded in unique ways that others may not entirely understand but being wounded is part of the human condition. While we are unique in the *ways* in which we are wounded, we are not unique *because* we are wounded. When I remember that, I am more willing to stop trying to avoid my wounds and flaws. I become a little more open to exploring those wounds with curiosity and accepting that they are part of the human condition. It also helps me extend a grace toward others in their flaws.

There is something valuable that happens when we stop trying to hide our wounds and protect ourselves from pain. This idea is poetically portrayed in the classic children's book, *The Velveteen Rabbit*. The wise Skin Horse explains to Rabbit the process of becoming authentic or "Real."

> "Real isn't how you are made," said the Skin Horse. "It's a thing that happens to you. When a child loves you for a long, long time, not just to play with, but REALLY loves you, then you become Real."
>
> "Does it hurt?" asked the Rabbit.
>
> "Sometimes," said the Skin Horse, for he was always truthful. "When you are Real you don't mind being hurt."
>
> "Does it happen all at once, like being wound up," he asked, "or bit by bit?"
>
> "It doesn't happen all at once," said the Skin Horse. "You become. It takes a long time. That's why it doesn't happen often to people who break easily, or have sharp edges, or who have to

be carefully kept. Generally, by the time you are Real, most of your hair has been loved off, and your eyes drop out and you get loose in the joints and very shabby. But these things don't matter at all, because once you are Real you can't be ugly, except to people who don't understand."[3]

Learning to let vulnerability into our lives and accepting the pain that is part of our journey isn't an experience of becoming soft, weak, and emotionally needy. It's an experience of becoming more human, more "Real."

Our willingness to recognize the fears of vulnerability and engage in that battle anyway affects our ability to mourn. Though the terms are often used interchangeably, there is a difference between grief and mourning. Grief is the *internal* experience after a loss, while mourning is the way we express that grief *outwardly*. Mourning while we grieve is one of the ways that we build harmony of mind, body, and spirit after a life-changing loss. Finding ways to express the truth of our hearts is a lesson on the road to authentic and peaceful living.

It is in that outward mourning that the rubber meets the road when we're discussing grief and vulnerability. The internal experience that comes with losing a child is deeply personal, intimate, and sacred to our lives. Conveying these most intimate and painful feelings of grief may be the height of emotional exposure. There is a tremendous amount of uncertainty and risk in that outward expression of our broken hearts. We don't know how the people in front of us will respond. We don't know if they'll be able to acknowledge our pain in a way that is helpful, or whether they'll say something that makes us feel little, or inadequate, or judged. To put a piece of ourselves in the hands of another, to be dependent on the people around us... *that* is vulnerability.

Yet, despite our resistance to allowing ourselves to feel vulnerable, we as humans are built for connection. Relationships are a necessary part of a meaningful existence. The arena of grief is one that should definitely not be entered alone. These battles are too big to do without the support of other people.

Recruiting Coaches

As I began to understand that this crushing weight wasn't going anywhere and I was going to have to learn to live with the ever-present absence of my son, I developed a hunger for resources. I knew I was not the only parent who had lived through the loss of a child. Other people had figured out how to live the life of a bereaved parent and I wanted to learn from them. I wanted to hear stories and perspectives that might help me find a way to be able to tolerate being in my own skin again. I wanted to know where other people found their little lights of hope in this darkness. If I was going to live well again, I knew I was going to need coaching.

Books were one of my favorite resources. I couldn't get enough of them. The stories of parents who had survived the death of a child validated the depth of pain that I felt, normalized the crazy feelings of grief, and helped me see that there was a real possibility to live well in the aftermath. I learned to see that even though I was forever changed, I wasn't ruined. The stories of others helped me find language to describe my experience, which in turn, helped me to better understand it.

The books that described death and dying helped me feel less afraid of what dying was like for Lachlan. I also read a myriad of books on heaven and on near-death experiences, each one offering some comfort into where my baby was now. Religious books offered perspective on how a good and all-powerful God could coexist with a world where children suffer and die. I read books that described the spiritual connections that remain between the living and the dead, and those strange and beautiful coincidences that people can't help but interpret as a "hello" from their loved ones on the other side.

Each new story, new author, and new perspective offered a nugget of wisdom and understanding. I held onto each of those nuggets as something on which I could start rebuilding the crumbles of my existence. Though the arena of grief is unique for each individual, and there is no "how-to" playbook that fits everyone, these stories were like written coaching manuals that helped me start to build my own playbook.

While books and written materials have been an essential element for me, as humans built for connection, there is nothing more valuable than finding people who can, and will, be part of our healing. However, that can sometimes be hard to do because in bringing our grief to others, we give up control and predictability in the experience.

Sharing our grief with others can be scary. Yet, we *cannot* hide, cover up, or avoid this vulnerability. When we try, our attempts to protect ourselves come out sideways as addictions, broken relationships, and heightened feelings of depression and anxiety. We do not get to choose whether we will feel vulnerable. We *do* get to choose how we will engage with that vulnerability.

Not everyone can stand alongside someone who is grieving, help them dust off, wipe away the blood and tears, and then give real, gentle, and meaningful feedback. But when we find the right people, we'll know it. It is priceless to find those sacred connections to people who can allow us to share our experiences and who can engage in those deep, painful, and powerfully meaningful conversations.

Most beneficial are the people who have the gift of *accompanying us* in our grief. Those with this gift are good at simply being present and walking beside us as we wander through the desert. It is normal to struggle intensely with the expectations of other people as we grieve. Sometimes well-meaning people want to instruct the process and "fix" our sadness as soon as possible: "If you would just do 'this' or stop doing 'that,' then you would be better." However, grief is not a problem to be fixed. Deep sorrow comes hand-in-hand with deep love.

Grief is not a problem to be fixed. Deep sorrow comes hand-in-hand with deep love.

The *Understanding Your Grief* support group guide by Alan Wolfelt[4] emphasizes this necessity of *companioning* each other in our grief. A companion doesn't come as an expert to teach, direct, or lead. They don't frantically push us forward, analyze, or impose order and logic. Rather, a companion comes with a gentle and open heart. They are genuinely curious about our experience, there to learn from us, willing to be still, and can simply bear witness to all the hard battles within.

As David and I started the search for people to invite into our corner, we began with a trial of counseling. The counselor was great; he was warm, thoughtful, and empathetic. David and I both appreciated the time set aside to talk about Lachlan, but we were able to talk about our grief regularly at home. We went to counseling with an underlying hope that we would find ways to remove the pain; instead, the counseling further revealed that this burden wasn't going to be taken away. Counseling could be a place to help process the grief, but it wasn't going to take this weight from our shoulders. Before long, we felt like the counseling sessions weren't really offering anything more than what we could do with each other and the people we loved, so we stopped going. For some, professional counseling is a vital piece of their processing; for others, the safe space to do that work is available right at home.

A kind and thoughtful family member did some legwork to help me hunt for resources. He provided us with the information for a local Compassionate Friends support group for bereaved parents. In our search for support, we attended a handful of these meetings.

There was always a wide spectrum of attendees. Often, we had the youngest deceased child. Others were there after their teenagers died in accidents or by suicide. Some even had adult children who died after chronic illness. I walked away from those meetings with a better understanding of the spectrum of parental grief. There were so many similarities in the thoughts and feelings that all of these parents had to wrestle through, yet each story was uniquely its own.

There seemed to be a sliding scale spectrum of what parents grieved for most intensely. On one end, for the parents of the youngest children, they largely grieved the things they would never know about their children, never experience with them, and the memories they would never create. There would never be a first day of kindergarten, a favorite sport, or a high school graduation. On the other end of that scale were the parents who had lost older children. They grieved for who their child was and missed the quirks of their child's personality. They also grieved the secondary losses of the people and things their child brought into their lives. These meetings gave me a great opportunity to feel less isolated in the depths of my grief.

In addition to the Compassionate Friends group, we found an

infant loss support group that met once per week for six weeks, led by a thanatologist, a counselor trained specifically in grief and death. This was a small group of four sets of parents—all who had lost children in late pregnancy or infancy. At first I found it intimidating to walk into a room with a small group of strangers with the idea that I was going to be talking about the most intimate, vulnerable, and painful experience of my life. David and I walked in with some hesitancy, but it didn't take long for that apprehension to dissolve. I was amazed at how deeply we could touch and sift through so much in such a short time. It turned out to be a safe space with other people who were living a similar experience and a guide to walk with us as we dared to look into the pain that comes with the loss of a baby. The infant loss support group became like a little coaching seminar, a place to learn about grief and take away tools to bring into the everyday, real-life experiences of navigating this new and unpleasant world.

In the general population, outside the haven of a support group, my loss made me feel like a sudden social outcast. People were afraid to make eye contact, or if they did, it was with a glance of pity. Everywhere I went, I could feel the whispers around me. Some people were afraid to approach at all; others did, but with a terrible awkwardness. Navigating social interactions after a significant loss is just hard.

C. S. Lewis describes this phenomenon by saying:

> An odd byproduct of my loss is that I'm aware of being an embarrassment to everyone I meet. At work, at the club, in the street, I see people, as they approach me, trying to make up their minds whether they'll 'say something about it' or not. I hate it if they do, and if they don't. . . I like best the well brought-up young men, almost boys, who walk up to me as if I were a dentist, turn very red, get it over, and then edge away to the bar as quickly as they decently can. Perhaps the bereaved ought to be isolated in special settlements like lepers.[5]

Outside the safe space of home or a support group, I felt horribly uncomfortable to even think about talking openly about my dead child, yet the thoughts of Lachlan and his death were so pervasive and intrusive that it was almost more uncomfortable *not* talking about him. I remember one of the first times I really felt that strain. I was internally being consumed by thoughts of Lachlan, but also feeling a social pressure to keep that pain to myself.

My mom was coaching a high school track team, and they had come across the state for a meet a few weeks after Lachlan had died. David, Westin, and I joined them for their team dinner at an Olive Garden restaurant. The group was mostly made up of excited and squirrelly high schoolers who were happy about getting to travel with the team. I assumed the other coaches knew of Lachlan's death. I didn't know if the kids knew or not.

No one spoke of our loss. There was no hug, no "sorry to hear of your loss," no asking how we were holding up. The interactions were all very normal, light conversation. A high school team dinner didn't feel like the place to bring up dead babies, so I sat there pretending to participate normally in the meal, all the while being smothered by the proverbial elephant in the room. *Did no one else notice the suffocating presence of this elephant? Why didn't any one of them say anything at all?* No one brought it up, so neither did I, and I sat in an internal torment, faking a socially acceptable smile.

That experience was the first lesson for me that if this was something that I wanted to talk about, I was going to have to lead the way. People we knew more peripherally weren't likely to bring it up, and even many of the people who loved us dearly didn't know how to initiate conversation about Lachlan, or death, or grief. Most people, even though they were thinking about us and wanted to be supportive, did not know what to do or say. They were afraid that bringing up Lachlan in any way would make it worse and that it would remind me of my loss and might make me cry.

I did not blame others for not wanting to bring up those hard topics. Before Lach's death, I *was* one of those people who didn't say anything at all because I didn't know what to say when other people had experienced hard things. I was silent not because I didn't care, but because I didn't know what would help. I definitely didn't want to make anyone feel worse. I was afraid of those hard conversations and afraid of the vulnerability that was necessary to say something.

Now that the hard things were mine, I *wanted* to talk about Lachlan and how much I missed him, but when I left the comfort zone of my home, I didn't know how to go about breaking the silence. I had no idea how to bring it up or talk about those things in a way that wasn't weird. I was worried that I would be seen as attention-seeking, or like I was throwing my own pity party. I also didn't like the thought of making people feel uncomfortable. I hated the perpetual awkwardness.

Sometimes though, not saying anything backfired too. I remember one specific conversation with someone that I knew peripherally. She warmly dove into happy everyday conversation about life and kids. I, not knowing what else to do, just played along—until the bomb dropped. She asked, "You had a baby, right? How old is he now?" I stood there shell-shocked in a long and painful silence. My thoughts were spinning wildly as I was trying to figure out how to answer this innocent question without making a fool of us both.

There was no gentle way to say it, so out it came: "He died." The exchange was miserable for both of us. She felt absolutely terrible for not knowing and for asking about the baby in such a nonchalant way. I imagine she left wondering what other things she might have said that would not be fitting for a conversation with a mom who had just buried her child. I felt terrible that the facts of my life made her feel so awful.

In that conversation, I learned quickly that trying to pretend Lachlan's death didn't happen had dreadful potential to backfire. I was going to make people uncomfortable whether I brought up the topic voluntarily or whether it came out later, and I definitely felt better when I opened the door to talk about Lachlan more openly. I began to experiment with ways to talk about him and my grief.

More than learning any phrases or techniques to make it easy, I learned that those conversations were much more dependent on the individual to whom I was speaking than the words I said. David and I lovingly coined the term "squirmers" for people who were clearly uncomfortable talking about our loss. These are the people who, when the topic comes up, get a deer-in-the-headlights look in their eyes, they start to fidget, and you can almost see their minds racing as they frantically search for something to say. Inevitably, they throw out some clichéd statement that is more likely to be a little offensive than helpful, and walk away as quickly as possible.

But there were other people who *could* talk with comfort and ease about death, dying, and all the enormous emotions that went with it. They asked open-ended questions and they weren't afraid to hear the answers. They didn't have notions about how I *should* be feeling, or what I *should* be doing. They were genuinely okay with hearing about it and walking beside me. They let me be right where I was, without ever giving the impression that I should think or feel any differently than I did.

These people were true treasures in my healing process. These were the people who I invited into my arena. There was so much to think about and process. The work of integrating our losses can happen just by having the freedom to talk it out. Author Jordan Peterson explains this critical need in this way: "People organize their brains with conversation. If they don't have anyone to tell their story to, they lose their minds. Like hoarders, they cannot unclutter themselves. The input of the community is required for the integrity of the individual psyche. To put it another way: it takes a village to organize a mind."[6] If I hadn't had the courage to experiment with ways to break the silence, I would have never known what a blessing these people could be to my battle.

My mind was like a tornado-strewn village. Utter devastation and chaos. In the painfully slow progression of rebuilding, the people I felt were most valuable in giving me a place to talk, process, and pick through my psyche generally fell into one of two groups.

One group was the handful of friends and family who loved me and had the ability to talk openly without expectations for me. They knew my history, my personality, and where I was coming from. They loved me, loved David, and loved Lachlan. They were also hurting because of Lach's death, but even though they had more skin in the game, they were still able to come to us openly and share in our experience without expectation or judgment.

The second group included other bereaved parents. Though I identified most with the people who had lost children of similar age to Lachlan, I learned quickly that many bereaved parents had something unique in the way they could speak about the death of a child. These were the surprise strangers who became vital to my healing. They weren't afraid of those discussions. Through many conversations over a cup of coffee, other bereaved parents became the village that helped me organize my mind.

It was interesting—sometimes a delightful surprise and sometimes a sour disappointment—to learn which people were ready and able to be part of our support team and which ones were not. This is a common story in almost everyone's grief experiences. Some of our closest friends seemed to disappear. People we expected to support us had little to say. We would, for example, have a conversation with them, and next to none of it was about Lachlan and his death. They were "squirmers," and our new state in life put them at a loss for how to be with us. We were left to wrestle with the disappointment of having people we loved who wouldn't, or couldn't, step into this arena with us.

It stung when people I loved couldn't offer the support we hoped to receive from them. Over time, by reflecting with curiosity and an open heart on what might be keeping them from supporting us as we'd hoped, I began to understand. For some, they didn't have children and weren't in a position to grasp the depth of our pain. For others, our grief hit too close to home. Sitting next to a friend grieving the loss of her child makes it all too real that your own child could die too. It puts you unbearably close to that crushing pain and leaves you feeling completely helpless. We naturally avoid situations in which we feel intense pain and helplessness. Pulling away is a normal protective mechanism that often happens without much conscious thought. I understood they weren't trying to hurt us.

On the other hand, there were casual acquaintances who could have easily kept their distance yet chose to draw close to us anyway. These unexpected people became amazing pieces of our support team. They became little lights in the darkness of grief. These are the people who were not afraid to look when I was on the ground of the arena, face down in the dirt, bloodied and broken. My pain didn't scare them. They were able to ask questions openly and bear witness to the answers. They lightened my emotional burden, like Simon of Cyrene, and helped me for a moment to carry my cross. They were the coaches who gave me direction, offered guidance, and walked with me in the self-discovery that was necessary to unclutter the chaos in my head.

There has been a cultural shift and society is just beginning to understand the value of being able to acknowledge our losses, talk about our loved ones who died, and mourn outwardly for as long as we need to. Back in 1980, my husband's beloved Aunt Mary Lou had a 17-day-old son die unexpectedly in his sleep. The culture was different then. Death wasn't something to be talked about. The loss was something to pack away and "forget" about. As I was meeting David's family, I only knew of OJ, the baby who died, as a name whispered in small groups behind closed doors. I clearly picked up the unspoken message that this was not something we talked about. Though I didn't entirely understand why, I did understand that the baby was not to be spoken of.

When we were driven to mourn in a more outward way after Lachlan's death, it also became an opportunity in which the tightly-packaged box of loss, grief, and pain from OJ's short life and death was cracked open for his mama. For the first time, after 30 years, she was able to mourn the loss of her baby boy, integrating his life and death into her way of living. This new approach became an avenue for meaningful discussion and tremendous healing for their whole family.

By opening conversation about Lachlan and his death, we also opened the door for OJ's death to be mourned too. When OJ died, the family packed away his things, put away his pictures, and didn't talk about him in order to protect Mary Lou from the constant reminders of that pain. They were following the advice of the "experts" at the time. How they responded, though coming from a place of love, had created more pain rather than relieving it. Mary Lou, responding to the cues around her, felt like she was supposed to live as if OJ's life never happened. She understood their gestures as an expectation that her child and her grief were to be hidden. The dichotomy between what she felt and what she was able to express only exacerbated her internal unrest.

This story demonstrates the value of communicating to our loved ones what kind of support feels most helpful. Even when the people around Mary Lou loved her deeply and only wanted to help, they didn't understand that they were actually making it more difficult. We *have* to be able to communicate to those closest to us what we need, what is helpful, and what is not. We didn't know that in previous generations, but we are learning a lot about the value of mourning from the brave women who have endured a silent grief.

Even though we are emotionally raw, it is important to make efforts to communicate our needs patiently and gently. Chances are pretty good that, even when people are "screwing it up," they have no underlying intent to make it worse; they just don't know how to help. But we can *teach* our supporters what we need.

Our supporters might need to know that it means a lot to us to see our child's picture still displayed, to hear his name spoken out loud, or for them to acknowledge the days that might be particularly hard for us. They might need to hear us say that we prefer to count our deceased child when we're talking about how many kids we have. If there are things that they are saying or doing that add to our pain, that needs to be communicated too—gently.

Most of these hard and vulnerable conversations will be with people who are in our innermost circles. It is likely, though, that there are also many people in the periphery who think about you often, and want to express their love, but just don't know how.

The *Water Bugs and Dragonflies* story[7], and the hope it inspired that Lachlan was alive and well just above the surface, led us to adopt the symbol of a dragonfly for Lachlan. It was a symbol of hope for our own hearts, but inadvertently, it also happened to give others an easy way to communicate their thoughts that would have otherwise gone unspoken. There are a lot of people in my life who might not ordinarily bring up the topic of Lachlan's death, but when they see dragonflies on something, they will often send the item, or even just a picture of it to communicate their thoughts of us and our boy. Each time those things come my way, even though they are small gestures, I am deeply grateful to know that I am not alone in remembering Lachlan's existence. I've seen many other families use symbols like butterflies, owls, cardinals, lilies, turtles, hearts, and even Bigfoot, with the same effect. This is one more way that we can help the people around us show their support.

Armed with a trust in our ability to know our own needs, the tools of courage and surrender, and a few trusty companions, we can start finding a way to live the life we have, even if it is not the life we dreamed of. We can take the next wobbly steps forward holding tightly to the popular words of the serenity prayer:

God, grant me the serenity
to accept the things I cannot change,
courage to change the things I can,
and wisdom to know the difference.

Download a free version of the accompaniment journal at www.aThousandPoundsBook.com

7

The Work of Pruning

Transformation isn't sweet and bright. It's a dark and murky, painful pushing. An unraveling of the untruths you've carried in your body. A practice in facing your own created demons. A complete uprooting before becoming.

VICTORIA ERICKSON

We can't expect to step into a battlefield and think we won't come away a little beat up. If we really want to engage, we have to be willing to shed some blood, sweat, and tears. We all carry ideas, beliefs, and attachments that prevent us from growing. These attachments are like tree suckers—those little unwanted shoots that grow from the base of a tree. Tree suckers develop when the tree is under stress or has been injured. If you never address them, they will sap the water and nutrients away from the rest of the tree, negatively affecting the tree's life and wellness. The more promptly they are pruned, the better. The longer they last, the more they will interfere with the healthy core of the tree. These unhealthy and unsightly shoots will continue to pop up while the tree remains under stress and often require regular maintenance.

This chapter describes things within me that I needed to prune because they, like the energy-stealing tree suckers, were sapping my energy and stealing the full and authentic life I was seeking. They are the parts of my being that are unsightly and unhealthy when they are left unchecked. There are common elements of our human existence that get in the way of our ability and our willingness to be vulnerable, to mourn, and to build connections. When I actively work against these things and prune them back, I slowly find a more peaceful way of being.

Pruning ourselves is hard and uncomfortable. It involves cutting out and removing the parts of ourselves that get in the way of our flourishing. In order to optimize our growth, we have to be willing to part with things we are attached to. Pruning not only improves the well-being of the tree, but also protects those around it. A dead branch caused by unmanaged tree suckers threatens to fall at any time, tearing down power lines and wounding innocent bystanders who stand too close. Similarly, if we don't want to hurt others because of the parts of our hearts and souls that are dead or wild, we must be willing to see those parts and then cut them away.

We can have the perfect intention to integrate, heal, live peacefully, flourish, and grow, but we can't forget the need for patience. In a garden that is under stress and overgrown with weeds, the gardener must be delicate and patient in uprooting them. If he is impatient, tearing at the weeds with abandon, he will also uproot what is good, and true, and beautiful. In order to restore the beauty, the gardener must be gentle and attentive, watering and fertilizing what is good, cutting back what is bad, and studying the fruits to know what stays and what goes. It can be tedious and meticulous work.

Expecting to do it all at once is overwhelming and frustrating. This process requires taking a break when we need it but never being afraid to step back into the mess, to endure discomfort, and to get closer and closer to our goal of restoring beauty. Let's push up our sleeves and start some of the dirty work.

In my journey to integration, I have been able to identify nine big tree suckers that were inhibiting my ability to grow:

1. The desire to numb my feelings
2. The need to uphold the image of being strong
3. The fear of shame
4. Feelings of guilt
5. Untended anger
6. The tendency to compare suffering
7. Feeling bitter toward others
8. A tight grip on control
9. Judgments and expectations for others

Noticing the Tendency to Numb

With an overwhelming flood of negative emotions, the desire and natural response to numb those feelings, and to try to protect ourselves from that pain, is strong. We live in a society that doesn't know how to experience negative emotions and teaches us that the way to deal with the hard stuff is to push it way down deep somewhere, to drink it to oblivion, to distract ourselves with social media, or to "keep busy" to avoid those moments where our thoughts might wander, and we might have to experience our pain. We might eat, or exercise, or work in excess, seeking the little dopamine bump as we run from the things we don't want to feel.

The problem is that we cannot numb only the negative emotions without dampening our whole experience of existence—including the good things we *want* to feel. If we want to be on a path toward living and loving to the fullest, numbing (however we choose to do it) sets up a big brick wall that barricades us from our destination.

> *Numbing the pain for a while will make it worse when you finally feel it.*
>
> J. K. ROWLING (DUMBLEDORE)[1]

If we aren't paying attention, we can mindlessly try to escape our emotions in all kinds of ways. It's the glass of wine with dinner that turns into two or three, the safety net of medications that alter our mood, anxiety, or energy levels, the bowl of ice cream, the impulsive purchases, the endless and mindless social media scroll . . . you name it. None of these things are bad in and of themselves, but when we use them to hide from our emotions, they become the little tree suckers of our souls.

Many of the things we use to numb our emotions are also necessary daily activities, so we have to approach them with a level of mindfulness and a willingness to be aware of our internal movements. We have to take a moment to turn inward and ask: *Am I shopping for a necessity, or am I shopping to make myself feel better?*

With a family history of addiction, even though I wanted to have a few drinks to "take the edge off," I was petrified that would be my path to a drinking habit that spiraled out of control. I was so on guard for this, that I avoided alcohol altogether for quite some time. It's all the other little behaviors that I had to be most mindful of and learn to observe my motivations for doing. When I am uncomfortable, I tend to fill my schedule with all kinds of "important" projects that keep my mind busy and the conversation on the task at hand. This is something that will require constant attention for as long as I live.

Learning to notice where I numb my feelings in my grief has also helped me to notice where I numb other negative emotions that come with being human. Finding ourselves in numbing behaviors isn't something to beat ourselves up about—it's just an internal movement to be aware of. The stronger the negative emotions, the stronger our desire to escape that pain is going to be. We simply need to notice. And when we do, we can take a moment to explore the emotions that we're aiming to drown. Then we lean into that, even if it is just a little. If leaning in is still too much, we can simply stand still and stop running away from it. Baby steps are still steps of progress.

Redefining Strength

"You are so strong." "I don't know how you do it." "I could never live through that." I hated when people said these things. They were meant to express the unimaginable depths of pain in trying to live through the death of a child, but my thoughts always reeled back and protested: *Yes, you could, because you're not given a choice.*

I wasn't given a choice in whether I would live through the death of my child. If I could have chosen for my heart to stop beating with his, I'm pretty sure I would have. I just wasn't given that option. I was standing there, still breathing, and still moving through life, not because of some internal strength or courage that other people don't have, but because I didn't get to choose that my life would go on despite the fact that my son's did not.

To hear the words "you are so strong" when I was barely hanging on—struggling to breathe and survive in the only way I knew how—was so hard. Those words, while meant as a compliment, were painful to hear because the depths of my pain and the crumbles of my spirit did not feel seen. The internal me, who was barely hanging on, was overlooked. All that was seen was my shell standing in an upright position. Nothing about this felt like strength or courage. I was being dragged through life protesting all of the pain with every fiber of my being—brutally tortured by my new existence, but still alive.

My name, Brianne, is the feminine form of Brian, which means "strong." My whole life I've loved that and identified with that. *Strong* had become part of my identity. I was always physically stronger than most of my peers and I loved how fitting that seemed. I had all kinds of ideas and attachments to what it meant to be strong. It was a word of power, accomplishment, and admiration. Now, those things were nowhere in sight. Maybe that's why hearing people say I was strong carried such a sting.

In grief, we can think we are supposed to be strong for the people around us. Culturally, we are fed the image that being emotionally "strong" is an act of stoicism. I thought that being strong meant being the person who could control and minimize her emotions, who could carry on through her normal daily activities as if nothing happened, who could be the shoulder for everyone else to lean on, and who didn't *need* other people to survive.

I desired to be that person. I wanted to be strong. I wanted to be seen as someone to look up to for my ability to endure. I didn't want to be a needy, emotional mess. I wanted to show the world that I was not weak, and that I could carry on even in difficult circumstances.

It seemed the only hope in being able to live out that version of "strong" was to stuff my emotions, to pretend life was normal, and to avoid and numb all the enormous feelings that stole every ounce of that kind of strength from me. But trying to live that way didn't work. It only added to my pain.

> *To share your weakness is to make yourself vulnerable; to make yourself vulnerable is to show your strength.*
>
> CRISS JAMI

When I tried to be stoic and strong, pretending to the rest of the world that I was fine, internally I was still being crushed under my feelings of grief. And then, when my weakness made its appearance anyway, I would beat myself up for not being able to be "strong." I finally decided I couldn't keep pressuring myself to be strong. Instead, little by little, I began to redefine "strength."

The story of the Christ-child is a perfect example of this new vision of strength. This is a story of the all-knowing, all-powerful, creator of the universe who came to earth in human form. As a *baby*. If there is any human who is needy and dependent on the people around him, it is a small child. A baby's very existence depends on the ability of other people to meet his needs. If this God is all-powerful, He could have entered into human flesh in any way He wanted. He could have been huge, powerful, and 100% independent. Yet, instead, He entered as tiny, vulnerable, and completely *dependent*. Even when we have a hard time understanding how vulnerability and strength go hand-in-hand, a story like this can help us trust that there is a hidden truth there to discover.

Let me introduce you to what "strong" means to me now. I have a college teammate who has stage IV breast cancer. Kassidi is a living example of my new definition of "strong." Her metastatic disease continues to grow despite her treatment. Back in the day, this girl wasn't just any athlete. She was a national qualifier in the throwing events. She was strong among the strongest athletes. Now, as the disease takes over her once-powerful body, "strong" has morphed in her, too. She lives in constant pain, her body continues to weaken, and her physical strength has dwindled to the point that even simple activities of daily living have become a challenge. In many ways, she is weaker than she's ever been. But when she shares parts of her story, I sit in silent awe. She engages in her story with truth, authenticity, courage, and hope.

Authentic strength is much more than what we can get our bodies to do or how much emotion we can strong-arm into silence.

From Kassidi, I am reminded that authentic strength is much more than what we can get our bodies to do or how much emotion we can strong-arm into silence. She shares pieces of how hard this journey really is, the heartache, the disappointment, the pain of watching your once strong body become so diminished. But that's not all. From that dark and humble place she also has the courage to see the beauty around her. She sees the joy of the ordinary, everyday things. She finds meaning and love exchanged in every relationship. She sees with clarity what is truly important, and she lives fully, even as cancer is stealing from her the life she once had. By telling her story, she is a reminder to me of what is really important in life—to see and cherish the people in my life and the ordinary joys around me. By telling her story, she encourages me to see the world through a different lens and inspires me to dare to live fully. That is strength.

This authentic strength of spirit is one of the great paradoxes of life, because I am quite certain it can only emerge from a place of deep weakness, emptiness, loss, and suffering. Authentic strength is deep and powerful. This strength is not the corruptible strength of a powerful mind and body, but rather it is like the unchanging strength of the ocean. It is a deep and constant strength that goes so much farther than what the eye can see. This kind of strength finds a way to renew itself while subtly, but vitally, affecting the entire world. This strength can easily go unnoticed if we are looking through a worldly lens, but this authentic strength is a source of life for all of humankind.

I have laid to rest my old definition of strength. Now, to describe strength in its most authentic form, I would say it is the courage to be present to your pain and loss, to acknowledge fully how much and how deeply life can hurt, and still maintain the courage to remain open to the world around us. It is to understand our own wounds and weaknesses. This real strength is not measured by our ability to *avoid* vulnerability, but rather in our ability to *be* vulnerable. Even in the presence of pain, strength dares to look beyond what hurts to see the beautiful things that life continues to hold. It is to be fully present to both the beauty and the suffering of life, and to be willing to engage and acknowledge them both. From a place of suffering, there is a powerful opportunity to bring life to the world around us. If we invite grace into our ashes and dare to use our pain to bring life to others then, in what feels like our weakest moments, we will discover an inner strength that defies and outshines the worldly definition of what it means to be strong.

SENDING AWAY SHAME

Another pruning battle to face is that with shame. When I first heard the word shame, I thought: *Why would I experience shame? I did nothing wrong!* When I dug a little deeper, I saw those feelings dotted all over my grief experience. Shame is that feeling of wanting to withdraw, shrink, or hide when we feel like we are "not enough" or that we are flawed. Shame interferes with our capacity to feel love, belonging, and connection to others.

Parents are supposed to protect their children and keep them safe. When a child dies, there is some level of shame in the failure of that basic task of parenting. It doesn't matter whether or not I had any control over the events surrounding my child's death. Since a primary goal of parenthood is to raise our children to adulthood, I failed in the job that was most important to me. We hear it all the time: a parent casually comments at the end of a tough day with their kids, "Well, at least they're still alive." Those words make me want to shrink and disappear because I can't say the same. That's shame.

> *While we can't always remove the reminders of shame that show up on the doorsteps of our souls, we can refuse to answer the door.*
>
> VICKI COURTNEY

There is also shame in having grief that interferes with our ability to be attentive and to parent our living children in a normal capacity. I felt a lot of shame about not being able to be present to Westin, my toddler who still needed a parent. I tried to play with him to soak him in deeply, to cherish every second with the child I could still hold in my arms, but it seemed beyond my capacity when I was grieving so deeply. I wanted to, but I just couldn't. Instead, he got more screen time than I would normally allow because, day after day, we were trying to survive. Shame often comes from the place of feeling like we are "not enough." I definitely did not feel like enough when I was parenting in survival mode.

I have also spent time with parents who have lost an only child. Their experience of shame sometimes extends from the piece of their heart that appreciates the freedom of not having to work every detail of their life around the needs of their child anymore. It feels wrong to have that freedom again, and it often feels shameful to appreciate any part of it.

Many shame triggers come from social situations that can feel like a steel trap, with sharp jaws on either side, leaving us with no escape. In these circumstances, no matter what we do, we're going to be uncomfortable. One place I found this inescapable shame was in the grief bursts that happened outside the safety of my house. Out of nowhere, I would be overcome by a sudden and intense wave of grief. In those moments I wrestled uncomfortably with the decision to let that pain be seen or find a way to hide it. Either way, there was a level of shame. I felt some shame or embarrassment in crying or showing my unexpected distress to the random set of people around me—but those feelings of shame were equally attached to having to leave quickly to keep that emotional flood unseen, as this made it obvious to others that I didn't have the strength to hold myself together. Either way, there was no escape from feeling a sense of shame.

Another shame trap is present in deciding when, or how, we go back to work. There can be shame in *going* back to work and being able to function in your job, as if our ability to function communicates that the loss isn't that painful. However, there can also be feelings of shame in *not* being able to go back to work or to function in a normal capacity, as if that communicates emotional weakness or brokenness. In a similar trap, there can be shame tied to re-engaging in any part of life, doing things with friends, finding things we enjoy, smiling, laughing, or being happy in any way; and on the flip side, shame surfaces when we are not ready to go back to those things yet. No matter what we do, shame rears its ugly head.

A shame trap can clamp down in the way we choose to mourn. By mourning and remembering in an outward way, we run the risk of having people think that we're stuck in our grief, that we can't move forward, or that we're seeking attention. If we put up some walls so our grief is unseen and we don't outwardly express our grief, we're opening up the door for people to think we're not dealing with our grief and we're denying ourselves some of the most valuable opportunities for the real integration and healing that could happen.

Even now, I still find that no-win trap is also present in the shame attached to making other people feel uncomfortable when I simply mention Lachlan or his death, but I also feel terrible about not acknowledging Lachlan simply to protect the other person's feelings. Even when an opportunity does present itself to be able to talk about Lachlan, the shame trap is often still there. I've felt shame in discussing his death in a way that might come across as too emotional or dramatic, but I've also felt it in not being emotional enough. A conversation with anyone who is not part of our innermost circle is a conversation that's ripe for feeling judged about the level of our emotional response. Too much emotion and we aren't dealing with it well, we aren't stable, and we don't have much emotional resilience. Not emotional enough, and we're considered cold, in shock, not dealing with our loss—or much worse, it might bring into question the depth of our love for our child.

I stumbled across a phrase that has helped tremendously in communicating to other people that there is more to the story than they can see. The phrase came from a lovely woman I met who had a transformative experience in the Peace Corp. When I asked her to tell me about her experience she said, "It's such a big experience that it's really hard to talk about." I took that immediately to understand that there was more to it than one conversation could hold. I knew that no matter what she felt up to telling me in that moment, the conversation would be vastly incomplete. I thought the phrase was brilliant, and took it for my own use in the conversations with people who are brave enough to ask me about Lachlan, but who are not close enough to me that they will ever have the opportunity to really understand the depths of my loss. When I start a conversation about Lachlan or his death by saying, *"The loss of a child is such a big experience that it's hard to talk about,"* I am telling them succinctly and clearly that there is way more under the surface than what can be shared in one conversation.

One of the most common questions for bereaved parents to wrestle with is how to answer when someone asks how many kids they have. Bereaved parents bump into this uncomfortable situation all the time. This question is in the lineup of first things to ask when we meet someone new: *How many kids do you have?* This shame-trap feeling is largely what makes it difficult to figure out how to answer the question. No matter how I answer, I feel awkward and uncomfortable.

If I answer that I have six kids, but don't define that I'm only raising five of them, I feel a bit of shame because my family doesn't operate as a household with six children. If I answer six, and qualify that one of them is deceased, then I incite that feeling of shame from making the other person uncomfortable. There is no surer way to bring a nice conversation to an awkward screeching halt than by mentioning my dead child. (A forced sympathetic reply is equally awkward.) If I answer that I have five kids, it feels like I am denying that my child ever existed, and there's shame in that, too. I have found no way to escape the discomfort when someone asks me how many kids I have.

The most helpful thing for me in the struggle with shame has been to simply identify what I am feeling. There is no way for me to completely avoid Shame, but I don't have to invite him in for dinner either. I can wave, acknowledge his presence, *"Hey, Shame, I see you,"* and then keep walking. It's easy to ruminate over these situations, stewing over what we should or shouldn't have said, and what the other person should or shouldn't have said. We kick ourselves or point fingers at other people, trying to assign blame for what felt awful and uncomfortable. Rumination has never helped me feel better nor has it helped me avoid feelings of shame the next time either.

Ignoring the feelings does not work. Shame can be pretty persistent and will keep tapping on our shoulder until we notice. Tap, tap. Tap, tap, tap. Shame is like a kid tapping at me while my attention is focused on something else. If I try to ignore the child, he keeps tapping or gets more aggressive and starts pulling at me. I find I react to that persistent tapping in one of two ways. Either I pretend the tapper is not there until I can't take it anymore and blow up, or I stop what I am doing momentarily to acknowledge the tapper, address the need, and send him on his way. The latter always works better for everyone involved. Shame is a tapper that needs to be acknowledged so he can be sent on his way. Don't worry, we have plenty of opportunities to try out this approach. Even if we've acknowledged and sent him on his way once, he'll be back.

GUILT: THE MASTER GARDENER

Guilt seems to be a very common opponent in the heart of almost every bereaved parent I've spoken with, regardless of their child's cause of death. Whether the death was actually connected to some parental oversight or not, guilt gets its turn in the boxing ring. Each parent has a unique set of things that contribute to their feelings of guilt. These tend to be things we wish we had done differently, words we said or didn't say, or things we didn't recognize in time to save our child. Some of us have bigger giants of guilt to face than others, but however big the giant, the fight is unavoidable.

The moments that I missed with Lachlan were what prompted the most guilt for me. Through most of Lachlan's life, I wrestled with working-mom guilt. I was not at peace with the amount of time I spent working. I felt like my kids were being raised by child care staff more than by me. I argued to myself that it was temporary, and that I needed my job to support our family while David was going to school. With this arrangement, a large portion of our family time was at the end of our long, busy days, when David and I were both tired, and the kids were whiny because they, too, were tired and hungry. I would race home from work to feed them and put them to bed, not getting nearly enough day-to-day time to sit and enjoy my boys.

Working, in itself, is not something to feel guilty about. It can even be argued that we have a moral obligation to work (which includes caring for our families and any kind of volunteer efforts). Work is how we provide for our families and have the financial means to take care of the people we love. The trick with work is finding the right balance because, while the financial means to take care of our families is important, it is also important to be present to the people we love. It is easy to chase the dreams of what we could do with more money, higher positions, or more influence, while we slide the importance of being present to our families to the back burner. Dwight Eisenhower spoke to this idea when he said, "Most things which are urgent are not important, and most things which are important are not urgent." Why is it easier to tell our families we won't be there because our boss needs us than to tell our bosses we won't be there because our families need us?

How often do we step back and evaluate our work-life balance and whether our current job is what's *really* in the best interest of our family? It's easy to justify how and why working more can help take care of our physical needs—we can provide a better home, better school, better food, better clothes. We can go on vacations and retire early. For me, I was in a place where I was driven by wanting to establish a career, to meet and exceed the expectations of coworkers, and to minimize our school loan debt, which would set David and me up for a lifetime of better financial freedom.

Even though I was nudged by feelings of guilt that my work-life balance was off, I ignored them. When Lach died, the consequence of ignoring that tug was a hard and startling slap in the face. All at once I saw what I had missed. The reality was that I had missed so much of my child's life for the pursuit of money and status. I would have been happy to chip away at that student debt for a lifetime to have spent more time present to my boys. Instead of being a useful tool to my employers, I would rather be known and seen, truly and deeply, by the people who love me no matter how much money I make. I would rather be available to make my kids feel known and seen than make the extra money needed to send them to a nicer daycare. My guilt in my work choices comes from not taking the time to *really* evaluate what was of the deepest importance to David and me, and how we could improve the way we were living that out.

> *There are two kinds of guilt: the kind that drowns you until you're useless, and the kind that fires your soul to purpose.*
>
> SABAA TAHIR[2]

I also feel guilt and regret about my lack of presence in the moments that I did have with Lachlan. He didn't sleep well and when he was up during the night, I did not appreciate that quiet time together. I was frustrated and annoyed, anxious that my lack of sleep was going to make the next day that much harder to get through. I was impatient and just wanted him to go back to bed. Now, in his absence, I would give anything to be up all night with him in my arms, breathing in deeply the scent of him as he nestled into my shoulder.

I am especially plagued by my lack of presence in his final morning here. That day, I behaved as I normally did, with my primary focus being on where I had to go and what I had to do next, rather than who I was with. That particular morning stings because it was my final opportunity with him and I missed it. I sat nursing him that last time feeling rushed to get out the door, and annoyed that he was more interested in watching Westin run around than in the job at hand. I barely said goodbye as I darted out the door. If only we could have some do-overs. I would have hugged him like I meant it, planted a kiss on his forehead as if I wanted it to stick there all day long, and I would have told him how very much I loved him. I realize it is not feasible to live every moment as if it were the last time we'll see the people we love, but I do think it is feasible to be more present to them on a day-to-day basis.

Guilt, while an uncomfortable feeling, is a healthy and helpful feeling that is meant to prompt us to change. Guilt is not the opponent, but the messenger that shows us where there is pruning to be done. The people around us can often try to brush away and deny these feelings of guilt: "Don't feel guilty, there was nothing you could do." "It wasn't your fault." "It was only an accident." And while all of that may be true, denying the feelings of guilt often serves to exaggerate them more than diffuse them. Dr. Joanne Cacciatore, a champion of grief advocacy, explains: "Many bereaved people struggle with issues of guilt and shame. This is particularly true in cases of traumatic grief and, especially, when a child dies or when one person is directly responsible for another person's death. Just the process of staying present with shame and guilt in a safe space can help to neutralize those emotions' potency. In such a place, we can abandon the need to judge feelings as *right* or *wrong*, *good* or *bad*. This alone has the power to diffuse and dilute them."[3] Having a safe space to process and to talk about where and how we feel guilty about the circumstances of our child's death, without being denied those feelings, is important in bringing them down to size.

If we allow ourselves to recognize where guilt is coming up, we can then allow those feelings to inspire us to grow. Guilt can prompt us to live in a more integrated way, slowly coming to resemble the person we really want to be. However, we also have to be aware that we can misuse our guilt as a weapon to relentlessly beat ourselves with.

Ultimately, my experiences with the guilt attached to my grief have led me to live in a different way than many of the people around me. I often feel like I'm working against the grain of culture in how I choose to go about my work-life balance. I still want to be excellent in my work, but I have created much clearer boundaries around when I am available to do that work. This has meant that I put significant time and effort into contemplating the idea that a job is just that—a job. I will give 100 percent while I'm on the job, but I now remember that the work is primarily the means to an end, not the end itself. If the schedule and the demands are not a good fit for my family's needs, then I must be willing to walk away, even from work that I love, in search of something that fully supports what is most important to me.

The guilt I have experienced about my lack of presence during Lachlan's life continues to be a driving force in my desire to improve my ability to be present to the people around me. Every single moment is dripping with goodness, truth, and beauty which are just waiting to come into our awareness and it is up to us to direct our minds to be still and notice this beauty in the present moment. In order to really be present to this beauty, I have to constantly wrestle against daily distractions and the fear of what I might realize about myself when I listen in the silence. This battle for presence might be a never-ending one, but I want to be intentional and grow in my ability to sit, to wonder, and to breathe in the presence of the people I love, and to always remember that the time we will share on earth is limited.

Taming Anger

Another big and dark emotion to contend with is anger. This is one of the five stages of grief identified by Elisabeth Kübler-Ross in her 1969 book *On Death and Dying*. Her work was groundbreaking and opened a door of valuable insight into the commonalities of emotion in the grief experience. One of the primary criticisms that she received was that grief did not happen in neat and orderly stages as her theory seemed to describe. This was not the intent of the model. The "stages" described are simply meant to be understood as pillars or touchstones of common experience and emotion in grief.

The emotion of anger can often show up before we even know why we're angry. We feel that strong emotion and then, in natural human thinking patterns, we start looking for places to direct that anger. Sometimes, we are angry at the health care teams that we believe should have been able to intervene in a different way to prevent the death. Our anger might be directed toward the people who were closest to the child when he died, and in our natural tendency for magical thinking we feel like they should have seen, or known, or been able to prevent the death by the knowledge that has only been gained in hindsight. Sometimes there is true fault, and that creates a whole separate realm of difficult emotions to work through. God, too, is often the recipient of our anger that is searching for a place to land. Sometimes our anger is justified. Other times, if we break it down, the natural anger that we feel in our grief is landing on others unjustly.

My first and most direct feelings of anger were toward the officer who prevented me from entering the daycare, the team who took Lachlan out the back door and out of the facility without my consent or knowledge, the daycare staff who didn't initiate CPR the instant they found him unresponsive, and the team of detectives who were limiting the access to our boy. As we went, I found myself wrestling with anger toward the friends who did not respond like I thought they would or weren't as supportive as I needed them to be. My primary and longest-lasting anger was toward God for "taking" my baby away from me.

My husband has been the best teacher for me in being able to work through my feelings of anger. David has an almost unnatural ability to put himself in the shoes of others and then look at the world through their lens. When I take a moment to do that, it isn't hard to see that people are probably not being inconsiderate, rude, hurtful, or incompetent on purpose.

When I consider the role of the officer, his job was to protect the perimeter of the daycare. When a death occurs in a daycare setting, the police have to be particularly cautious to correctly follow all the protocols and directions in case there is foul play. He was probably directed by a supervisor that he was to let no one into the building until it was cleared. The officer wasn't trying to add to my agony. He was trying to protect all the other children in the facility, to keep the space clear so the medical team could do their job, and to prevent any interference with the investigation that would need to take place. The detectives probably had been called to other cases when the death of a child *was* the result of foul play. Their primary job is to protect the community and to be able to investigate thoroughly and accurately. When I put myself in their shoes, I saw the chances are high that they weren't trying to make it harder for me either. Their goal would have been to be thorough and accurate to make sure that the daycare facility was a safe place for children.

The investigative team probably gave direction to the medical team for Lachlan's body to be brought to the hospital for a thorough medical exam before he could be released to us. As far as the daycare staff not initiating CPR immediately, I realized that too could depend on the circumstance. The way we respond to an unresponsive person who is still warm and flaccid is different than how we respond to a body that is clearly deceased. There was really no place for blame or anger at the medical or daycare teams either.

When I push myself to see God through that same lens, I can find perspectives and an understanding there too that makes room for His goodness in a world where people—even children—die. This wrestling with God is a big enough issue to be worthy of a whole chapter of its own—or maybe even a book.

We often think of anger as a negative emotion and something that nice people shouldn't feel. But anger is a natural part of the human experience. There is nothing wrong with having feelings of anger. This big emotion, when used rightly, fuels us to search through and identify problems and then drives us to make them right. Anger is an emotion that helps us make sense of what went wrong.

> *I sat with my anger long enough until she told me her real name was grief.*
>
> C. S. LEWIS

We do need to handle our anger with extreme caution. If we don't pause to reflect on these feelings and give ourselves space to tame the rage, then we may add insult to injury. We don't want to create more pain by firing hurtful and unjust comments and actions toward others. We can grow in our mastery of this emotion by using it to fuel big questions and drive the righting of wrongs, by digging deep to understand where it is rooted, and by deciding what to do with it only after the rage is tamed.

Doing Away with Comparisons of Pain

Grief is a time that we especially need a community around us, and there is nothing that causes feelings of separation more than *comparison*. Comparison is a thief of joy and drives an impenetrable division between us and those around us. When we are comparing our pain to the pain of others we become disengaged from the people around us. We begin arguing to ourselves that no one can possibly understand what we are going through, so rather than building connection we create deeper isolation.

The death of a child is often spoken about as "the ultimate loss." Grief therapist David Kessler told a story of his own encounter with losing a child and the realization that this kind of loss cannot be truly understood until it is experienced personally. He had lived through several of his own big losses, including the loss of his mother as a child, but in regard to the death of his son, he shared:

> I have two sons, and I was lecturing on the east coast and got a call that my younger son had died. It is the worst call you can ever get, at least it was for me... I couldn't believe it. I got home and canceled everything, and just tried to survive. It was just so heartbreaking... I was putzing around just trying to survive, and breathe, and figure out what to do. The pain was so great ... I've had a career, *forty* years of counseling parents... I wanted to write them all a note and say, "I had no idea how bad your pain was."[4]

While the loss of a child brings a grief that is in a league of its own, it doesn't have to be a loss that separates us from the rest of humanity. Thus, I have a love-hate relationship with the idea of "the ultimate loss."

On one hand, the phrase "ultimate loss" validates the depth of this pain. In the first years after Lachlan's death, I wanted (and maybe even needed), to defend my loss as being the worst thing that could happen to someone. It helped me to know that it was okay that I wasn't okay. The loss was an extraordinarily heavy burden and my grief is one that not everyone can understand. Viewing my loss as an "ultimate loss" helped it feel more acceptable that it was taking me a really long time to get my bearings and helped me grasp that there was a good reason for me to never feel like the same person again. It also helped me understand that while all grief is important, it is not all the same.

Even amongst other bereaved parents, I still found ways to let comparisons create walls between me and the people who could have been my greatest sources of support. I couldn't see outside the walls of my own suffering and pain. For a while, in a contraction of grief, I latched onto thinking that my loss was worse than others'.

I reasoned that my loss was worse than other infant deaths because Lachlan had lived with us for nearly a year, and our lives were intimately integrated with his. He was old enough that his personality was starting to blossom, yet he hadn't lived long enough for me to learn what that would actually look like, or to discover which things he would love to do.

Parents who lost an older child, I told myself, had many memories to hold onto. Their child was independent enough that they probably had parts of their day that felt normal without their child's presence. Lachlan was still a baby and I was intimately involved in all his cares. I thought about what he needed 24 hours a day and actively made those things happen for him. When he died, there was no part of my day, awake or asleep, that was untouched by his absence. The only thing that could be worse than *my* loss, I thought, would be losing more than one child. When I allowed myself to diminish the losses of others, I also inhibited my capacity for connection.

The insolent thoughts that minimized the painful experiences of others were followed by pangs of shame. I didn't want others to minimize my grief, yet I found myself with thoughts that minimized theirs. *How would I ever find space in my heart to hold the painful stories of others without putting them on the chopping block of comparison?*

When I was experiencing those thoughts that elevated my own

experience of pain, while minimizing the losses of others, I wouldn't have dared to admit that out loud. It was a self-centered way of thinking, and part of my heart knew that. Now, I can step into the vulnerability that comes with admitting to those thoughts because I know that this self-centeredness is part of the natural contraction and expansion of grief.

We cannot stay in the contraction forever, but we must draw inward to understand the uniqueness of our grief before we can turn outward and be ready to hold space for the stories of others. Ultimately, this phase of comparisons was a valuable stage in my growth. These comparisons helped me define and understand the things that were unique to my grief and were the deep points of my pain. Though there were benefits to making a pit-stop for comparisons, it wasn't a place I could stay if I wanted to grow in my ability to love others and connect to people in meaningful ways.

Your suffering only matters if it connects you to the suffering of others, if it heals them too.

GEOFFREY WOOD[5]

Clinging to this idea of "the ultimate loss" on one side of the coin validated some of my experience, but on the flip side, those words were a root to the comparisons that were building walls and separating me from the rest of humanity. If I was going to live my intention of a life of love, joy, and connection with the people around me, I was going to have to tear those walls down.

Shifting my perspective on this took me a lot of time and reflection. When we're in the hole of our own grief, it is impossible to see anything but the walls that make up that hole. It is not until we dig ourselves out and stand on the surface with the rest of humanity again that we see those holes are everywhere. The holes are different sizes and shapes, but they appear throughout the landscape. Pain, suffering, and loss are universal experiences. All we have to do to experience them is live long enough. I have learned by observing with curiosity and an open heart that each loss is wholly unique, with some parts that make it harder to bear than other losses and some parts that make it easier.

Now, I can honestly say I am grateful that I did not have to watch my child suffer through a long illness and agonizing medical treatments. I am grateful that his death was not a preventable accident or at the hands of someone else. If I had been given the task to choose the cause of death for my child, I would have chosen for him to pass away just as he did—peacefully in his sleep.

There is a family I know and love whose daughter died of a brain cancer. One day as we were exchanging stories they expressed how horrible it must have been for us to have experienced Lachlan's death without any notion that it was coming; while I, on the other hand, was able to witness their agony of having to walk through a long journey filled with many uncertainties and painful medical treatments.

Every single loss is unique in its pains and its consolations. Rather than clinging to our differences, I find it more helpful to respect and honor those differences in a space that's free of comparison. If I look for the common experiences and the threads that overlap, I find my heart welling up with feelings of empathy, connection, and love. With time, and in the natural movement of post-traumatic growth and expansion, I have been able to open my heart to human suffering in a much wider array of experiences. I am again capable of feeling empathy for the life challenges that others are facing. That empathy was not possible when I was clinging to the idea that "my suffering is worse than yours."

Until I learned that comparison is a common pattern for those who grieve, I felt like there was something wrong with the selfishness of my response. Dr. Joanne Cacciatore points out from her experience of leading support groups: "People often initially attend a group seeking another person whose story closely resembles their own. They want an image of self in some other. Even so, many experience a gradual softening of the heart toward those whose stories are different. And the ability to expand our sense of empathic connection grows."[6] With time and a slowly growing openness to the hearts of other sufferers, our ability to connect to stories that are different from our own grows, and with it, our capacity for true empathy and meaningful connection.

I have slowly grown in my ability to bear witness and honor the suffering that is different from mine. I have not had to struggle through a marriage that is falling apart and wrestle with how to guide my children through adjustments of a broken home. I have never had to watch my child suffer through extensive medical treatments and illness. I have not been betrayed in situations of physical or sexual abuse, or felt the hopelessness of addiction or the helplessness and frustration of infertility. I haven't had to bury the spouse I planned to grow old with. I haven't had to suffer from any major physical illness of my own or had to face a terminal diagnosis. The list goes on and on. Many have to suffer silently because their struggles are not socially acceptable to admit or talk about.

The more I have reflected on my initial feelings of having experienced the "ultimate loss," the more I realize how unfair that assessment might really be. I expected to raise Lachlan and then send him off to spread his wings, with hopes that he'd live close enough that David and I could see him and his family on a regular basis. If I pause to consider what it would mean for my life if I had buried my husband instead, I see that I would have said goodbye to the person I expected to come home to every night for the rest of my life, well beyond the next 18 years, to the person God gave me to share the joys and sorrows of living with, to the person who is my security, my primary support, my teammate, my traveling buddy, the father of my children. With a little more readiness to look at a different situation openly, it's hard to say that one loss is worse than the other. They're simply different.

My suffering is something I can talk about. Many people suffer alone and in shame: twisted and broken relationships; drug, alcohol, or sexual addictions; mental illness; feelings of worthlessness and hopelessness; shameful mistakes that were made in the past. Many live with these things and suffer silently, being unable or unwilling to reach out to other people for help. Upon learning of these kinds of struggles, people don't generally bring a casserole and swoop in to offer their support. Rather, the sufferer often finds himself ostracized and estranged more than loved and supported in their quest for healing and recovery.

Even now, on days that I start to feel sorry for myself, and feel some sort of entitlement to sympathy, I am slapped in the face by another terribly tragic story that puts my perspective back in its proper place. There is no real "ultimate" loss. There is only suffering from different experiences and circumstances with different battles to be fought and won. We could ask almost any person we meet to tell us the hardest things they have been through, and our hearts would be broken by the stories we would hear. Suffering is part of the human experience. A willingness to soften to this idea is a willingness to share in meaningful encounters with the people around us.

Eliminating Bitterness Toward Others

Holding onto our comparisons of pain extends to create a generalized bitterness toward so many people. This is something that I hated feeling. Bitterness is a coldness and judgment toward others and it was turning me into exactly the person I didn't want to be. I stewed and was upset by everyday ordinary things that people did.

If other people were short with their kids, or appeared unkind to them in any way, I was angry and frustrated. If parents complained about a tough day or tough moment with their kids, I wanted to put them in their place by reminding them how lucky they were to have their child alive. Hearing people complain about *anything* was extraordinarily grating and I wished whatever they were complaining about could be the worst thing of my day, too. *How could they not see how petty those things were and let them go?!* These feelings of bitterness popped up all over the place and were one of the hardest parts for me in stepping back into the world.

As my sufferings mounted I soon realized that there were two ways that I could respond to my situation: either to react with bitterness or seek to transform the suffering into a creative force. I decided to follow the latter course.

MARTIN LUTHER KING JR.

Bitterness was part of the comparison pit-stop. Frustration with the ordinary complaints of others helped me see how much and how often we tend to complain about insignificant things. While there was something good in that recognition of petty complaining, I could also feel the wedge it was creating in my ability to be open-hearted toward others. I didn't want to be upset with everyone who, in a normal way, expressed their frustrations about something hard in their lives. Just because their struggle wasn't the death of a child, didn't mean that it wasn't something uncomfortable or difficult.

Emotions are neither good nor bad. They just are. We have very little control over what we feel. What we do have control over is how we respond and what we decide to do with those feelings. I had the option to continue to justify my feelings, separating myself from the people around me, or I could take control of my self-talk, and remind myself that we are all humans in different places in life, who experience pains and frustrations in a lot of little ways. Even though I had a primary pain that drowned out almost every other discomfort, I knew that I, too, still experienced those littler discomforts, and that one day, those little things might feel bigger to me again.

Over the years that bitterness has faded. For me, it didn't change because of some sudden "aha" moment. The change was a product of time coupled with a desire to become more empathetic to even the little discomforts of others. Our human hearts hold a tangle of good and evil, or in this case, bitterness and love. Bitterness is a weed that will choke out love if we let it. We have the power to make intentional choices that will keep our little resentments in check. When we are willing to recognize where we are feeling bitterness we can start weeding it away. As we work to prune away bitterness we create space to let love grow to its full potential.

Cutting Back Our Desire to Control

I am slowly learning that trying to control things that are not really mine to control is just a way of trying to protect myself from pain. If we feel some sense of control, no matter how falsely that is, we are trying to prevent ourselves from feeling our vulnerability. Then, when we find we're vulnerable anyway, we are not only wounded, we are also shocked and horrified that the wound was even possible.

This aim to surrender my sense of control, and in doing so, learning to open myself to uncertainty and vulnerability, was one of the hardest things for me to work through after Lach's death. One of the places I particularly noticed this struggle for control was in how to parent my living children.

Especially in the first year after Lachlan's death, I had wild swings in how much control I was trying to hold onto. There were times that I worried myself excessively about every tiny thing, aiming to micromanage and helicopter parent in an attempt to control the environment and minimize the risk of anything bad happening. That was exhausting for me, and it didn't feel healthy for the kids either.

One moment in particular sent my sense of control into a tailspin. Westin and I were home together, and I needed to jump in the shower. Typically, if there were cartoons on, he would reliably sit and not budge for extended periods of time—more than enough time for me to rinse off. On this day, I turned on the TV and took a quick shower. When I turned the water off, I heard unusual sounds coming from Westin and hustled out to check on him. I found that he had climbed up the back of the couch to the shelving ledge on the wall, had wrapped the cord from the window blinds around his neck, and had it pulled so tight he was struggling to get free.

I was horrified. I was still reeling from the death of one child, and another had nearly hung himself on our window blinds. I had to work a little to free him from the tangle. Westin was fine aside from the rope-burn on his neck. I, on the other hand, was not so fine. I had heard stories of children injuring themselves, or worse, with window blind cords, and I had minimized that risk to the best of my ability. I had followed recommendations and cut the cords as short as possible to still allow them to function, and yet even in a controlled environment with safety precautions in place, and in only a few minutes without direct supervision, my child was in a potentially life-threatening situation. My efforts to control could not protect him.

So then the pendulum swung the other way (probably in attitude more than in actual practice). I saw clearly that I have very little control over how this life plays out. I can do everything right, and my child can still die. There's no way a parent can directly supervise their children 100% of the time. Every parent who has left the room to come back and find new crayon artwork on their walls or the entire roll of toilet paper strung out knows that. I thought, if my efforts to control every tiny thing weren't going to prevent tragedy, why bother with worry and diligence at all? My child could get cancer no matter what I do. I could glance the other way, and he could dash into the road to be hit by a car. And then there are the parents who do not make many efforts to follow standard safety recommendations, and their kids grow up just fine. So, I would think: *Why bother trying? Fate seems to be random acts of the cosmos anyway.* The pendulum of control swung back and forth many times, from hyper-control to throwing all desire for control to the wind.

The battle for control also showed up in deciding whether to have more children. For me, the control was centered on a fear of having to live through a loss like this again. For other parents, the battle for control may be in the desire to have more children quickly to bring the gift of life back into their lives as soon as possible.

Life is to be lived, not controlled; and humanity is won by continuing to play in face of certain defeat.

RALPH ELLISON[7]

I laugh at myself a little bit now, and at my desperation to control and calculate risk. But the threat of living through another loss and the uncertainty that comes with bringing life into the world was very real to me. David and I had always dreamed of having a big family. But after Lach died, I was petrified to put my heart on the line again. The more children I had, the more likely that another one of them could die, and I would have to live through this hell again. I wasn't sure I could ever dare to put myself in that position. It didn't matter if they died as babies or as elderly people. Parents aren't supposed to bury their children. I searched for statistics that would tell me the odds of a child dying before their parents. I could never find one. I resorted to scouring obituaries to find out whether the deceased was "preceded in death" or "survived by" their parents in order to calculate my own statistics. That didn't prove to be particularly helpful for me either.

Slowly, the swings of the pendulum became less wild as I navigated my way through this new world of uncertainty—this world that was making a point to show me that I did not have as much control as I thought, or wanted. As I spent time wrestling with learning what is mine to control and what is not, I began to find more peace.

I settled in with an understanding that there is a reasonable level of prudence and safety that is wise. We can't throw all caution to the wind just because the people we love could die even when we aim to control every tiny thing. On the flip side, it is equally ridiculous to stifle the experience of living, to never take a risk, to avoid adventure, essentially placing ourselves and our families in a prison of caution trying to escape the inescapable fact of our human mortality.

What has been helpful for me in finding a balance is asking myself, "If the worst happens, and someone dies, will I be able to look back at the situation and know that I did my best with what I knew in the moment?" People we love will die. When they do, will I be able to grieve with some level of peace, knowing that I couldn't have changed the outcome with what I knew at the time? This question helps me to make standard, sensible, and prudent choices, even when they are hard—but pulls me back from being so cautious that we can't live full and rich lives.

As far as daring to have other children despite the risk, I eventually came around to embracing the fact that the love and experience of being Lachlan's mom was worth all the pain that I experienced with his death. Since that was truly how I felt about the experience with him, I knew that it would be true with other children too. Yes, there would be unavoidable risk and uncertainty, but there would be enough love to make it worth the risk. For Lachlan's birth announcement, we chose a quote by Elizabeth Stone: "Making the decision to have a child—it's momentous. It is to decide forever to have your heart go walking around outside your body." In his death, that risk became reality. Yet, in that risk, I experienced a love that I know with certainty transcends even death.

Our desire, impulse, obsession, and drive to control ultimately comes from an intolerance for uncertainty. Human nature is repulsed by the uncertainty that comes with living, but if we want to harness our desire to control the uncontrollable and live with peaceful hearts, we must find a way to leave space in our lives for uncertainty. Author Jacques Philippe states: "We find it difficult to do this, because we feel a natural revulsion for situations we cannot control. But the fact is *that the situations that really make us grow are precisely those we do not control.*"[8]

If we can't find a peaceful space for that uncertainty, we will always be fighting anxiety, fear, and the need to control. The reality is that to live this life means to live in a world full of uncertainty. When we dare to peer into the circumstances of our existence, we see that our environment, our relationships, our careers, our health, the movements of our emotions, and our very lives have no guarantees. Any of those things can change drastically in an instant.

Recognizing where I was striving to control things that weren't mine to control has done wonders in helping me loosen my grip and open my hands to be ready to receive the people and experiences around me. When I am not clinging to control I feel more freedom to appreciate what I have in the moment and to find a little more ease in my way of moving through the world.

Pruning Judgment and Expectation

Grief is an unbelievably lonely journey. It is one that must be done in our own way, in our own time, dealing with our own issues and pains, one at a time. While we can connect with others in meaningful ways by sharing our experiences, our thoughts, and our needs, we can never share the entirety of it. This leaves a deep chasm of internal experience that is untouched by the world around us. And that can feel very lonely.

Just as we want other people to be open to us and our pain, to hear without judgment, and to trust our intuitions about what we need to get through our grief, we also have to extend that courtesy to the other people in our lives who are also grieving. This can be so hard to do.

Emotions are raw, we are hanging on by a thread, and we are getting through each day in the only way we know how. That naturally limits our capacity to be open and understanding with other people. Yet, if we don't stretch ourselves by trying to be gentle and understanding with others, we are likely to add relationship turmoil to the pain of our grief.

When we are in the trenches of grief, we naturally develop personal and strong convictions about how grieving and mourning need to be done, what is helpful and what is not, what constitutes "dealing with it" and what constitutes grief avoidance. In deep grief, we have our own new and acute needs that force us to lean on the people around us and we have an expectations that others will step up to meet our needs.

Sometimes the needs of our spouses, our parents, and our closest family members are different from our own. Our loved ones are not always willing or able to meet the expectations we have for them. These conditions are ripe for conflict, frustration, and resentment. As I navigated these feelings, it first helped to be intentional and mindful about giving other people the benefit of the doubt. Relationships were a little better when I started with the assumption that the other person was exactly where they needed to be. If I took a moment and imagined God Himself whispering in my ear that they were really doing the best that they could, I found myself instantly setting my boxing gloves aside.

When we let go of all expectation, there is peace.

KIM ENG

I often longed for David to be in the same place I was and to approach every challenge in the same way I did. I wanted him to see and to meet all my needs. That is too much to ask of a grieving person. Our relationship was better when I learned to share what we could of our experiences, but to leave room for him to have his own ways, his own needs, and his own methods. Our differences in needs have shown up in how much to talk about Lachlan's death, how much time to spend alone or with others, how quickly to go back to work, whether counseling is helpful, and which mourning rituals bring comfort.

From within, we know we are working through our grief in the best way we know how, even when it is messy and ugly. We know we don't get it right all the time, but our grief is foreign and terribly difficult terrain. We want the people in our life to support and encourage us with gentleness and without judgment. We will often get closer to those kinds of interactions if we make our best efforts to communicate openly, leave space for different styles of grieving, and know with confidence that there are many paths to finding healthy integration of this loss into our lives.

It was helpful for me to leave room for other people to screw up too. Seeing us grieve so intensely is an enormous and helpless pain for the people who love us. It is easy, when we are overwhelmed with huge, ripe emotions, to have even our best intentions come out wrong and end up being more hurtful than helpful.

In my grief, one of my battles was to fight that interior voice wanting to point fingers and assign blame. I had to learn to quiet the voice that says things like, "Why can't they just be like this?" "Why won't they just do that?" "Why can't they just be the x, y, or z that I need?" "I don't think they're grieving the way they should . . ." The list goes on. In this battle, I had to see how I might be wrong in my own judgments and expectations of the people, recognizing that my way may not be the only *right* way.

We've heard the saying, "*Expectation is the root of all heartache.*" I had to learn to keep the expectations I had for others in check, remembering that most frustrations and resentments stem from unmet expectations. It was helpful as I learned to communicate clearly and gently, and then be willing to expand my circle of support to find other people who could fill in the gaps where I still had needs to be met. This does not mean we can't challenge someone about their methods. I *want* the people who love me to suggest other ideas to help me grieve. When they do, I also want them to understand that I may not be ready to give their suggestion a try, or I might completely disagree with their assessment. If that is how I want others to approach me, it is reasonable for me to approach others in the same way. In pruning our judgments and expectations of others, we not only improve our own experience of healing, we also take care of the people we love by allowing them to grieve and mourn in the ways that best meet their own needs.

8

Becoming Friends with the Enemy

Do I not destroy my enemies when I make them my friends?

ABRAHAM LINCOLN

While there are many battles in this grief journey to be actively fought and won, there are other elements in this arena that cannot be fought into submission. I hated these parts of my new existence, but nonetheless were here to stay. At first, they felt like huge barriers that I would never be able to work around. It's a funny thing though, that as I learned to let them be, to stop fighting them, to stop judging and berating myself for experiencing them, and to extend myself grace, compassion, and understanding, these barriers began to shrink to a manageable size.

Ten primary enemies felt like insurmountable challenges, and I grappled with them fiercely but could never strong-arm them into defeat. These enemies required me to accept their presence in my arena.

1. The question of *What if?*
2. Wondering *Why me?*
3. The unknowns surrounding death
4. Wishing I could know what my child would be like now
5. The presence of uncertainty
6. Post-traumatic memories
7. The threat of tears
8. A lifetime of secondary losses

9. Knowing that memories fade
10. The emptiness of time and space

What If

Every bereaved parent I know has faced the opponent of *What If?* in the arena of grief. Our minds tend to ruminate on every possible real or imagined scenario that might have prevented the death from occurring. Lachlan's diagnosis was SIDS (Sudden Infant Death Syndrome), a diagnosis that is made only after a thorough medical and environmental review reveals no apparent cause of death. SIDS is a terrible and misfortunate thing and there is no known way to predict or prevent those deaths. By medical exam there was no fault to anyone, but I still had feelings that led me to wonder if I could have changed the outcome. *What If?* still found a place in my battlefield. My thoughts were plagued by that unanswerable question. My mind raced constantly with the things that I could have, or should have, seen or known—or just intuitively felt by motherly instinct—that may have prevented Lachlan's death.

I thought: *What if Lachlan's death was associated with swings in stress hormones due to the emotionally and verbally abusive nanny we had just fired? What if his cold was more serious than I thought? What if his death was due to something metabolic that I should have noticed as he was being introduced to new foods? What if it was related to the food allergies we had recently discovered? What if it was a heart arrhythmia that could have been detected and prevented? What if I had gone to the daycare to pick him up when I considered it earlier that morning? What if going to get him would have interrupted that nap before he died? If I had listened to that hunch to go, maybe I could have prevented his death. I thought that breathing monitors and sensors were an expensive Band-Aid for high anxiety moms and were unnecessary, but what if he had had an alarm that would have indicated the problem as it was happening? Would that have opened up an opportunity for medical interventions to actually make a difference? Aren't moms supposed to have some sort of sixth sense that gives them an acute awareness of their child's well-being? Wasn't I supposed to sense in some way that my child's soul was leaving his body? Why didn't I have that?*

The what-if game is mentally exhausting and its presence is largely beyond our control. The list of real and imagined what-if questions can be long, and there is no way to answer any of them with certainty. Yet, with our human despise for uncertainty and natural unwillingness to rest in the unknown, our minds continue to run scenario after scenario on endless repeat, searching for answers that we will never find.

This abrasive enemy slowly began to shrink in size when I realized that the questions are a completely natural process. Endless what-if questions weren't surfacing because I could have changed the circumstance or did something wrong. It was just a natural part of grieving. Once I understood that I wasn't crazy for having these thoughts over and over, I was less judgmental about it and started to simply let them be. When my thoughts began to play the what-if game, rather than fighting myself and my thoughts or believing they were going to lead me to an answer that would satisfy my heart, I just let them run their course and trail off, as they always did, into the unknown.

> *There are simply no answers to some of the great pressing questions.*
>
> BARRY LOPEZ[1]

Once that string of what-if questions had run its course, I would find closure to that run of thoughts by reminding myself that I would have gone to the ends of the world, and even given my own life, to change the outcome. If there could have been any way for me to know, predict, or prevent what was going to happen, I would have done anything in my power to keep my baby alive. *I did the best I could with the information I had available to me at the time.*

In talking to other bereaved parents, I learned that this reassurance is helpful in many circumstances surrounding a child's death. It is helpful to the parents who fought with their teen shortly before she took her own life. It helps the parents who lost their child to cancer, wondering what they could have done differently to change the outcome. It helps the parents whose three-year-old snuck out through the doggy door while he was supposed to be napping and drowned in the backyard pool. It helps the parents of the child who died suddenly after a short viral illness, wondering why they didn't bring her to the doctor sooner, or why they didn't push for more intervention, even when by all outward appearances she seemed to have an ordinary viral bug. All these parents would have gone to the ends of the world and exchanged their own lives to keep their children safe. But they did the only thing that any of us can do: the best we can with the information we have available at the time.

The unanswerable what-if questions are uncomfortable to rest in, but rest can eventually come through the reassurance that we did the best we could with the information we had. Hindsight is always 20/20, and it is not a fair fight to blame ourselves for things we did not know at the time.

Though uncertainty will always remain in whether we could have done anything different to prevent our child from dying, we can rest in the certainty of our love. We can rest knowing in our heart-of-hearts that we would have given *anything* to change the outcome if that power had been given to us.

WHY?

Why? is a close cousin to *What if?* The questions of *Why?* stream just as quickly and often. We are hardwired to find meaning in the circumstances around us. Our brains fill in the gaps of information with stories that create meaning.

That instinctual search for meaning occurs in even the normal and everyday life events. Whether we hear a story on the news or through the rumor mill, or have an awkward interaction with someone we know, our minds immediately start working to create backstory, context, and underlying intentions. As humans, we can create elaborate stories to fill in the gaps in our knowledge. We seek to eliminate uncertainty, usually without having any conscious realization that we are doing it. We don't like to be left with any uncertainties and when our thoughts are left to their own devices, we are often quick in our attempts to eliminate the unknowns.

Even little kids will develop stories to create meaning from their experiences. Since the time Lachlan died, we have had many discussions with Westin about how we don't know why Lachlan died. His body just stopped working. One day, when Westin was about five, I found him sitting in the living room, staring intently at a picture of Lachlan. When I asked him what he was thinking, he said with some level of confidence: "Mom, I think I know why Lachlan died. Do you see that little red spot under his eye? I think it has something to do with that."

Westin's little brain was searching for clues to explain why his brother died. I had to break it to him, that while he made a good observation, the red spot wasn't why Lachlan died. The spot was there because a tear duct wasn't open yet and the constant drainage and wiping had irritated his skin. My little five-year-old boy had to settle back into the loathsome feeling of uncertainty. We writhe in our own uncertainty, and that pain is amplified when we can't spare our children from that discomfort either.

This need to assign meaning or cause is often the root of hurtful things that are said to bereaved parents. People want to pin down what was different about the situation that caused the death of the child. By assigning certainty where there is none, it is easy to create a false sense of security to protect our hearts from feeling the vulnerability and fragility of life. It's this inability to sit with uncertainty that makes people want to "reassure" us that "God has a plan for everything"—a statement that is usually anything but helpful to those who are living in the throes of the deepest pain imaginable. *I'm not sure I want a God who "plans" such horrendous pain.*

I must have asked myself a million times: *Why me? Why him? Why us? Why now? Was this some sort of slap from God because I wasn't as good a person as I thought I was? Maybe I needed to suffer to pay for my sins. What did we do to deserve this? Did God do this just for the good that can come from it? Was Lachlan being saved from some greater pain later in life? Was his life's purpose already complete? If he was going to die in his sleep, why didn't it happen when he was two to four months old like most other SIDS babies? Why? Why? Why?*

> *To ask the right question is already half the solution of a problem.*
>
> C.G. JUNG

Over time, I began to figure out that these questions were not helping me. There were no answers to any of them, and in the way I was framing these questions, they were only amplifying my pain. Rather than continuing to ask, *Why me?* I started to pose a new question, *Why not me?*

With that, the hole of my grief began to slowly open up. This new question helped me see that I was not singled out as the only one to experience such a painful loss. Mothers have had to bury their children from the beginning of time. Some cultures delayed naming a baby until well after birth because the infant mortality rates were so high. Across history, more than one-fourth of babies died before they reached their first birthdays, and almost half of all children died before they reached adulthood. Even as recently as 1960, almost every fifth child died. Today, the global infant mortality rate has decreased to a fraction of that: now only 2.9 percent of infants die before their first birthday, and only 4.6 percent of kids die before reaching age 15.[2]

So, while mortality rates of children have plummeted in recent years, I am among *many* women across time who have had to bury a child. The loss of a child is not a unique experience. I am privileged that I am living in a time when child mortality rates are so low that I could reasonably expect to raise all of my children to adulthood. There is nothing unique about me, or Lachlan, or my family that would exclude us from the possibility of suffering as the rest of humanity does.

It is easy to think that cancer, death, tragedy, and sickness only happen to "other" people. No one wants those things to happen and we don't often expect or plan for them in our own lives. As a culture we spend very little time considering that we are just as prone to the sufferings of life as anyone else. When we hold an underlying attitude of invulnerability we can then feel singled out and insulted when we experience the harder things of life firsthand.

Slowly, I started to hold a bigger picture for the suffering of humanity, seeing that it touches every individual in some profound way during their lifetime. Suffering touches some people more deeply than others, but often with no rhyme or reason to who experiences what. In considering *Why not me?* my ego began to shrivel enough to see that I was not unique or protected from the sufferings that come to all of humanity. As I started to see through the mirage of my invincibility armor, I began to feel less indignant that I (and by extension my family) had to experience profound loss and pain.

Asking *Why?* in an exhausting and unrelenting fashion is a normal part of the healing process of traumatic grief. Those unanswerable questions come by instinct and impulse for a long time. As we come face to face with this enemy, consider letting those questions have a place at the table. It's okay to befriend them. Thoroughly seeking the *why* is part of how our brains begin to integrate, make sense of, and understand our pain. The *why* question helps us evaluate what could have been done differently, and what was truly beyond our ability to influence or control.

For me, the shift in perspective came not in trying to eliminate the *why*, but in adding two more questions: *What Heals You?* and *Why not me?* Intentionally asking ourselves *what brings healing* helps capture the little things that *are* bringing a moment of comfort, peace, or hope. The question, *Why not me?* helps us surrender to the universality of suffering that is part of the human experience. These questions will not take away the pain we are experiencing, but together they orient our hearts in a direction that helps us build more peace in our lives.

Uncertainties of Death

It's not until we are backed into a corner and forced to look mortality in the eye, that we typically find ourselves thinking, wondering, or learning about death. We carry uncertainty and fear surrounding the circumstances of death, especially as parents in our desire to protect and comfort our children. The fact that I was absent in Lachlan's moment of death was another avenue of torment for me. *What if there was pain or fear for him in dying, and I wasn't there with him?* Although he was in a room with other people, no one was really *with* him in those moments. There is also the agony of questions about what happens after death: *Where is he now? What is that like? Is our separation as painful for him as it is for me? Babies need their mamas!*

> *It is the unknown we fear when we look upon death and darkness, nothing more.*
>
> J. K. ROWLING (DUMBLEDORE)[3]

Parents have a need and longing to know that their kids are okay. When they are not with us, we go to great lengths to ensure that they are entrusted to people who will take good care of them. Even when we trust our children are in good hands, parents wonder what they are doing, how they are doing, and what their day has been like. Having a veil between life and death that leaves a lot of uncertainty about what is on the other side, creates an agony in a mother's heart.

I craved and longed to find answers to these questions about death, dying, and the afterlife so I began to delve into stories of near-death experiences. I read many of them and the glimpse into those personal accounts that told of overwhelming peace and love brought me comfort. Each was told in a unique way with unique details which gave me some assurance of their authenticity. While each story is unique, there is clearly a golden thread woven through all of them that communicates that death is an experience of deep, total peace and love. In most stories of near-death experiences, the authors describe a longing to have stayed on the other side, but also felt an understanding that there was a divine purpose for their return to earth.

Three stories in particular gave me great comfort. The author of *90 Minutes in Heaven*[4] was in a car accident but experienced no pain in the moment of death. He described the experience as being pulled from his body even before the moment of impact. When he regained consciousness in the hospital, he was in plenty of pain, but in the moment of death he felt none. This story gave me hope that Lachlan did not necessarily suffer pain and fear in his moment of death. The second story was written by a neurosurgeon who had doubted the validity of an afterlife until he had his own near-death experience. His memoir, *Proof of Heaven*[5], weaves his scientific understanding of brain function into his personal account of a near-death experience. He articulated how his experience was outside what science can explain by simple firings of the brain. This gave me one more layer of confidence that there really is a life after death. Lastly, in the book *Heaven is for Real*[6], four-year-old Colton had a near-death experience after his appendix ruptured. My aching heart found comfort in hearing the stories through a child's lens. I appreciated learning about his confidence in what he experienced, his stories of meeting family members that he didn't even know he had, and his descriptions of what he saw while he was there.

Each story on its own may offer little in knowing the truth or validity of the near-death experience—maybe it's a rare experience or maybe it's made up entirely. While we read with caution, knowing that there are people who will tell such tales with their own underlying agenda, there are also peer-reviewed scientific studies and collections of data on the phenomenon. One source is the Magis Center which has an extensive online collection of information on scientifically validated near-death experiences. Their summary of the evidence is: "The most conservative interpretation of NDEs [Near Death Experiences] is that some aspect of human consciousness is non-physical and continues after physical death."[7] The stories of near-death experiences are similar across cultures and times, which gives me confidence in the stories. We can trust and find comfort in the likelihood that, after death, our loved ones are experiencing transcendence and love with freedom from their physical limitations.

One significant battle in the arena of our grief is the arrival of the autopsy results. The final results often take months to be available, and usually come with an enormous load of anticipation and anxiety. The autopsy can both satisfy our need to understand what happened and reveal to us things that we wish we did not have to know.

Autopsy results are written in cold medical language, which is particularly difficult to read when it is referring to someone that we love. The arrival of that paperwork is one more thing that communicates the finality of death. Autopsy results have the potential to reveal our worst fears, the potential to put our fears to rest, and the potential to leave us with unanswered questions. It's hard to say which is worse—the known or the unknown.

The pathologist who did Lachlan's autopsy diagnosed his death as a SIDS death, which meant there was nothing identified on autopsy or in the death scene investigation to reveal a cause of death. However, there are still causes like heart arrhythmias that cannot be identified on autopsy. In my desperation to know what could have been missed and how a potential missed diagnosis could affect any living children, I called the local pathologist to talk through my questions and concerns.

The pathologist was very kind in taking my call, and was as gentle and thorough as possible in talking through my concerns. One of my concerns was Lachlan's age. Since he was older than most babies who die of SIDS, I asked how could we know it wasn't something else? The doctor explained that there is a lot of wiggle room in deciding which term to use for the final cause of death, especially in the terminology for infant deaths. He said that if he had done Lachlan's autopsy, he would have called it SUID (Sudden Unexplained Infant Death) rather than SIDS because of Lachlan's atypical age, even though being under a year old, Lachlan still met the criteria for a SIDS death. Although there was nothing wrong with the existing diagnosis, the pathologist's willingness to reveal his opinion to me opened my eyes to the uncertainties that remain even when we think we are getting answers.

The terminology used for the final cause of death makes an enormous difference in how the loss of a child is processed and internalized. The autopsy results reveal and/or lay to rest our worst fears.

There is no clear standardization as yet for the nuances of how infant deaths are classified. On autopsy, there is no difference in the physical findings between one that is labeled SIDS and one that is diagnosed as a positional asphyxia. The determination is based primarily on the findings of the death-scene investigation.[8] Sometimes there is a clear environmental problem and asphyxia really is the likely cause, but other times the findings are more subtle and that diagnosis is more of a reasonable guess than an answer of certainty. There are a handful of different terms that coroners might reasonably use as their diagnosis for sudden infant death.

A whole new battleground is created in the heart of a parent by the autopsy and what it does and does not reveal. Sometimes the terminology makes parents feel at fault. Sometimes it reveals a medical cause that indicates the death could have been prevented. Sometimes it leaves parents with no real answer at all. No matter what the autopsy says, it almost always creates big feelings to think and wrestle through.

The SIDS diagnosis left me with a mixed bag of feelings. Unknowns are hard. They leave potential for an underlying heart, brain, or metabolic disorder that could not be seen on autopsy. Especially with a history of other unexplained deaths on both my side of the family and David's, the concern for an undiagnosed cause will always remain. While it is hard to not have an identified cause of death, the unknown also gives me things to be grateful for. There is relief to know there wasn't an obvious medical cause that I, especially as a medical provider, could have seen or prevented. It also means his death was not the fault of someone else, and did not leave me grappling with enormous feelings of blame.

In the end, wrestling with the autopsy findings is another lesson in the curriculum of grief. It is learning to surrender our hearts to living with what we have been given. It is learning to forgive the humanity of others. And it is learning to rest in the uncertainty that remains.

What Would He Be Like Now?

One of the privileges of parenthood is seeing your child grow through every stage and phase, and to walk with them as they grow, change, and develop. A longing to know what Lachlan would be doing, what he would look like, and what he would love started almost immediately after his death—and as far as I can tell, the longing will never end.

> *I will always wonder who you would have been.*
>
> UNKNOWN

At the time of his death, Lachlan had been on the verge of walking and his ability to communicate had been growing rapidly. Within weeks, I wondered if he would have taken those first steps and what he would have been doing or saying. As time went on, my wonder continued in which books and toys would have been his favorite. I wondered if he would have latched onto cars and trucks like his brother, or if his love for balls would have led to a love of sports.

On any given day, I know how old he would be if he were still living, and I look at other kids that age with wonder . . . *What would Lachlan be doing? What would his interests be? How would he interact with his siblings? Which of these kids would be his friends? Would he be good at school? Sports? Music? How tall would he be? What color would his hair be?* Not being able to know even these basic things about my own child is heartbreaking.

Lachlan was the first of four grandchildren born to David's parents that year, so we have three other nieces and nephews who are close to his age. I've found it bittersweet to watch them grow. At every step along the way, I've loved to see how big they are, what they are doing, and how their personalities are developing. I have a special wonder in watching those three kids, yet in that wonder, there is also a sharpening of the ache and longing for my boy.

I hated so much not being able to know what my own child would look like. When Lach would have been about three, I paid a team to do an age progression photo in hopes of getting a glimpse of what he might look like. The younger a child is, the harder it is to be accurate in an age-advancement photo. While there was something interesting about seeing the possibility, the photo was still just that: a possibility, a guess—a decent guess, maybe, but still only a guess. The photo didn't take away the uncertainty. It didn't fill the void. It didn't give me the satisfaction that I was hoping for.

Without any basis for the idea, I love thinking that when I get to heaven, I might be granted the gift of greeting Lachlan as a baby, just as he was on the day he died, and getting to watch him grow into adulthood. In accounts of near-death experiences, most people in heaven are described as being in their 30s. Yet there are also accounts of children being in heaven. Maybe, just maybe, the children are waiting for their parents to arrive before their growth continues. This way their parents can experience the gift of watching them grow into adulthood. I love the idea that this gift, given to parents on earth, may still be granted to me in heaven.

Embracing Uncertainty

Finding peace with all of the questions posed in this chapter boils down to finding a way to embrace uncertainty. In the questions that torment the mind of the bereaved, learning to embrace uncertainty was a final step for me in bringing those enemies down to a manageable size.

When we cling tightly to our fears about the unknown, we are promoting the growth of that fear and anxiety. By feeding seeds of fear, doubt, and uncertainty, we are growing restlessness and irritability, and we are strengthening the desire to build walls of protection around ourselves. However, when we loosen our grip on *needing to know* and leave room for uncertainty, for mystery, and for the unknown, we become less consumed by that void.

The theological virtue of hope is the patient and trustful willingness to live without closure, without resolution, and still be content and even happy because our Satisfaction is now at another level, and our Source is beyond ourselves.

RICHARD ROHR[9]

As we create space for that uncertainty, we start to trust in faith again. We become less fearful of the world around us. We become less judgmental. We find the courage to walk into the unknown to live and love more fully. The enemy of uncertainty doesn't ever go away, but something shifts when we stop fighting and instead consent to its presence. Its presence is like a stone pillar—ominous looking yet harmless once we stop banging our heads against it.

Post-Traumatic Memories

Oh, the dreaded flashbacks! I have never found statistics on how many bereaved parents experience this phenomenon, but most of the bereaved parents that I have talked to have struggled with flashbacks. They are one of the most distressing parts of grief. Out of the blue, or triggered by the smallest thing that we didn't know would be a trigger, comes the flash of memories—and not just memories, rather a *reliving* of those horrific moments. Heart racing, sweat beading, the sights, the sounds, and the smells become just as present as they were the first time. We are reliving the most traumatic and painful moments of our existence. These are moments that, more than anything, we would like to forget rather than relive, yet they present themselves over and over again without warning.

There are a million things that can trigger the panic-stricken flashbacks. One of the first reliable triggers for me was the flashing lights of emergency vehicles. This trigger worried me because, as a health care provider, it didn't seem particularly functional to be triggered so intensely by the flashing lights. Flashbacks also came from driving the road that brought me into view of the daycare center, the smell of fresh-cut grass, a funeral procession crossing my path, a kiss on the cool forehead of a child in my arms, or my cell phone ringing while I am at work.

In his best-selling book *The Body Keeps the Score*, Bessel van der Kolk describes how the brain and body are physically and measurably changed by traumatic experiences. Understanding that there is an actual physiological process that happens, and that the flashbacks are not just "all in my head," brought me reassurance and comfort. *I'm not crazy. What I'm experiencing is real, and even normal, in the given circumstances.*

Flashbacks are a physiological process of my brain and body. Knowing that, I can feel less critical of my thoughts, my emotional capacity, or my mental toughness.

In *The Body Keeps the Score*, van der Kolk describes how traumatic memories differ from other memories: "For most people the memory of an unpleasant event eventually fades or is transformed into something more benign. But most of our patients were unable to make their past into a story that happened long ago."[10]

> *It is not the power of the flashback, rather the power you give it.*
>
> DR. BILL TOLLEFSON

Let's try a little thought experiment to see this clearly. Consider something that was benign but unpleasant from your past that you will always remember—the time you broke a bone, or were scolded by the teacher, or had a friend say something hurtful. Notice how those memories are stored. You can think about them as past events, remember the feeling without actually feeling it now, and retell the story with a sense of distance from it. Notice how this unpleasant memory differs from what you experience in a flashback. Memories are ultimately benign. They pose no real threat to the present moment, but in a flashback of a traumatic moment, we experience that memory as if the threat is still immediately present.

Looking back to the opening chapters of this book, in which I told the story of Lachlan's death, I realize that I told it largely in the present tense. As I tap into those memories, his death wasn't something that *did* happen, but it becomes (like it always seems to) something that *is* happening. That is a defining characteristic of a traumatic memory.

There are measurable changes that happen in our brain and body when we are experiencing a flashback of a traumatic memory. Functional MRI studies[11] show that our brains light up differently in a flashback compared to typical memory recall. Thoughts, sounds, and images can trigger an intense reaction from the amygdala, or the emotional center of our brain. This reaction of the emotional center sets off a hormonal cascade that makes our bodies react in alarm. This flood of stress hormones sends our bodies into a fight or flight state of alarm, with increased heart rate, breathing rate, and blood pressure—even though we never entirely lose the sense of where we actually are. It's a dual existence of sorts. We know where we are in the present moment and are simultaneously experiencing and re-living the threat of the trauma.

There are a couple of elements that contribute to making these traumatic experiences extraordinarily difficult to communicate to others. Functional MRI studies[12] done while someone is experiencing a flashback show that Broca's area (a primary speech center of the brain), goes offline. In addition, the right side of the brain shows primary activity during a flashback. The right side of the brain is where emotional experiences are stored with the sights, sounds, and smells that trigger them. The inactive left side of the brain is primarily responsible for helping us organize our thoughts, make sense of them, and be able to find the language to communicate our experience. Van der Kolk explains what happens when the two hemispheres of our brain are not working together:

> When something reminds traumatized people of the past, their right brain reacts as if the traumatic event were happening in the present. But because their left brain is not working very well, they may not be aware that they are reexperiencing and reenacting the past—they are just furious, terrified, enraged, ashamed, or frozen. After the emotional storm passes, they look for something or somebody to blame for it...
>
> Even years later traumatized people often have enormous difficulty telling other people what has happened to them. Their bodies reexperience terror, rage, and helplessness, as well as the impulse to fight or flee, but these feelings are almost impossible to articulate. Trauma by nature drives us to the edge of comprehension, cutting us off from language based on common experience or an imaginable past.
>
> This doesn't mean that people can't talk about a tragedy that has befallen them. Sooner or later most survivors . . . come up with what many of them call their "cover story" that offers some explanation for their symptoms and behavior for public consumption. These stories, however, rarely capture the inner truth of the experience . . . People who are very upset sometimes say they are "losing their minds." In technical terms they are experiencing the loss of executive functioning.[13]

Learning what is actually happening in the brain and body is helpful but I personally don't care to hold the view that "I *have* PTSD." That label communicates that my trauma is a larger part of my existence than what it really is. It seems to say, "I'm wounded beyond repair." It feels more accurate and less defining of *who I am* to say, "I have a traumatic memory." That statement acknowledges the fact that I continue to wrestle with a traumatic event—and it leaves room for more of "me" outside of the traumatic memory.

As we are facing this enemy in the arena, the battle becomes figuring out how to live with such a distressing symptom. There are varying degrees of PTSD (Post Traumatic Stress Disorder), and some people will need to seek professional help to work through those memories and flashbacks. This is not a sign of weakness, but rather a sign of wisdom to understand that traumatic memories create a physiological change, and we may need a trained professional to help rewire those memories into something that is more tolerable to live with.

We can also do a few basic things on our own that will, over time, dampen the intensity of the trauma response. I'm not convinced that I'll ever be 100% free from the potential of a flashback. Even now, I will have unexpected circumstances, sights, sounds, or feelings that will bring me right back to those most horrific moments of Lachlan's death. When they do, instantly the stress response flares—my heart races, my breath quickens, my throat tightens, and my eyes well up with tears. The first thing that helps me get through a flashback is to remember that the string of memories and bodily responses that occur will run its course, and in a matter of a few minutes, will fade. It feels awful while it is happening, but it doesn't last forever. Once that emotional storm passes, I know I will reenter the same state of missing my little boy that I live with day in and day out. The second thing that was a reassurance to me, when flashbacks were new and intense, was the knowledge that they wouldn't always be as overpowering and frequent. I just had to get through them while they were there, and trust that over time they would decrease in intensity and frequency.

Ultimately, dealing with flashbacks is a process of growing in mindfulness. Mindfulness is a brain exercise that helps us learn to stay in the present moment, to improve our self-awareness, and to be able to put a degree of separation between ourselves and our thoughts. It is a particularly good method for helping us step out of the "fight or flight" mode, and is a powerful tool for calming the hyper-aroused emotional centers of our brains. Mindfulness can be a tremendous technique for reestablishing some sense of control over our internal chaos. While mindfulness may not be able to entirely eliminate this enemy of traumatic memory, it can help us achieve the goal of learning to live in its presence. We can learn to let our traumatic memories be, without letting them hijack us.

We can learn to let our traumatic memories be, without letting them hijack us.

Many of the therapeutic methods offered by professionals are also things we can work through in our own time and at our own pace. Therapists often use some form of exposure therapy or desensitization that involves revisiting and leaning into the very things that make us most uncomfortable. If we slowly, but intentionally and mindfully, refuse to walk away from situations just because they stir up negative emotions (while simultaneously being gentle with ourselves and not forcing ourselves to do more than what we are ready for) we are essentially taking a self-guided journey in exposure therapy.

One of the final things that has been helpful for me in bringing this enemy down to size is simply improving the integration of those memories. Integration involves being intentional about seeking opportunities to continue to process and reprocess what has happened. Every time I make an effort to find language for my experience, I am building the connections between the right and left hemispheres of my brain. This can be done in a lot of ways such as talking it out with a trusted friend, journaling, or simply reading the words of others.

I can't describe how many self-discoveries and new understandings of my own grief have come about simply by writing and by pushing to find the words to depict my experience. It can be writing to myself, writing to others, or writing to the world through social media—whatever feels right in the moment. My writing was quite disjointed for a long time. Finding any words at all was hard work. It has been a slow and continual process to deepen my ability to see and understand my own inner workings. Each time I tell my story, each time I write about an aspect of my experience, I am adding to the healing that comes through integration.

I am given a new opportunity to work on that integration every spring when so many difficult feelings bubble to the surface as the anniversary of Lachlan's death draws near. I've found it interesting how, even now, my body reacts to my grief often *before* I am conscious of what is happening. As springtime rolls around, often by mid-April, I find that I am feeling restless, irritable, tearful, and more emotionally labile, before I have even started counting the days to that dreaded anniversary of his death. Only after pausing to figure out the source of my tension, do I recognize it as a grief reaction.

This phenomenon is often part of the package deal of traumatic memories. It is documented as "anniversary reactions." Environmental cues are coded in the wiring of those traumatic memories telling us when to be "on guard" for threat. The layers of our brains, even below the level of conscious thought, start warning us of potential danger. For me, that coding is attached to the grass turning green, the warm spring breezes, and especially the blooming of the trees. These anniversary reactions can be unsettling, yet there is power in identifying and understanding what is happening.

Understanding this phenomenon puts me back in control of how I want to respond. I'm not just a victim of my own inner workings being dragged mercilessly by emotions and feelings that I can't understand. I can use the rise of my grief to observe with curiosity how I feel, to better understand what the triggers are, and to see where I might need more intentional emotional work. When I approach with openness and curiosity, I have the power to respond thoughtfully rather than just react mindlessly to my experience. Ultimately, triggers do not have to be viewed as an enemy to avoid. The external triggers aren't *creating* our pain, they are *pointing* to it. They show us the areas within us that are still in need of some integration and healing.

Even with these tools, I still have moments that catch me by surprise, and an occasional flashback will be triggered, or an anniversary reaction will be stronger than anticipated. I no longer walk in fear of this enemy. I know that even if it does make an appearance, I will experience a temporary increase in my pain, and then return to baseline.

With time, training, patience, and curiosity, we can grow in our capacity and confidence to carry the long-term effects of a traumatic memory.

TEARS

I clearly remember the moment I surrendered my fight against tears. Our culture teaches us that tears are a sign of weakness. "Be strong" and "your loved one would not want you to cry" are common phrases we hear when we bare our emotions. Even at funerals, we hear things like "don't cry for me." We are encouraged not to cry even at the rituals designed for mourning!

For a long time, I felt like I was always on the brink of the floodgates being unleashed. I put so much effort into trying to hold myself together, to blink back tears, breathe around the knot in my throat, and put on a mask that was presentable to society. I held an underlying belief that my tears needed to be controlled.

> *But there was no need to be ashamed of tears, for tears bore witness that a man had the greatest of courage, the courage to suffer.*
>
> VIKTOR FRANKL[14]

The day I befriended this enemy of tears, I was standing in a children's clothing store, browsing the rack in search of something for Westin. The pain of not needing to purchase a coordinating outfit for Lachlan brought a crushing wave of grief. I was so exhausted from constantly fighting my own emotions that I just couldn't do it anymore. In that moment, I let go and let the tears fall. While I wasn't freed from the self-consciousness of being seen with a tear-stained face in a public place, I no longer cared to fight it anymore. And as those tears fell, my body began to relax, my internal wrestling stilled, and I was able to move forward with the task at hand.

Over and over again, in a million blunt and subtle ways, we are taught that tears are not acceptable. On that day, I learned it is not so. On the contrary, tears are sacred, and they are healing. For both men and women, they are a sign of genuine strength, courage, and humility. Tears are a symbol of authenticity. They are a product of love. Tears are not shameful. They are beautiful. As I've slowly learned to embrace vulnerability for the authenticity it brings to my life, I've also become more comfortable with letting tears hit my cheeks when they are begging for a release. Having the courage to let tears fall is to be vulnerable and to be seen. They water the ground that grows meaningful relationships. Like a waterfall that feeds a still pool at its base, tears are the waterfall that contributes to an internal stillness.

Tears are sacred and they are healing. They are a sign of genuine strength, courage, and humility. Tears are a symbol of authenticity and a product of love.

There are many biblical references that allude to the sacredness of tears. One of my favorites is: "You keep track of all my sorrows. You have collected all my tears in your bottle. You have recorded each one in your book" (Psalm 56:8[15]). Padre Pio, a twentieth-century saint and mystic, said, "Your tears were collected by the angels and were placed in a golden chalice, and you will find them when you present yourself before God."

Even in the ancient wisdom of the great saints and philosophers, the value of tears is not overlooked. Saint Thomas Aquinas lived during the thirteenth century and is considered one of the all-time greatest spiritual thinkers and philosophers. He pointed to tears and mourning as a valuable remedy for our sorrow[16]. He essentially confirmed for me what I was starting to uncover on my own. He said the first reason tears are helpful is that when we are hurting emotionally, and we try to keep that pain all bottled up inside us, our souls tend to become even more intent on that sorrow. If we allow the pain a path of escape, rather than turning in on ourselves, we can begin to turn our attention outward and in doing so, we lessen the inward sorrow. He also noted the comfort that comes from the honesty of showing on the outside what we are feeling on the inside. When our actions match our internal disposition, that congruency brings a serenity to our being.

Tears have an additional, hidden value. An article in *Smithsonian Magazine,* "The Microscopic Structures of Dried Human Tears,"[17] shows intriguing images of how tears of different purpose or emotion differ dramatically in what they look like when they are dried. The chemical makeup of tears differs, depending on their purpose. The basal tears that lubricate our eyes differ from reflex tears produced when something irritates an eye, and these are also different from emotional tears.

Emotional tears contain stress hormones including a neurotransmitter that is a natural painkiller. Tears inspired by different emotions all differ in their chemical makeup.

As grievers, our need to cry can vary widely. For some, tears are not a primary mode of emotional release. If you are not a crier, that is perfectly okay too. Your grief is processed differently. Some grievers will find that their lack of tears is troublesome to the people around them. People may see that as a sign that they are not grieving like they should. As with many elements of grief, any visible behavior is only a tiny tip of the iceberg of emotion and tells us little about what is happening under the surface. My point is not to insist on the necessity of tears, but to recognize the inherent value of them, so that when they rise to the surface, we can embrace them with gentleness rather than fighting fiercely to hold them back.

Secondary Losses

What might have been. . . That is what weaves the loss of a child like a thread through the remainder of our life. But it's more than that. It's not just what might have been, because this thread includes what *should have been.*

It's fun to play with "what might-have-beens." My husband talks about how he was a great golfer as a kid and wonders what kind of golfer he could have been if he hadn't given it up when he was little. Maybe David could have won state championships, or gotten a college scholarship, or been the only guy who could beat Tiger Woods. "What should-have-beens" are different. They are more like an Olympic qualifier who had the best jump in the world, was well-trained and well-rested, and felt prepared to compete at the top of his game—but then was unable to compete due to circumstances outside his control. He had that medal! He was there, and it heartbreakingly slipped through his fingers. There is no way to tell exactly how the events of the day would have unfolded, but it was going to be a great day.

Lach was here, and he slipped through our fingers due to circumstances beyond our control. There is no way to tell exactly how the events of his life would have unfolded, but it was going to be something great. The lingering effect of that loss is much bigger than a simple, casual wondering of "what might have been." The loss of a child is losing something of the future, and it comes with a deep and guttural longing to know how the world would be different if our child was still here. This ache and longing are dotted through the rest of our days, woven into the ordinary and insignificant moments of daily life and into the desire for their presence in all of life's big occasions.

The losses that come after that primary loss are the secondary losses that linger for a lifetime. They are the ripple effect. Those ripples touch our being in every way, physical, social, emotional, intellectual, and spiritual. While I don't always dwell on them, those secondary losses are everywhere.

Shortly after your death, I realized I'd lost so much more. Suddenly, I felt lost, confused, shattered. I realized so much of who I was and who I ever wanted to be was based on having you by my side.

RACHEL BLADO[18]

One of the chief secondary losses for me is the loss of what Lachlan would be to his siblings. My husband has a brother who is just 15 months older than he is. They grew up doing everything together. Kevin has been David's built-in best friend since they were babies. David and I always dreamed of having kids close together to give them the opportunity to have built-in best friends too. With Lachlan's death, there is a perpetual gap in my stair-step children that can never be filled. While the kids all love each other, an age difference of four years puts them at different phases in life, and those relationships tend to be different than the ones between siblings who are closer in age. With the death of Lachlan, my kids lost a brother, a friend, a playmate, a confidant—not just during childhood but for their whole lives.

I also find the secondary losses in the hole that's left in his spot in a bedroom, in the car, and at the dinner table. It's the missing backpack and an empty hook. It's missing his first day of every school year. It's never seeing his jack-o'-lantern grin as a seven-year-old. It's his absence in every elementary Christmas program. Christmas programs are so hard! Parents and children are excited, all the parents trying to capture their pride-and-joy on film while the children do their thing on stage, all dressed up in their finest—and everyone else is unaware that a child who belongs there is missing.

The secondary loss is felt when there is one less sleepy-eyed boy in his Christmas jammies grinning as he makes his way to the tree to see what Santa brought. It's one less soccer game on Saturday. It means I have to pack Westin's hand-me-downs into a box to sit on the shelf for a couple of years (instead of going straight into Lach's dresser). Instead of sending him off to middle school in his new uniform, I bought a memorial brick with his name on it to be placed on the school grounds. I miss the relationships that should have been with his cousins, grandparents, and friends. I know that as time moves forward without him, I will continue to grieve in all the places he is missing, like in the absence of proms, graduations, a wedding, and the grandchildren that will never be.

Except in circles of grievers, I'm never referred to as "Lachlan's mom." I miss that too. I miss the fact that our family picture will never accurately represent all the children I hold in my heart. Someone is missing. The incomplete image of our family is always hard. It is not how the photo is supposed to be. When we have a formal family picture taken, I like to bring a dragonfly prop to mark his spot in the photo. That's more for me than it is for anyone else. I don't do this to forever call attention to our loss, as I worry some people might think. Rather, it helps create a better reflection of what my heart feels when I think about our family. It brings more peace and comfort for me to acknowledge his place than to leave it out, and so I honor what my grieving heart needs.

The pangs of grief and longing that accompany the endless supply of secondary losses are aches that are here to stay. They are an enemy to befriend. There's no way to make that better or to fill that hole in a way that will satisfy my heart. While I can appreciate the depth, the empathy, and the wisdom that have grown within my spirit because of my experience with loss, I also miss the innocence of my life before this ache—that, too, is a secondary loss.

These "should-have-beens" still make me miss him so much it hurts. Part of the work of grief has been to learn to accept the inevitable secondary losses, and the tears that sometimes come with them. The pang of these secondary losses is a permanent part of my journey and part of that thread that will continue to run through my days. In learning to befriend that ever-present awareness of loss, I have learned to embrace the ache as part of what connects me to my little boy. The ache reminds me of what an irreplaceable part of my life he was and always will be. Missing our deceased loved ones might be our heart's way of reminding us that we still love them—and it is comforting to know with certainty that even death cannot stamp out our love.

Fading Memories

One of my biggest fears in the beginning of my grief journey was the fear that I would forget Lachlan. It was nauseating to think that I would forget the details of how he looked, what he did, the expressions he made, how he smelled, how he felt in my arms . . . that I would forget *him*. I understood, as a human confined to the forward movement of time, that there was no way around the effects of time on my memory. The details would fade and morph, and the harder I tried to cling to them, the more distorted they seemed to become. I hated that. Trying to remember him by using pictures threatened to reduce my memory to what was captured on film and left out so much of him that was unrecorded. There was no way to perfectly preserve all of what I wanted to be able to remember.

C. S. Lewis wrote the following lament about trying to remember his wife, who he refers to as H:

> Already, less than a month after her death, I can feel the slow, insidious beginning of a process that will make the H. I think of into a more and more imaginary woman. Founded on fact, no doubt. I shall put nothing fictitious (or I hope I shan't). But won't the composition inevitably become more and more my own? The reality is no longer there to check me, to pull me up short, as the real H. so often did, so unexpectedly, by being so thoroughly herself and not me. . .
>
> Today I had to meet a man I haven't seen for ten years. And all that time I had thought I was remembering him well—how he looked and spoke and the sort of things he said. The first five minutes of the real man shattered the image completely.

> Not that he had changed. On the contrary. I kept on thinking, "Yes, of course, of course. I'd forgotten that he thought that—or disliked this, or knew so-and-so—or jerked his head back that way." I had known all these things once and I recognized them the moment I met them again. But they had all faded out of my mental picture of him, and when they were all replaced by his actual presence the total effect was quite astonishingly different from the image I had carried about with me for those ten years. How can I hope that this will not happen to my memory of H.?[19]

I was with Lewis in understanding the reality that my memory of Lachlan would not remain precise, which prompted me to preserve what I could in the only way I could think of. I got a special journal and wrote down everything about him that I could think of. I kept that journal near, and every time I thought of another detail, I wrote it down. I went around my house using regular household items to prompt my memories: The clock on my nightstand—Lach routinely woke up when it shone 11:00, 3:00, and 6:00. The handles on the chest at the foot of our bed—he loved to sit in front of those and flick at the handles to make them clatter as entertainment while he was waiting for me to get ready for the day. The shirts in my closet with the beads and the ties along the neckline—he made me laugh when he drooled all over my shirt, assertively attempting to get those beads into his mouth.

I couldn't stand the idea of forgetting these little things, but I knew that time would snatch many of them away from me. There was no way to record every detail and mannerism, so even this journal felt vastly incomplete. However, I was comforted knowing that at least some of those memories not preserved by a photo were securely written down. That journal helped minimize the fear of what time would do to my memories.

While I was still wrestling intensely with this fear of forgetting him, I had the opportunity to talk to another bereaved mama who was about ten years out from her loss. I remember clearly from that conversation the blessing it was to hear her say that not a day had gone by, in all that time, that she didn't think about her son. I felt a huge, internal sigh of relief at hearing those words. They helped me to grasp that, while the details might fade, I would never forget Lachlan and he would never, ever fade to a distant memory that I only thought of once in a great while. He would remain very near and very present to my heart every single day for the rest of my life. As the years from my loss have added up, I've found this to be very true. There are plenty of stories and memories of Lachlan that we love to keep alive by retelling and revisiting them, and though many of the details of the memories are not as crisp as they once were (and I do mourn that too), I remember *him* just as much as if he were still a living member of our household.

> *Shortly after your death, I realized I'd lost so much more. Suddenly, I felt lost, confused, shattered. I realized so much of who I was and who I ever wanted to be was based on having you by my side.*
>
> RASHIDA ROWE

I hated the enemy of fading memories. There were two primary things that helped me make peace with its presence in my arena. The first was considering that quirky nature of memories—like what Lewis described in seeing the man ten years later. The details are very much stored within our subconscious, even when we cannot recall them. The instant we see them again, or find an occasion that prompts a memory, we find that the details were not gone at all. They were all still there, just below the surface of our conscious memory. I am comforted by knowing that many of those faded memories of Lachlan are not really gone, only dormant, and they have the potential to be reawakened with just the right prompt. I hold onto hope that they will all reemerge in their fullness at my first glimpse of Lachlan when I leave the confines of time to enter into eternity.

The second thing that helped me make peace with this enemy was in learning that, while the details have become fuzzier over time, Lachlan is just as much part of us, a part of me, and a fact of the world as he ever was. I was not open to seeing that he was permanently a fact of the world when I was clenching my fists onto those memories that felt like grains of sand slipping through my fingers. The tighter I gripped, the harder they were to hold onto. When I loosened my grasp, I began to see that Lachlan would not ever leave my life entirely.

Returning to Lewis' reflection on his wife, this is how he explained this same understanding:

> And the remarkable thing is that since I stopped bothering about it, she seems to meet me everywhere... [There is] a sort of unobtrusive but massive sense that she is, just as much as ever, a fact to be taken into account... It is as if the experience said to me, "You are, as it happens, extremely glad that H. is still a fact. But remember she would be equally a fact whether you liked it or not. Your preferences have not been considered."[20]

Lachlan remains a fact of the universe no matter what my memories or feelings might be. Therein lies my comfort. Before I came to understand the permanence of Lachlan's place in the world, I writhed in the foreboding shadow of this enemy as he threatened to snatch my little boy from my memory. I now stand taller, knowing with certainty that those threats are empty, and the power of that enemy is only a whisper of what it tries to claim. While I can't remove this enemy from my arena, he does not have the power to take the memory of my child, nor the fact of his existence away from me.

Emptiness of Time and Space

It's amazing how unbearable the roar of silence can be. The silence that wasn't meant to be, and the freedom of time that was uninvited . . . these create a roar that cannot be escaped. To be in a place where thoughts can wander is terrifying, because inevitably they wander into the darkest and most difficult corners of our being. In our brief period of counseling, I remember being asked what the hardest part was for me in that moment. I answered, "That he is everywhere, but nowhere."

The silence from the crib at night. The silence from his car seat. Silence from his high chair. Silence from his play space. Even in the activities of caring for Westin, caring for one child instead of two created a roaring silence. Not having to divide and multitask those jobs left a palpable and distracting emptiness. That feeling of emptiness extended over absolutely everything.

I could do nothing about this feeling except acknowledge it, and appreciate the significance of that one tiny person's meaning in my life. There is nothing untouched for the rest of my life by his absence. This leaves me with awe at the power of love.

Grief is the loudest silence I've ever heard.
ANGIE CARTWRIGHT

Humans are pretty adaptable creatures, and the physical life around us is constantly changing. We normally adapt to these differences with little thought. Yet my inability to adapt to Lachlan's absence proves to me that there must be something beyond what we see here on earth. My soul wouldn't continue to ache with such intensity for my child if there wasn't something to yearn for. His absence leaves me with a persistent reminder and longing for what might be beyond this present life, a place where we can be together again with no threat of separation.

This feeling was powerfully expressed for me in the movie *Interstellar* in which the main character says, "Maybe [love is] evidence, some artifact of a higher dimension that we can't consciously perceive...Love is the one thing that we're capable of perceiving that transcends dimensions of time and space. Maybe we should trust that, even if we can't understand it."[21]

When we are thrown into the arena of grief and mourning, the first glimpse of the army of threats is overwhelming. However, as we learn to approach each of them, albeit with wobbly legs, we find that the enemies, once identified, are not nearly the threat they initially seemed to present. Yes, each of them is something to approach, to study with curiosity, and to identify. When we have the courage to do that, we find the threats that had put us into an anxious and restless fight-or-flight mode are not nearly as foreboding as they first appeared. When our fears, irritations, and uncertainties are brought down to size, a whole new world opens up—a world of being able to grieve with a softer heart, with more gentleness, more forgiveness, more self-acceptance, and more peace.

9

Lessons to Learn

His grief he will not forget; but it will not darken his heart,
it will teach him wisdom.

J. R. R. TOLKIEN (ARAGORN)[1]

The last chapter highlighted many of the things that couldn't be changed about my experience. I could only see and accept them for what they were, and then learn that they did not have to be *all* of my existence. Some difficult things in life always stay put, but there is a lot of beauty in the life and love that can be woven right in and around those difficult parts. The last chapter was like preparing rough and ugly ground, removing rocks and weeds, and tilling the hard and unforgiving soil.

In this chapter, we'll start watering, nourishing, and protecting the delicate new sprouts of life as they begin to emerge. I'll walk through the things I actively did to make it more tolerable to live in my own skin. These are the lessons I've learned along the way that have helped me grow and connect in a deeper way to myself and the people around me:

1. The necessity of honoring my own needs
2. Taking care of my body is part of nourishing my soul
3. To be intentional about protecting our marriage
4. To foster gentleness in all my relationships
5. The benefits of practicing gratitude
6. How to surrender to suffering and then embrace it
7. Finding balance between holding on and letting go

8. Becoming whole by integrating my loss into my life
9. The gift of ritual
10. How to love someone who is no longer physically here

Honoring My Own Needs

Grief has been my primary teacher on the necessity and the splendor of honoring my own needs. Up until Lachlan died, I had lived my whole life mastering the skill of people-pleasing. I was good at setting aside my own needs and desires in order to step up to the plate of expectation—even when it might become a source of resentment for me.

> *When we truly care for ourselves, it becomes possible to care far more profoundly about other people. The more alert and sensitive we are to our own needs, the more loving and generous we can be toward others.*
>
> EDA LASHAN

After Lachlan died, at first, I found myself always scrutinizing my own behaviors, wondering if I was behaving as people expected a bereaved parent to behave. It was hard to assess, though, because people seemed to have differing opinions on the "right" way to respond. This was way too big, way too deep, and way too complicated.

There was no clear "right" way to respond, and I didn't have the energy to try to figure it out. I was busy just trying to hold on in the only way I knew how. At the same time, it seemed that if I appeared too sad then people worried I wasn't coping well. If I was too stoic, people worried I wasn't really grieving and that I must still be in shock. Talking about my feelings and my loss regularly, people worried that I was stuck in my grief. If I didn't talk, they worried I was shutting myself in. I was worried that if I did any "normal" activities people might think I was okay, or "over it." If I excused myself from normal activities and gatherings, I worried that people would think I was having a total breakdown.

For the first time in my life, I found it necessary to excuse myself from tending to the expectations of others. There was no way to people-please through my grief. When I was using everything I had just to get through the day, somehow I couldn't care anymore what other people thought I should be doing. My grief pushed me out of my comfort zone and forced me to examine my own heart and my own needs like I had never needed to before. Like an unsteady fawn, I started taking steps to tend to those needs, rather than going through the motions that I assumed others thought I should be doing.

My grief pushed me out of my comfort zone and forced me to examine my own heart and my own needs like I had never needed to before.

Social pressures can often add an extraordinary burden to our heavy grief. Dr. Joanne Cacciatore points out, "Many grievers feel implicit or explicit social pressure to 'feel better' or 'move on,' and the incongruence between the messages of how they should feel and the inner wisdom of what they actually *do* feel causes many to doubt their own hearts. This lack of alignment between self and the other is one more way in which *avoidable* and *irrational* suffering is imposed on grievers in the middle of *natural*—which is to say unavoidable and rational—suffering."[2]

I was recognizing for the first time that no one else could know what I needed to get through this. I had to let my own heart be my guide, rather than the expectations (real or imagined) of others. If there was something I couldn't do on a given day, I gave myself permission not to, even if someone expected me to do it. I started finding the courage to tell other people what I was up for and what I wasn't, *honoring* my own needs rather than ignoring them. Grief was an ugly crash course in authenticity and self-exploration.

I also had to learn the uncomfortable lesson of building healthy boundaries with the people around me. Some days it was just hard to be around people, even when they wanted to support us. Rather than taking phone calls or visitors when my heart needed silence, I started letting myself decline those interactions. On the days I needed company, I welcomed the interactions and even reached out for them.

I started to allow distance to grow in the relationships with people who were increasing my pain (usually unknowingly), and I hoped that those relationships could be re-kindled when my heart was ready. Interestingly, leaving a temporary distance in a relationship that was strained because of my grief did more for preserving the relationship than a forced, continued interaction would have.

I saw with new eyes how my interactions with people were affecting my ability to cope with my grief. It was important to recognize which people were helping me feel loved, supported, and witnessed, and which people left me feeling exhausted, hurt, or unseen. It became an act of courage and self-care to acknowledge what I needed and to tend to my wounded heart like I would a wounded child. One of the rules in Jordan Peterson's *12 Rules for Life* is to "treat yourself like someone you are responsible for helping"[3] and that's finally what I was doing.

The old me would have argued against tending to my own needs first. I typically ignored the standard advice of putting on our own oxygen mask before we help the others around us. Taking care of my own needs first always seemed selfish. *We are called to give until it hurts, aren't we?*

It was the curly-haired angel in disguise that I introduced in the opening chapters who substantiated for me the authentic beauty of healthy boundaries. She has a big and generous heart and shares her time and resources wherever she can. But she is also willing to say "no" if what is being asked of her doesn't work well. As a recipient of her generosity, something unexpected happened for me in hearing her say "no" when I came to her with a request. It did not leave me feeling unsupported, but instead gave me confidence in our interactions. I knew I could trust that if I made a request, I would not be imposing. She wouldn't say "yes" and then hide an underlying resentment or annoyance. When she said "yes" it was a true, authentic and resounding "yes." I felt at ease accepting her generosity, knowing that she wanted to be doing what she was doing. By the ease and confidence with which she declined requests that were not a good fit for her, she became a powerful witness to how amazing healthy boundaries can be for both the giver and the recipient.

I saw for the first time that healthy boundaries, rather than being selfish, build an authenticity and a genuineness. Boundaries allow me to give generously with my whole heart, not just a few nice outward actions that are marred by a secretly resentful disposition. I saw yet again the value of living with congruency in my thoughts, feelings, and actions, and how that inner consistency is a powerful asset in quieting my internal battlegrounds. In the chaotic state of a grieving heart and mind, even the slightest movements toward peace and stillness are infinitely valuable.

Even though I am now tasting and seeing the value of honoring my needs, I still feel the marks of the people-pleasing chains that held me for so long. I still feel uncomfortable when I have to say "no" to something that is being asked of me, even though I know that brief moment of discomfort will lead to a longer-lasting peace from not overcommitting. I would not be surprised if most people feel the same appreciation and respect toward the boundaries I'm learning to keep, that I felt toward my angel in disguise who introduced me to how beautiful and powerful boundaries can be.

Another challenge was letting go of the self-criticisms that came with my unique set of needs. Every person has a unique and individual set of needs based on their own experiences, personalities, and perceptions. It has taken practice to learn to trust my intuition about my personal needs. I had to work at finding compassion and forgiveness for the weaknesses that have come through my wounds. Especially in my grief, I had to learn how to be compassionate with myself. Initially, when I just couldn't do the things I thought I should be able to do, I added insult to injury by berating myself for the weakness. As I learn to extend compassion and gentleness toward my own weaknesses, I create a more peaceful internal space.

Because of the wound of losing a child during sleep, I know I have more anxiety than the average parent about when, how, and where my babies sleep. I get frustrated and a little panicked when other people don't adhere to safe sleep recommendations with my babies or theirs. If I'm not aware of my feelings and being compassionate toward myself, I resort to scolding either myself or others. Some days I berated myself for not being able to *just be normal*. Other days, my anxiety was pointed toward others, and I was quite reactive when people who knew our story chose to put their babies in unsafe sleep environments. It felt like a slap in the face—like the gravity of our loss was not enough to inspire them to be intentional about using a sleep environment that might reduce the risk of it happening to them.

When I find myself all wound up, I pause and remember that I have been through something that is extremely painful and not an average part of everyone else's life experience. It is normal to feel reactive to circumstances that are similar to those that caused our deepest wounds. When I remember that, I can extend myself some grace. If I need to check on my babies an extra time or two, or put a sleep monitor on them, or change the position or the place of their sleeping to let my heart be still, I give myself permission to do so. When I am compassionate and gentle with myself, I can tend to the needs of my wounded heart without scolding myself for being "an anxious crazy person." Instead, I remember that this is simply part of being human. I also have to extend that same grace to others, remembering that they too have their own unique set of needs and experiences that drive their decisions.

In learning to befriend my human weakness, the other area that I have wrestled with is the everyday experiences of raising kids. When I think about the hard moments with Lachlan, I would give anything to go through all of them a million times if I could have him back. I am acutely aware and sorry for the times I was less of a parent than I wanted to be with him because I was tired or frustrated.

Ironically, with my living children, I still find myself frustrated and short-tempered at times. How can I long for the hard moments with Lachlan, and at the same time want to be done dealing with the defiant child who is looking me in the eye? It's part of the broken nature of being human. While I hated feeling frustrated after a hard parenting day, I learned to extend compassion to myself here too. It is possible to know the value of life and how much I would give for each of my children *and* be tired, frustrated, and at my wit's end.

A conversation with a friend who had been in a life-threatening motorcycle accident left a mark on my heart and helps me remember to honor the unique needs that follow a traumatic experience. In this conversation which took place years after her accident, she told me of the anxiety she was feeling about an invitation to go on a long motorcycle ride with a group of friends. She wanted to go along, but being on a bike for long stretches brought up the worst of her traumatic memories. She's not a person to shy away from the hard stuff, but she was afraid this ride was more than she was ready for. She was afraid that she would become too anxiety-ridden to stay on the motorcycle and would end up embarrassing herself and ruining the trip for everyone else if she couldn't do it.

We talked through how we felt when we offered ourselves compassion around our traumatic experiences. We tapped into the peace that comes with giving ourselves permission to feel whatever it is we are feeling, and allowing ourselves to do whatever it is we need to do to get through that. As the conversation unfolded and she gave herself permission to have anxiety about a long bike ride, a door opened for her to respond to that anxiety differently. Instead of trying to wrestle the fear into submission, she brainstormed ways that she could live with its presence. In the end, she gave herself an easy way out when she needed it and spent much of the trip following her friends by car. By approaching with self-compassion, she was able to both honor her needs *and* enjoy the company of her friends.

The last reflection on honoring our needs is regarding the standard advice to avoid making any big life changes for at least a year. I did not go back to my job after Lachlan died. I had been wrestling with my work-life balance for a long time before he died. Not going back to the job meant I could set aside that battle for balance and use that time to attend to the new, bigger battles that came with such intense grief. It was a big shift for me and our household. It clearly went against that advice of not making any big life changes—yet it was exactly what I needed.

There is a layer underneath this standard advice that is more important to consider before we make big changes. That deeper layer is to understand what is driving us to make the change. If movements of peace come with thoughts about moving to a new house or changing jobs, it's probably a good thing to have the courage to follow through on those desires. However, if the desire for change is coming from a place of impulsivity, fear, or avoidance, we're better off sticking to that advice, stay put, and work through those difficult emotions rather than run from them.

Grief has pushed me to see and honor my own needs, so that I can be well enough to engage more fully with others. It has taught me to give myself permission to create and maintain healthy boundaries so that I can be free to give of myself generously. In the process of rebuilding something beautiful from what is broken, it is necessary for me to understand where the sharp edges lie so that I can work with them, respect their presence, and gently soften them as I go. Rather than throwing out the parts of me that feel broken, I can appreciate the broken pieces and use them to create a stunning new mosaic of life.

The Connection of Body and Soul

The connection between the wellness of our mind and body is a Pandora's box that the scientific world is only beginning to crack open. We are just scratching the surface of exploration and discovery, learning how significantly our mental, emotional, and spiritual state can affect our physical status, and vice versa.

> *Our body is like armor, our soul is like the warrior. Take care of both, and you will be ready for what comes.*
>
> ST. SYNCLETICA

Even before scientists took a dive into understanding these intricate connections, the wisdom of the great saints Aquinas, Augustine, and Ambrose had outlined this. In his remedies for sorrow, Aquinas (referencing Augustine and Ambrose) includes weeping, pleasure, sharing sorrow with friends, contemplating the truth, and the physical care of our bodies through naps and baths.[4] I have discovered the power of each one of these on my own, and learning of Aquinas's prescription for sorrow reinforced their value.

Over time, I have become an advocate for the necessity of balance, both in grief and in all of life. What balance looks like is different for each person, but holding onto a "both/and" principle is helpful for me as I'm seeking balance for myself. This "both/and" principle means we don't have to choose one thing *or* the other, one way *or* the other. We find balance and peace when we discover that we can have *both*. We can have this *and* that—even when on the surface they appear to be opposing forces. For example, it was essential for me to lean into the hard emotions and do the work of grief, but it was just as necessary to give myself rest and to embrace little moments of lightness and joy.

Athletic training programs are built to account for the necessity of rest. Recovery days are an essential piece of the growth. We cannot hammer hard, day after day, with gruesome relentlessness and expect that we won't end up injured instead of growing. Without rest, we run into burnout. We lose clarity. We stop moving forward. We hurt so much that our efforts are blunted. The book of Genesis tells us that after creating the world, even God rested.[5] Both ancient wisdom and principles of physiology support the necessity of rest. In Aquinas' list of remedies, three of them pertain to the work of grief and two of them to rest.

Part of our nature as human beings is that *both* body and soul are part of our existence. Even though we tend to think of grief as being a purely emotional and psychological process, it is not. It's a very physical experience too. That means it is also essential to take care of the physical parts of ourselves.

When I learned that Aquinas recommended hot baths, I was amused that one of the means of comfort I had stumbled upon had been an advertised form of grief therapy for centuries. When I took bath after bath in the months after Lachlan's death, I had no idea what the ancient wisdom had to say about it. All I knew was that my body ached all the time and there was something soothing, quiet, and contemplative about soaking in a pool of hot water. All I knew was that caring for my physical body brought moments of comfort to my aching soul.

Research studies are beginning to reveal the physical impact of psychological and emotional stressors. *The Body Keeps the Score* outlines a number of these identifiable physical changes that can be seen and measured after someone experiences a traumatic incident.[6] I've mentioned the broken heart syndrome in which we can see cardiac changes that mimic a heart attack after a stressful event. We know that exercise, sleep, and dietary choices can all have a measurable impact on our mental health too. Exercise is known to release the chemical messengers of endorphins, serotonin, norepinephrine, and dopamine. All of these work together to help improve mood, reduce stress, and help us sleep and eat better. A healthy diet also helps our bodies function, repair, and recover optimally. It reduces inflammation, improves our immunity, and helps us just physically feel a little better.

When we're in the deepest parts of our grief, there might be nothing we can do to sleep well, but adding exercise and good nutrition is likely to help us improve the sleep we do get. Sleep is essential to restore our energy, improve our mood, and bring healing to our bodies. Being adequately rested improves our ability to deal with our stress, gives us more energy to get through the day, and decreases our cravings for sugar and caffeine.

Sleep often felt like a break from the constant oppression of my grief (which, on the flip side, imposed a risk of wanting to oversleep as an escape method). For some, sleep will be nearly impossible to find. There are some studies[7] that suggest a short-term sleep deprivation after a traumatic event can have an antidepressant effect, but if that difficulty sleeping is prolonged, it is worthwhile to seek professional help to break the cycle of insomnia.

When we are in such deep grief, it's hard to care about anything besides that grief, including taking care of ourselves. I wasn't particularly interested in maintaining my physical health. Part of me even thought, *Good. If my physical health is lousy, then maybe I'll get to join Lachlan sooner.*

When I chose to try to be intentional about exercise, sleep, and my food choices, it was much less about wanting to be "healthy" and more about needing those things as stress-management tools to lighten the unbearable load, even if it was only in the tiniest increments. When I implemented self-care, my internal chaos felt a bit more manageable.

In college, I competed in track and field, so intense exercise had become a stress reliever for me. For most of the grievers that I spend time with, however, self-care doesn't usually include a hard five-mile run. When just surviving through a day takes Herculean effort, finding ways to implement self-care happens in baby steps. In the beginning, physically taking care of myself sometimes meant that I pushed myself to take a shower, get dressed, and go outside for ten minutes. Taking care of ourselves means we choose to follow through on one little thing at a time.

Maybe self-care is foregoing the trip through the drive-through and eating something a bit healthier instead. Maybe it's going for a walk around the block. Maybe it's taking some time to sit in nature. We are all in different places physically when we are thrown into the depths of grief, so how we respond physically will need to be tailored to our individual needs. However we decide to do it, taking care of our physical bodies gives our souls moments of comfort, hope, and refreshment.

Our efforts to give ourselves a little care and tenderness include giving ourselves permission to take breaks from our grief, to do something we enjoy, to spend time with someone we love, to be engaged in lighter activities, and—dare I say it—to give ourselves permission to laugh.

I lived for a long time wanting to cling to my grief and sadness. Grief and sadness were the most powerful evidence that someone important was missing from my life. I worried that by loosening my grip on my sorrow, I might also lose the only thing I had left of Lachlan. I worried that I would be betraying him in some way. If I let go and did something I enjoyed, I was worried that I was saying I was okay without him.

Like it or not, I stumbled into moments of "rest." I had a toddler at home who brought an innocent lightness, laughter, and joy to our household, whether I felt ready for them or not. Westin's sweet innocence was infectious, and I couldn't keep myself from laughing with him from time to time. That laughter felt odd, foreign, and came with self-inflicted criticisms and judgments about whether it was "right" for a bereaved mom to laugh at anything. Even so, there was also something uplifting and healing in those moments. They brought little rays of hope that I could still possibly find joy, purpose, and a reason to live a wonderful life.

In those first years without Lachlan's physical presence, I didn't know how to connect to him if it wasn't through my grief. I worried that he would slip even further away if I wasn't holding tight to the pain of his absence. Only little by little did I begin to understand that my love for him was permanent.

By clinging to my grief, I was clinging to a shadow of my love for him. There was something truer, more solid, and more permanent in the love that remains than the grief I was clinging to. It turns out that it has been okay, and even better, for me to love Lachlan by engaging in the life that is left for me, by loving the people who are still here, by enjoying the little pleasures of this existence even though he is gone. Allowing myself to embrace these moments is one of the ways I continue to honor my love for Lachlan.

One quick decision to loosen my grip on sorrow did not set all my grief aside so I could live and love joyfully, but I slowly learned to give myself permission to appreciate moments of joy and pleasure. I was not dishonoring him or forgetting him, but rather bringing my remembrance to a higher level, and recognizing the beauty of a love that does not die. Being able to embrace the joyful little moments isn't a betrayal of the love for our child. It's an elevation of our love. When we think about the most meaningful moments of connection with others, they are the sweet, happy, and ordinary moments. That sweetness can still be our primary connection to our children, even after they die. Rather than losing my connection to Lachlan, seeking the love rather than the sorrow has allowed me to deepen my connection to him.

Our pain is softened and eased with moments of pleasure and joy. It turns our attention to the good that remains. That pleasure is found in the good company of a loved one, some lighthearted entertainment, or doing any little thing that brings joy. It turns out that Aquinas was right, and pleasure really can soften our pain. It is important to do our grief work, to make intentional time to sit with our pain, to process, and to mourn out loud—it is also important to balance that work of grief with rest, pleasure, and care for our bodies.

Protecting Our Marriage

Marriage can be amazing. It can also be really, really hard—even when life is good and everything is going right. Grief is unique to everyone and is influenced heavily by our personalities and coping mechanisms, by our gender, by our relationship to the person we're grieving, by our past experiences with grief, and by cultural expectations, to name a few.

No relationship is all sunshine, but two people can share one umbrella and survive the storm together.

ANONYMOUS

We also hold deep-seated beliefs on what grief should look like for ourselves and others. When we find something that is soothing for our souls, we expect it would be equally helpful for our spouse. When we know one another intimately, and we are grieving the loss of the same person, it is easy for unmet expectations to drive a wedge between us and our spouse. I had to learn to stop and put my expectations for David under the microscope to keep them in check.

There are abysmal statistics floating around on how many marriages survive the loss of a child. My mind would jump to those stats every time my husband and I were having a hard time aligning and I would wonder fearfully if this was the beginning of the end. But even though there were hard moments, days, weeks, or even months—on the whole, I felt closer, more bonded and more connected to David. He was the only other person in the world who understood what it was like to lose *our* child.

For the record, the statistic that 80 percent of marriages end in divorce after the loss of a child is based on a poorly-done study from the late 1970s. A survey was done in 2006 by a nonprofit called The Compassionate Friends[8] that suggests the divorce rate among couples who have lost a child is closer to 16 percent. A scholarly article titled "A Child's Death and Divorce: Dispelling the Myth" offers a similar reassurance:

> In view of the commonly held assumption about a high divorce rate among bereaved parents, a thorough review of literature was conducted to determine what evidence exists. Evidence was found to indicate that a child's death can strain marital relationships, which may lead to separation and/or divorce in some cases; however, there is no conclusive evidence that bereaved parents are likely to divorce as a result of a child's death. On the contrary, it appears that the majority of marital relationships survive the strain brought about by a child's death and may even be strengthened in the long run.[9]

In the wake of losing a child, there are key elements that contribute to how a marriage will fare after such an enormous event. These include the strength of the relationship, the cause of the child's death, the coping skills of each partner, and the means of outside support.

When a marriage is strong going into the storm, it tends to fare much better than the ones that were barely hanging on before the death happened. Major life stressors tend to have a polarizing effect: the strong ones grow stronger, and the weakest ones just might break. What about all the other marriages that fall somewhere in the middle? If statistics report only 16 percent of marriages end after the death of a child, then the other 84 percent of marriages have what it takes to grow stronger together.

A lot of self-reflection is needed to preserve one's marriage through this stressor. The necessity for communication, respect, and forgiveness grows. Those are the same things we have to do on any regular day of marriage but, under the heavy weight of grief, the need is profoundly exaggerated.

We have to know where we are in our emotions and grief on any given day, or at any given moment, and find ways to communicate that to our spouse. We have to be able to communicate our needs, what is helpful, and what is causing pain. And then we have to give each other the space that is necessary to have our own emotions, experiences, and ways of finding hope and healing.

It is important to find a balance between connecting as a couple where we can, and also leaving room for each individual to meet their own personal needs. Grief becomes a powerful opportunity to practice an open curiosity toward your spouse. There is value in seeing our spouse first as whole: intuitive and capable of commanding his/her own experience of navigating through the darkness. Their darkness, though similar, is not identical to our own, so we trust that they are doing the best they can with what they have, and then support them exactly where they are—just like we want them to do for us.

Leaning into our tough emotions, and being willing to sit and reflect on them, is a path to identifying the roots of our feelings and desires. Once those roots are identified, we can then be intentional about tending to them. The way in which we choose to deal with stressful events will always impact our relationships.

It doesn't matter whether it's a change in job, status, or income; a major purchase; a birth of a child; a move to a new location; or an illness or injury. Negative stressors of any kind can trigger the sympathetic response of our nervous system and put us into a fight, flight, or freeze mode. This heightened sensitivity naturally makes us more reactive to everything around us. We nurture our relationships when we learn how to be very intentional and mindful of our emotional storms and triggers. When we are aware of our reactive responses, we can start to slow down, and choose our reactions differently by making thoughtful decisions rather than knee-jerk, fly-off-the-handle reactive ones.

Another essential element to keeping our marriages intact while we are grieving is a willingness to forgive. When both partners are under an extraordinary stress, fumbling through a vast and deep darkness, there will surely be mistakes and blindness along the way. There will be days that we are sensitive and reactive, days where we are aloof and withdrawn, days that we need to talk about the loss nonstop, and days that we just can't bring ourselves to go there. There are days when our feelings align beautifully with those of our spouse, and we can be a vital support to each other. There are other days when our needs are opposite and by trying to meet our own needs, we are exacerbating the needs of our spouse.

Before we start pointing fingers of blame out of frustration, first remember the core, the heart, and the goodness of our spouse, and acknowledge that they, too, are living through hell. Relationships are softer and healthier when we encourage our hearts to be gentle with the people around us. Especially with our spouse, we will maintain our connection if we are ready to forgive them when they cannot support us in the ways we want them to, or when they need more from us than we can give. Let us be quick to forgive them when they are not behaving as the very best version of the person we married, for they too are living under that unbearable and soul-crushing weight of grief.

The cause of a child's death is another area that can introduce a lot of tough emotions and another enemy to contend with. Especially if there are any feelings of blame or fault, we will have to work harder than ever at our willingness to see others in the best possible light, forgiving the shortcomings of their human nature. Though it can be extraordinarily difficult, it is possible. When I read the powerful accounts of families who have offered forgiveness to the murderers of their loved ones, I am reminded of the freedom and peace that forgiveness gives.

While it can feel like moving mountains to reach that place of forgiveness, the tremendous benefit of doing the work is also ours to enjoy. The benefit is a heart that is peaceful despite the lingering sadness of grief. Anger, resentment, and bitterness can never be contained and directed toward just one person. Clinging to our hatred or blame will trickle in subtle ways into every other aspect of our lives. If we feel we had some role in what led to the death, that blame might be mostly directed toward ourselves. Here, too, we cannot be unforgiving and

We cannot be unforgiving and merciless toward ourselves and think that those emotions won't find ways to spill over into our marriages and the rest of our lives as well.

merciless toward ourselves and think that those emotions won't find ways to spill over into our marriages and the rest of our lives as well.

When we are hurting intensely, we crave connection and support from the spouse we've dedicated our lives to. We long for them to see our vulnerability and wrap themselves around those tender spots, sheltering us from our pain and heartache. However, it's hardly fair to ask someone in their own dark night of the soul to step up to meet all our grieving needs.

Spouses can lean into each other as much as possible, but it is also necessary to find other people in our lives who can fill in the gaps. While obvious in theory, it was still easy to find myself frustrated and irritated when there were gaps left unfilled as I held onto an underlying expectation that it was David's job to fill them. This is where the value of a whole support network comes in. When we let other people share in our experience, we create a space for a variety of needs to be met. Every person we carefully choose to let into the arena of our grief will bring a unique gift to our process of healing, helping us avoid the temptation to rely too heavily on one person to be our Superman.

Several years ago, I wrote this letter, trying to capture what it meant to have David by my side through this grief experience. I wanted to encapsulate the sudden shift in our life, the love, the steady presence, the messiness, the forgiveness, the gentleness, and the grace that helped our marriage grow stronger through this trial.

Dear David,

I know that deep down, you know of my profound and true love for you. I'm not as good at saying it and showing it as I wish I were. You have been like a rock for me. Silent. Steady. Unchanging. Solid. Trustworthy. A place for me to rest. You keep me grounded. You lift me up.

It's easy to celebrate the joys of love when our world is as we think it should be. However, it can also be easier to take our love for granted during those good and easy times. In that marriage blessing we sing at church, there's that line, "In your joy and in your weeping, God be with you," that makes me cry. Every. Single. Time. It's probably because those aren't just words to me, they are life, and they are marriage. I understand the depths of what they are saying. "For better and for worse" is far better and far worse than what I ever imagined it would be when I made that promise to you.

"For better and for worse" is far better and far worse than what I ever imagined it would be when I made that promise to you.

Some of my favorite times of ours, are those years between when we were married and when Lach died. There was such an innocence about us. We were untainted by the sufferings of the world. We were following our dreams together and making them come true. I finished school, landed a great job, we had two beautiful little boys, you were well on your way to finishing up your graduate program. We were setting ourselves up perfectly for the life we always dreamed of together. Sure, there were some tough days, but the big picture was exactly as we had planned it from the time we were teenagers. The world as I knew it up until then, was a place where dreams come true. If you want something, you just work hard for it and it will be yours for the taking.

Then we went from the best of times to the worst of times all in one swift moment. When Lach died, that changed the world. In the moment that he died, you became not just a partner to skip down the yellow brick road with, but someone to cling to in the depths of fear and brokenness. You are the only one in the world who knew Lachlan like I did, and the only one who would miss him like I did.

You seemed to have a way of being what I needed. You talked with me for hours most nights about the little things we loved and missed about him, about what it feels like to grieve like this, about how our life might look from here. You were someone to hold me up when I couldn't take it anymore, and on the days that I needed to be the strong one, you let me hold you. You stood beside me and quietly supported me in all the things I needed to do in my grief, even allowing me the room to do the things that didn't make much sense to you.

We weren't perfect. We were stressed, irritable, helpless. I had read the statistics and that made me wonder if we had what it takes to make it through. The statistic of high divorce rates for bereaved parents scared my intellect, but my heart never felt like we were in any real danger of reaching that point. You forgave me when I couldn't be what I should have been, which in turn, gave me the courage and grace to forgive you. There was a profound sense of God being with us during that time. Two people trying to make a relationship work during times of unbearable stress are going to have a hard time holding it together. A two-stranded rope is much more likely to unravel under stress than a three-stranded one. Especially when that third strand is All-Powerful. Though the two of us were being pulled to a breaking point, having that third strand to cling to gave us the strength we needed to get through. Thank you for allowing God to be a part of our relationship. He fills in the gaps where we can't meet one another's needs. I see how essential it is for our marriage to invite God's presence in times of both joy and weeping.

It was easy to know that I loved you when times were good. I didn't really know how deep that love could go until I experienced it when times were bad. For better and for worse. I know we are bound to have more tough times ahead, but with you, both in joy and in sorrow, my cup runneth over.

All my love,

Bri

Gentleness in Relationships

We create space for gentleness, forgiveness, understanding, and healing in our marriages when we make an attempt to step outside of ourselves and see the world through the lens of our spouse (even when it takes everything we have to do that for just a brief moment). The same ideas apply to the other important relationships in our lives.

We add so much pain to the already-heavy burden of grief when we hold tight to the anger and frustration that bubbles up in response to other people not stepping up in the ways we thought they would, or when they are creating more pain for us by the way they are responding.

I found myself swirling with these hard emotions, hurt and disappointed, wondering why so-and-so did this, or why so-and-so didn't do that.

Here again, it is our human tendency to create backstory and assign meaning to situations as an attempt to eliminate uncertainty that often ends up feeding our agitation toward others. When what we are feeling is a negative emotion, it can be easy to assume the worst about why people are behaving the way they are. Once we've made up our story, we often stick to that original version, without challenging ourselves to retell the story in a way that makes the other person one of the heroes of the story rather than the villain.

> *People are illogical, unreasonable, and self-centered. Love them anyway.*
>
> KENT M. KEITH[10]

One of my first experiences of being stabbed by the pain of others' behavior was on the day after Lachlan died. My family had stayed the night at our house in the basement, and in a lighthearted moment, were laughing, giggling, and playing. David and I were so fresh in the most profound and crushing of experiences, and the sound of that laughter was incredibly unbearable for us. We sat upstairs, writhing at the sound. It seemed callous, rude, and inconsiderate. *How could you possibly laugh in the home of a child who just died?!* David had to step out of the house and go for a walk. I had to hold back from asking my family to leave.

I remained wounded by that sound for quite some time. Ever so slowly as the dust storm of emotions around that moment of laughter began to settle, I was able to be more charitable in how I saw that event. Being on a different level of the house than we were, my family probably didn't realize how clearly their laughter could be heard. The extreme heaviness in the house, I'm sure, was suffocating for them. Laughter and lighthearted moments can bring comfort, strength, and courage when we walk in and through the toughest experiences. My brother was a junior in high school at the time, so my parents were probably trying to find a way to take care of him in the smothering atmosphere of grief.

Using laughter and humor can be a tremendous comfort for many. There are whole books written to bring laughter to the experience of grief. Even in concentration camps during the holocaust, humor was used as a coping mechanism. In *Man's Search for Meaning*, Viktor

Frankl wrote:

> To discover there was any semblance of art in a concentration camp must be a surprise enough for an outsider, but he may be even more astonished to hear that one could find a sense of humor there as well; of course, only the faint trace of one, and then only for a few seconds or minutes. Humor was another of the soul's weapons in the fight for self-preservation. It is well known that humor, more than anything else in the human make-up, can afford an aloofness and an ability to rise above any situation, even if only for a few seconds.[11]

My family wasn't trying to be callous or hurtful. They were using a real and healthy coping mechanism during a time that was unbearably painful for them too. Laughter simply did not match my own needs in the moment.

I learned that finding charitable ways to assign meaning to the behavior of others helped me tamp out much of the anger, bitterness, and blame that had started to blaze. I had to retell my made-up stories about why our childless friends didn't show up. Instead of being aloof, cold, or uncaring, it was more likely that they were unable to comprehend and process the depth of what we were experiencing. The new version of the story helped preserve those friendships through the storm.

My revised back story for friends who had kids and didn't show up to support me, was that having a friend whose child died might hit *way* too close to home. Drawing near to me and my grief would put them eye-to-eye with the mortality of their own children. I could see how that would be an extraordinarily hard thing to do. It was harder for me to be angry with people for not stepping in when I considered how vulnerable and scary it would be for them to do so.

Occasionally people said insensitive things that left me wondering, *Why on earth would they say that?!* If I stopped to put myself in their shoes it wasn't hard for me to imagine a position wherein I could say something similar. A natural protective mechanism is to assign a reason for a nonsense tragedy. If we can create a gap between the tragic circumstances of another person and our own life circumstances, that imagined distance helps us feel protected from being a victim to the same fate. When the tragedy of a child's death makes it to the media, we want to read the story, and satisfy our underlying need to find out how the death happened so we can keep it from happening to our kids. Humans writhe at the thought of being mortal—and even more so when that mortality applies to our children.

It helped me to be more forgiving of the human weakness of others when I pushed myself to consider how our perspectives and needs differ due to our backgrounds, life experiences, personalities, and coping mechanisms. David and I were at ground zero of this loss, and while there were many people who suffered with us and were grieving for Lachlan too, they were not in the same place that we were. It's not fair for me to expect them to behave like they were.

Yet, while they were not at ground zero, they were still each having their own individual experience of loss and pain because of Lachlan's death. For example, the grandparents who were hurting and reeling from the loss of a grandchild, and at the same time were hurting from the pain and helplessness of seeing their own child hurting so deeply. Our siblings, our friends, our extended family, our coworkers, and even strangers who heard about our story—all of them encountered some sort of suffering and pain because of their witness to our story, and each of them experienced that pain in different yet very real ways.

That brings us to a very pointed discussion on forgiveness. I've circled around the topic a few times, but it is worthy of direct attention. It's easy to think that forgiveness is just for the big offenses, or for the times when people purposefully hurt each other. With that underlying definition of forgiveness, I didn't feel like I had anything to forgive. Yet, I was holding onto resentments toward God and the people in my life who didn't meet my expectations. As I was struggling with these resentments, a quote attributed to Nelson Mandela came to mind, "Resentment is like drinking poison and then hoping it will kill your enemies." To move toward a peaceful heart, I learned to take those places of tension within me, those points of pain and friction, and root them out.

How do we do this? First, I found that I *must* check the stories I told myself about other people and why they behave the way they do. Over and over again, when I recognize that tight, fiery tension of resentment in my chest and throat, I remember to pause and put myself in the other person's shoes. I ask myself, "What would it take for me to behave the same way?" And when I do this, it helps me retell the story in a more charitable way.

The other important recognition is that forgiveness is needed for more than the hurtful things that people might do on purpose. More often we have to forgive them for simply being human—for their oversights and mistakes, for having their own needs that are different from ours, for not knowing what to do or how to help, or for having their own emotions that create barriers between us. It's just as important to forgive the little things. If we don't learn to forgive even the little things, gradually a heavy pile of resentments will be added to the weight of grief that is already so hard to bear.

The Benefits of Practicing Gratitude

Gratitude changes everything. In the deepest grief, gratitude softens some of the edges, but when we're suffering so intensely, it can be hard and unnatural to find anything to be grateful for. Other people can't coax us into feeling grateful, and when they try, it can become a source of resentment, stemming from the impression that they want us to forget our pain and "move on." The attempts to point the bereaved toward gratitude are often expressed in "at least" statements: *At least you still have other children. At least you can have another baby. At least he didn't suffer. At least he's happy in God's arms. . .* There are certainly things to be grateful for, even in the midst of our deepest pain, but there is no "at least" in grieving. It is tragic. It is painful. It is disorienting. And for a while, it is all-consuming. When others try to minimize our pain and get us to "look on the bright side" it often has the opposite effect. The push to gratitude often increases our need to defend the depth of our grief.

The world is indeed full of peril and in it there are many dark places. But still there is much that is fair. And though in all lands, love is now mingled with grief, it still grows, perhaps the greater.

J. R. R. TOLKIEN (HALDIR)[12]

In the days, weeks, and months that follow the death of a child, it may feel impossible to see anything but the darkness. It's like standing in a bright room and suddenly the world goes black. It takes time for our eyes to adjust before we can even begin to start seeing the little lights of things to be grateful for. When others try to steer us toward gratitude before our eyes have adjusted, it's like having someone who is sitting in a well-lit room tell us not to be afraid of the dark. Their attempts at encouragement mean little when they've never experienced the terrors of this darkness. It's hard to imagine that they can even begin to relate to what we are experiencing.

It takes time for our eyes to adjust before we can even begin to start seeing the little lights of things to be grateful for.

This dance of grief and gratitude is a place where, again, we see the necessity of balance and the mystery of paradox. We tend to want to pick sides: either gratitude and happy *or* grief and sadness. Holding the tension of that paradox and honoring the "both/and" reflects more truth and healing than the idea of "either/or." The word *paradox* is defined as "a seemingly absurd or self-contradictory statement or proposition that when investigated or explained may prove to be well founded or true... A situation, person, or thing that combines contradictory features or qualities."[13] The mingling of grief and gratitude certainly fits that definition in my book.

For gratitude to find a place to grow, it has to come from within. Gratitude is a seed that doesn't transplant well. If we sit patiently in our darkness and trust that our eyes will be able to adjust, the little stars of light will start to emerge. Like the wonder, awe, and humility that grows from staring at a night sky, we will start to appreciate the magnitude and the depth of the experience of loss *and the profound beauty within it.* The first little star-lights seen are often things like appreciation for compassionate medical staff and funeral coordinators, for the abundance of support from people around us, for a few hours of sleep, for a Puffs Plus tissue that is less abrasive to our nose, for the person who is there to greet guests and make coffee, for a peaceful death, for the gift of having had the child in our life at all . . .

As I explored some of the research that has been done on gratitude for my own grief journey, I learned that there is a relatively robust database that gives a more objective understanding on the benefit of practicing gratitude. Whether the temperament we've been given is naturally optimistic or pessimistic, making an intentional effort to identify the things we are grateful for can make a measurable difference in the way we live and feel. In my exploration, I found that gratitude is strongly and consistently associated with greater happiness. Gratitude helps people feel more positive emotions, relish good experiences, improve their health, deal with adversity, and build strong relationships.

"How Gratitude Changes You and Your Brain"[14] is a study from Berkeley that attempted to tease out whether happy people are grateful or whether it is grateful people who are happier—the chicken and the egg debate for gratitude and happiness. The study reinforces that it appears to be the latter: grateful people are happier. The study subjects were people seeking mental health counseling and reporting clinically low levels of mental health. They were divided randomly into three groups. All three groups received counseling services. The first group was also instructed to write one letter of gratitude to another person each week for three weeks, and the second group was asked to write about their deepest thoughts and feelings about negative experiences. The third group did not do any writing activity. Compared with the participants who wrote about negative experiences or only received counseling, those who wrote gratitude letters reported significantly better mental health four weeks and 12 weeks after their writing exercise ended.

There are a couple of points I think are particularly notable in this study. First, the participants were not given a list of items and told they were supposed to feel grateful for those things. By identifying and writing the things they felt grateful for by themselves, the feelings of gratitude were allowed to sprout from within. Second, the improvement in mental health didn't happen overnight. After the first week, there was no significant difference in what the groups were reporting. The change took time and consistency. We can't expect to sit down once to make a gratitude list and think we'll feel better for the long haul. For a practice of gratitude to make a difference in the way we feel, we have to be consistent.

An article from *Happier Human*, "31 Benefits of Gratitude: The Ultimate Science-Backed Guide," outlines studies showing a measurable benefit that comes with a practice of gratitude. The article states, "Gratitude may be one of the most overlooked tools for increasing happiness. Research shows it is the single most powerful method of increasing happiness."[15] Some of the benefits of a gratitude practice that are demonstrated in this article that are particularly pertinent when we are grieving include: an increased sense of well-being and happiness; improved health, sleep, and energy; better resilience and ability to cope with stress and negative emotions; reduced self-centeredness and feelings of envy; improved relationships; deeper friendships; and better social interactions.

I remember feeling torn when Westin would do cute and adorable two-year-old things. I couldn't help but enjoy his sweet innocence, but in a moment of lightness or laughter, I felt a sharp stab of shame as if I was betraying my grief and my love for Lachlan. Little by little, my understanding grew. This was part of the process of discovering that Lachlan was so much more than the shadow of grief that was left in his absence. Looking beyond that shadow of grief to the things of his life that brought joy and laughter was not betraying my love for him at all. Rather, allowing myself to feel joy and laughter was another way I could honor the gift that Lachlan's life really was to me. I was learning the richness that came when I could embrace both the light and the darkness of my experiences.

Brené Brown uses a great metaphor in comparing moments of joy to twinkle lights:

> Twinkle lights are the perfect metaphor for joy. Joy is not a constant. It comes to us in moments—often ordinary moments. Sometimes we miss out on the bursts of joy because we are too busy chasing down extraordinary moments. Other times we're so afraid of the dark that we don't dare let ourselves enjoy the light. A joyful life is not a floodlight of joy. That would eventually become unbearable. I believe a joyful life is made up of joyful moments gracefully strung together by trust, gratitude, inspiration, and faith.[16]

One of the things I deeply grieved, and wished I would have appreciated more during Lachlan's life, is the little ordinary twinkle-light moments of joy. What a shame it would be for me to lose another loved one and have the same regret, saying I was too busy grieving to let myself enjoy the moments of light with the other people in my life.

I love the twinkle-light metaphor because it highlights the balance between the light and the dark. We aren't in any way ignoring the presence of darkness. In fact, by honoring the space for the darkness, the delight of the light is enhanced. Here again we recognize the beauty that comes with letting our emotions be as they are.

When something joyful pops up, it is okay to soak in that moment of light, appreciate it, hold it, and cherish it. It will soften the pain of the darkness and highlight the joys of a life shared. In moments of being grateful for the light, we hold the paradox of joy and sorrow, light and dark, living the spectrum of human existence in an integrated and whole-hearted way.

In moments of being grateful for the light, we hold the paradox of joy and sorrow, light and dark, living the spectrum of human existence in an integrated and whole-hearted way.

As the saying goes, "It is not happiness that brings us gratitude. It is gratitude that brings us happiness." With openness and a willingness to cultivate and practice gratitude in an intentional way, a positive impact is made on the way we grieve and on how we perceive the world around us. Gratitude is a powerful instrument in helping us guide our own experience.

Surrender and Embrace

If I imagine life as a river, I was floating along quite happily before Lach died and enjoying all of the sights along the way. The course was predictable, and I had a good idea about what was coming even if I couldn't see it. Then out of nowhere, Lachlan's death was like being blindsided by a steep and raging waterfall. There was no way to prepare for this, and I suddenly found myself under the water, frantic, disoriented, and scrambling for a breath of air.

Somehow, I emerged to the surface. Looking around, the new scenery was not like what it was before. It was ugly and gray now. I hated this new place. That waterfall became a permanent division that marked my life with a "before" and "after." I wanted to go back to what I had before, but every moment pulled me further away from the comfortable and predictable stream I had known and loved. Now, it seemed to take all my strength just to stay afloat, and the harder I tried to fight the direction of the river, the more exhausted and helpless I felt.

I desperately wanted life to go back to the way it was before, but no matter what I tried, I made no progress. At some point, I understood that surrendering to this grief experience and this new life was the only real option I had, and I let go. I stopped fighting it and let the current of grief take me where it would. The lesson of learning to surrender to my pain and then embrace it has been a big one for me. It has pushed me outside my comfort zone of control and predictability. I like to plan ahead. I like for things to go my way, and I don't adjust easily when plans change. Once I've decided what I'm going to do, I'll do that.

Surrendering to grief means to take each moment, individually, as it comes, without expectations for how I should think or feel. I found too many times that as soon as I started expecting to feel any particular way, I was blindsided by a different emotion. When I thought I wasn't strong enough to get through a particular day, I'd unexpectedly have a pretty good day. If I thought I was getting better and was moving to a better place, I'd be swept underwater by a swift current of sadness. Fits of anger came out of the blue, as did moments of feeling okay.

> *The secret is very simple. It is to understand that we can only transform reality fruitfully if we accept it first.*
>
> JACQUES PHILIPPE[17]

Internal resistance to what we are feeling and experiencing will leave us with constant interior restlessness. As I began to surrender to the journey, knowing I could never really predict it, I started to find peace again. My goal became not to create an emotion or to change what I felt, but simply to acknowledge my emotion for what it was and surrender to that. I still wanted the old scenery back but I learned to let go of that internal fight for it. This step of surrendering to the new and unwelcome life comes before we can begin to embrace it, but learning to

I finally understood that there is nothing wrong with my grief as it is. Happiness is not higher, healthier, or holier than grief.

surrender was the harder step for me. I finally understood that there is nothing wrong with my grief as it is. Happiness is not higher, healthier, or holier than grief.

Once I stopped fighting my own world of existence, an openness to embracing what I now had came more naturally. When my heart was ready to accept that going back was not an option, it opened to begin seeking the new beauties around me. They were subtle at first, but the farther I've traveled from that treacherous waterfall, the more beauty I've been able to find—the lessons of gratitude are very tightly mingled with these lessons of surrender and embrace. Author Joseph Campbell said it like this: "We must let go of the life we have planned, so as to accept the one that is waiting for us."

Letting go of the life I planned does not have to mean letting go of Lachlan—it simply means incorporating his place in my life in a different way than I had planned. I have to find new ways to connect with the boy who is no longer physically here. I have to be willing to live the life I actually have in the best way possible, not grasping and bitter that it's not the life I had planned.

When someone we love has died, we recognize that it is the ordinary moments we miss the most. This new understanding and appreciation for the ordinary can be a starting point for being able to find gratitude and joy in the life that remains. In her research, Brené Brown identified gratitude as a key component in learning how to live in a wholehearted way. In *Daring Greatly*, she says, "In fact, every [research] participant who spoke about the ability to stay open to joy also talked about the importance of practicing gratitude."[18] Some of the most important lessons that emerged from her data about gratitude and joy came from people who have also known sorrow and darkness. Because of that grief and darkness they have learned to appreciate the value of ordinary moments. Brown writes:

> Joy comes to us in moments—ordinary moments. . . Without exception, all the participants who spoke to me about their losses and what they missed the most, spoke about ordinary

> moments. "If I could come downstairs and see my husband sitting at the table and cursing at the newspaper . . ." "If I could hear my son giggling in the backyard . . ." "My mom sent me the craziest texts—she never knew how to work her phone. I'd give anything to get one of those texts right now."[19]

One of the primary ordinary gifts of this unwanted version of life is the new people that I have been introduced to because of Lachlan's death. New relationships and new depths of relationships were made possible only because of the unexpected course my life had taken. In the new course of this river of life, many of the people I found along the way were people I'd never expected to be part of my journey, but they really are an amazing part.

Another gift in embracing this new course of life was in recognizing that my subsequent children might not even exist in my life as I had previously planned it. Lachlan's death changed the timing of how we planned to grow our family and led our hearts through a wrestling match of deciding whether we could be open to putting our hearts on the line by bringing more children into the world. We may not have been open to having these new children that we love without the previous death of their big brother.

There are also gifts in the unique experiences that my children have by growing up in a house where someone is missing. There is groundwork laid for their understanding that death and pain are part of the human experience and that they can rise above that to create something beautiful. They are learning something valuable about resilience just by being part of a family that always has to be intentional about practicing it.

Lastly, when I embrace this new course by sharing my experiences out loud—by offering bits of comfort to newly bereaved parents, by working to make a legacy that acknowledges Lach's life, by leaning into my new capacity to share in the most difficult moments of other people's lives—I discover unexpected grace that creates meaning and purpose out of the pain. Plain-old, everyday, ordinary joys are visible again, and the joy of living begins to return with the willingness to embrace this new unplanned course.

Balance between Holding on and Letting Go

When someone whom we love more than life itself is torn from our lives, it is easy to want to cling to everything that reflects them in some way. It is easy to want to hold tightly to every physical remnant of their existence, to keep a tight-fisted grasp on what our life looked like with them here, so much so, that we can't even begin to consider a new life without them. It is normal to feel that way for a long time. It's part of our desperate desire to go back to the other side of the waterfall.

The idea of letting go of attachments to the life I had before Lachlan died brought an underlying fear that I would also be letting go of pieces of *Lachlan*. But trying to hold onto something that was no longer a possibility stirred up a constant resentment over my life not going as planned. No matter how much I longed for what I had before, it was something that I would never be able to change or get back. And so I began grappling with where I could hold on, and where I needed to let go.

One of the struggles was figuring out how to acknowledge Lach's place in our family without him here. I didn't know any people who had pictures of their deceased children on the wall. *Is that poor taste? Is that clinging to something that I need to move on from? Should I try to hold onto him and his place in our family, or is that something to let go of? Am I honoring him by making a point to keep him as part of who we are, or does that make me a crazy bereaved mom who just can't move on?* I wrestled with how to integrate a deceased child into the life and future of my family in a way that holds space for both what *was* and for what *is*.

Death may change the way a family looks, and it may change the way the family functions, but it does not change who belongs.

Everyone will come to a different conclusion on what is the right fit for their household. My conclusion was that even death does not change the makeup of a family. Death may change the way a family looks, and it may change the way the family functions, but it does not change who belongs. I wouldn't think twice about a picture of deceased grandparents on the wall. It is an acknowledgment of people who are loved and a recognition of where we come from. A picture of a deceased child is really no different.

There is a lot of grief work around learning to balance where to hold on and where to let go. I hold onto Lach's picture but let go of the insistence that his picture reflects the same growth as the other kids. I hold onto including him in our Christmas celebrations but let go of not getting to see his eager smile as he opens his gifts. I hold onto the legacy that he left here but let go of the fact that he didn't get to create that legacy all by himself. I hold onto knowing that he is part of our family forever but let go of having his physical presence in our midst.

Finding the courage to let go of the things I could not control or change did not mean that I had to let go of him at all. It meant I had to find new and different ways to honor his belonging in our family and that shift created space for new little joys to emerge.

How do we honor the enormous absence in our lives and also find ways to live the best version of the life that we now have? Are there ways to do both? How do we let go of the physical things that we cannot have back and still keep the child close to our hearts? It is natural to wrestle with figuring out how to love a child when their physical body is not here to have and to hold. When a body and soul are separated, we step into a new realm of learning how to love and connect to a world that is beyond what we can see, hear, and touch. Learning to loosen our grasp on what is no longer here opens our hands to receive new ways of holding onto them.

It is inevitable that time will erode the details of memory, but time cannot erode what is eternal. It cannot erode him from my heart and soul. My connection to Lachlan has shifted to become less about the memories of him (while those are still important) and more about the essence of him. I cannot love what he does anymore, so I am left to simply love *him*. He is still every bit as much a part of me as my other children are. I find him in the stillness. I talk to him in my heart—and often feel his wisdom, his love, and his reassurance. This nonphysical connection will never be entirely satisfying to a physical being. But this nonphysical love is still important. It demonstrates the permanence of that love, and leaves me with a hopeful longing for that day when we can be together again. Those are things worth holding onto.

In our grief, there is a dance between holding on and letting go. It is give and take. It is honoring the past while embracing the future. It is participating in the memory of what *was*—not abolishing that from our lives entirely but transforming it to fit harmoniously with the life that now *is*.

Becoming Whole through Integration

When something tragic and traumatic happens, it creates many big and terrible-feeling emotions. These emotions are taboo to society and they usually aren't in line with the person we want to be. With societal pressures for how we are "supposed" to feel, it often makes us want to take that pain, and every reminder of it, and tuck them away out of sight. We hope the emotions that feel unacceptable will just go away and simply fade with time like the smaller discomforts of life often do. Sometimes our families, not knowing what to do, think they are helping us avoid the tough emotions by not bringing up the cause of our grief. The loss is only whispered behind closed doors and, as time moves forward, it becomes harder to crack the seal of silence.

> *Wholeness is not achieved by cutting off a portion of one's being, but by integration of the contraries.*
>
> C. G. JUNG

When we allow ourselves to experience the pain of the loss, we may worry about how others will perceive it. *People will think I'm losing it. I should be over it by now.* We feel pressured to portray to others that we are okay. This is a common trap while grieving a painful loss. When we stuff our emotions it will often appear to others like we have picked up and moved forward. However, in truth, that grief-box in which we've tried to pack our pain away is overstuffed and constantly threatening to burst open and intrude on life as we know it. That grief gets compartmentalized and set aside. We try to keep it packed away and prevent it from interfering with life, yet it leaks out all over the place despite our best efforts. It intrudes in the most inconvenient times, and the presence of that untended grief becomes especially disturbing to us when it shows up in uninvited ways.

In the book *Bearing the Unbearable*, Dr. Cacciatore tells of an exercise that she did with one of her grieving clients. They did a personification exercise, and the client was asked to create a character that personified her grief. The client, Jennifer, created Helga, the perfect picture of the most horrific hag imaginable with hair, teeth, posture, clothing, and home that were fitting for this wretched character. When Jennifer came in for her sessions, at first she had no room to invite Helga in, but instead told of Helga's intrusive nature. Cacciatore writes:

> Jennifer would document Helga's cruelty, how she came over uninvited, how she broke things, how she destroyed Jennifer's house. One time, Helga barged in on a perfectly lovely time Jennifer was having in New York City. For many weeks, Jennifer continued to resist Helga's trespasses.[20]

Gradually, with the nudging of her therapist, Jennifer became curious and finally agreed to start spending a little time with Helga. The time spent with her was tentative at first, but little by little a relationship between the unlikely friends had been formed. As Jennifer spent more time with her, Helga became less terrifying. Before the therapy sessions were done, Helga had even gotten a makeover. With Jennifer's help, Helga began to stand a little taller, her hair grew, the gray faded, she got a new set of clothes and a facial. Helga became more like an old friend. Cacciatore concludes the story by saying:

> When Helga was ready for a change, Jennifer helped her. But first, Jennifer had learned to accept Helga just as she was because it wasn't just the grief that Helga embodied—Helga loved [Jennifer's deceased husband] too.[21]

When grief gets packed away and cannot be openly acknowledged, it is called "disenfranchised grief." This term is coined to describe when someone is being denied the right to grieve openly, whether by their own ideas or someone else's; they are denied their need, right, role, or capacity for grief, and find an inability to grieve openly. People find themselves in that place for a myriad of reasons, but whatever the circumstances that create a disenfranchised grief, the result is the same.

The burden of silence adds to the weight of grief, and the griever feels more alone in an already lonely journey. The longer and deeper the silence has been, the more ominous it feels to break the silence.

That grief becomes the shadow that depicts the outline of a beast—but if we have the courage to look closely, we find it's not so scary after all. It's not pretty. No one wants to have stories of loss, and pain, and suffering to tell, but when we dare to tell our stories anyway, we become whole, authentic, and integrated. I have been invited into the stories of a few people who have had to overcome this shadow-beast and broken the seal of an extended silence surrounding their loss and pain. It is inspiring to watch the courage that it takes to approach that grief after so long a time. My heart swelled at seeing the healing and freedom that came from their willingness to face those shadows.

One of these families had given birth to twin boys almost two decades previously, one rosy and healthy, the other stillborn. There was so much attention focused on the living twin and the joy of bringing a life into the world, that the grief of losing a life was hardly acknowledged by their support system. The death of a baby before we've even gotten to meet him or bring him home is a scenario that's ripe for a disenfranchised grief. As time passes, it becomes harder and harder to allow ourselves to mourn that loss. It becomes an awkward and clumsy conversation to discuss the missing sibling with the living ones. For this family in particular, almost two decades later, that grief for the twin who died was still present and waiting to be explored. When that box was opened, it was as raw as if it had happened yesterday. There was no way to find healing without traveling through that darkness and without opening that chronic abscess and allowing it to heal from the inside out.

In Chapter 6, I introduced you to Aunt Mary Lou, and the many years of silent stifled grief that she had to endure. When a door was opened that gave her a new way to grieve the death of baby OJ, the integration of that loss brought notable healing to not just her but to her living children as well. OJ's little sister, now an adult, noted that as kids, she and her siblings could sense that something was "off" each July (the month of OJ's birth and death), yet most of the kids never even knew of this sibling who lived before them. In finally being able to talk about that unspoken grief, there has been healing within the family dynamics, relationships are more stable, and love and acceptance are shared in a richer way. OJ's little sister helped me with a project to personalize candles for other families who had experienced a loss. As we were wrapping up, she shared, "I will tell you what. . .being OJ's younger sibling is an interesting concept because it's like missing something that you never even had. Doing these candles have been healing for me, without me even knowing I had something that needed to be healed. These are really much more than a candle with a name on them."

When we are able to grieve in an integrated way, we are free to acknowledge and hold a place for that person's space in our lives and hearts. We are free to discover new ways to acknowledge the place for our dearly departed in our lives even now.

To integrate is to combine one thing with another so that they become a whole. Sometimes integration is hard. It means we have to make room for our vulnerabilities, and we have to risk some emotional exposure. No one wants to *be* vulnerable—the feeling is a little yucky—but at the same time, we admire vulnerability in others. Daring to integrate the hard stuff is daring to be vulnerable, and there is no truer testament to courage and authenticity.

It is prudent to note that it is wise not to dump all of our most intimate feelings on people we have not yet established a trusted relationship. That scares people away rather than inviting them in. The right to hear our vulnerable stories is something that others must earn gradually.

David and I choose integration of Lachlan into our lives when we choose to keep his photos on display along with the others, when we say his name out loud as we pray, when we tell stories about his time here, when we speak openly with the other kids about their brother in heaven. We continue to acknowledge him as part of who we are when we do something special to remember his birthday and the anniversary of his death. His existence is woven into the fabric of our being when we allow our hearts to be opened and we choose to live differently because we know intimately how fragile life can be. When we live this way, our grief is not an overstuffed chest threatening to burst open despite all efforts to keep it locked. This box of grief, when integrated, is freely opened and closed as the circumstances of the day present themselves.

Integration is a process of connecting the feelings and emotions of our right brain with the language and reasoning centers of our left brain. By telling our story, by putting words to our experience, by sharing our thoughts and feelings, and by moving our bodies through activities of mourning, we create integration, connection, wholeness, sincerity, and authenticity.

The Gift of Ritual

Another meaningful way to create integration is in the rituals that we develop to honor our grief and that ever-present absence in our lives. I did not appreciate the value of rituals until I met with a bereaved mama who was an atheist. In my predominately Christian sector of the world, I hadn't had much opportunity to spend time with bereaved parents who had a belief system that didn't give them the strong hope of heaven that many other parents lean on in their grief.

> *Ritual is the antidote to helplessness.*
>
> SUKIE MILLER

I asked this mother to tell me about how not having religion or a faith in God has impacted her grief. As she described her experience, the primary thing that she talked about missing were the rituals that religion often gives. Where others move through rituals of mourning to recognize the grief and the loss, and to guide a process of laying a loved one to rest, she felt a sense of emptiness, not knowing what to do without those rituals. As someone who has grown up in and around all kinds of rituals, it hit me how much I have taken that gift of ritual for granted.

A study out of Harvard identified how enacting rituals helped people recover more quickly from their losses, big or small.[22] Moving through simple rituals helped people regain their sense of control and that brought with it a sense of hope. Involvement in rituals brought some benefit even to people who participated reluctantly.

Appreciating the gift of rituals was an epiphany for me. I suddenly recognized how significantly ritual helped us through those first days after Lachlan died. Funeral rituals are taught by our culture, and we are guided through the motions with a pre-existing understanding of what to expect. But then the funeral is over, and life begins without our child in our arms, our home, or even on our planet. After the expected rituals from our faith and community are finished, it can be equally important to develop our own grief rituals as we venture into our new and unfamiliar life. With intention and creativity, we can continue building meaningful grief rituals that will carry us through a lot of the tough days.

One reason the first few years of grief are so hard is that we have not yet established any long-term rituals for our grief. At first, this idea of creating our own set of rituals is completely foreign. What do we do to recognize the birthday of a child who no longer lives? How do we honor the grief that leaves us missing them so fiercely as we sit under the Christmas tree? What do we do to recognize the significance of the anniversary of their death?

For many years, every one of those big days came with a sense of dread. David and I knew it was going to be a hard day, and we didn't know what to do with it. Even as we were thinking through ideas, we didn't know if any of those things were going to bring comfort to the hard days. *What if they just felt weird rather than meaningful? Which people do we invite to participate in these rituals with us? Will it be too uncomfortable for other people?*

In the first years, every one of those days was a day of trial and error. We'd give an idea a try and then evaluate. *Was that helpful? What did I like about that? What would I do differently?* And then as our grief matured, our needs for those rituals also shifted, so they continued to morph because what worked once didn't necessarily feel like the right fit forever.

Holidays, birthdays, and anniversary days have become easier to bear now that we know what we can expect to do. These rituals that develop over time bring a calmness to my heart, a framework to build the day around, and the satisfaction of an outlet to express the undying love that continues for my boy.

We now have settled into a pattern of Lachlan-related rituals. Those rituals preserve the memory of him and eliminate a lot of the uncertainty around those hard days. We have rituals that are built around the nonprofit fundraising events that we host in the late spring. We have rituals built into how we celebrate his birthday and Christmas, how we honor his space in our family, and what we do on the anniversary of his death. There is something soothing about a predictable rhythm.

Our rituals are small and simple, but they honor Lachlan's place in our family and they offer a structure to help us through the days that are especially hard without him. These rituals are part of our efforts to continue to integrate his life with ours. Rituals create order in the chaos of our internal experience. While small in outward appearance, little rituals transcend the physical act itself to communicate our continued love.

I Love You All the Way to Heaven

My grandma died several years before Lachlan did. When she did, my extended family adopted an idea of "pennies from heaven" and took to the notion that finding pennies in meaningful spots was a "heavenly hello" from her. While I liked the thought of a continued connection to my grandma, and I wanted to be able to believe the pennies were from her, I couldn't bypass my skepticism or give myself the freedom to experience the joy and satisfaction that everyone else did.

Many of the penny findings could have been easily explained by a well-meaning person planting the pennies to be found. Others were little more than nice coincidences, but there were a handful of penny findings that were harder to explain away. For example, my grandpa went to bed one night and found a penny on Grandma's pillow. Then there was the time that he sat down in the pew in church that was the standard place for my grandparents to sit, and he looked down and found a penny next to him where she would have sat. Another time, as the family arrived at my grandparents' house for a holiday gathering, we found a penny on the front step where Grandma would usually stand to greet us. A cousin of mine opened a book that Grandma often read to her as a child and a penny fell out from between the pages. My aunt was having a particularly hard day, alone in her house, crying in the living room and wishing she could talk to her mom, and she heard a "clink" and watched a penny roll across the floor. Even with all those stories, I never could let my guard down and open-heartedly receive those things as a purposeful

> *In the Communion of Saints, we believe that our relationships are stronger than death.*
>
> FRANCIS CARDINAL GEORGE

connection between the visible and invisible worlds. Yet, as those things started happening to me after Lachlan died, my heart began to open to the idea.

It is prudent to hang onto some skepticism, and avoid the pitfall of becoming too attached to these signs. As grievers, we long deeply to find a continued source of connection. We desperately want to know that our loved ones are safe and well, and we can put ourselves at risk of being taken advantage of by those who would gladly put a price tag on "manifesting" a sign for our comfort. If we throw all discernment aside, signs can be a rabbit hole that quickly leads into the occult and to people who are willing to use the longing of our grief for their financial advantage. With hands and heart held loosely open, these communications come as free gifts. Guarding our soul and our pocketbook, we can still leave space for the mysteries of these encounters to touch our grief experience. The most genuine encounters will not need anything from us besides an open heart.

We connected to the symbolism of a dragonfly within days of Lachlan's death. Dragonflies, like butterflies, are a symbol of death and the hope of a resurrection to new life. They remind me that Lachlan is alive and well in a new and glorious form just beyond the veil of the physical realm. Dragonflies have also grown to take on meaning in regard to the personal growth I have experienced in and through my grief. Dragonflies are a symbol of transformation, and are well-known as an image of the growth, wisdom, and maturity that lead to changed perspectives and a deeper understanding of the meaning of life.

Dragonflies have been the most common way for little "hellos" from heaven to catch my attention. My first notable experience of this was during a walk with a neighbor in the early weeks after Lachlan died. We were walking a lap around the neighborhood, Westin riding in the stroller, when a dragonfly joined us. It flew smoothly and lingered steadily beside us for several blocks, making the turn at the corner right along with us. We both noticed and were bewildered at this dragonfly hovering next to the stroller for so long. Dragonflies typically fly in an erratic pattern, changing speeds and directions constantly, not in a smooth straight line for blocks at a time. Something about that dragonfly connected my thoughts to Lachlan's presence. And with that, I started to lower my shield of disbelief.

Over the years there have been dozens of notable dragonfly moments. There are plenty of times that I see dragonflies and enjoy them, but I don't read into the sighting as being a special "hello" for me, even though they do always make me think of Lachlan. There are other times, though, that the circumstances and the coincidences are just a little too uncanny to brush them off as purely accidental. They sometimes show up as a clear and pointed "hello" on meaningful days, or times, or places.

One instance was on what would have been Lach's eighth birthday. I woke up that morning, and in my first glance out the window, I saw a *huge* dragonfly resting on our back deck. Sometimes I try to take pictures of the dragonflies I see, but they almost always fly away before I can get a decent photo. I wanted to show David this dragonfly that greeted me first thing on Lach's birthday, so I took a picture through the window. Then I went outside, inching closer a little at a time to see if I could get a better photo. The dragonfly stayed put even when I stood only inches away from it, snapping away on my iPhone.

Interestingly, on that same birthday, my niece Leah, who was born three days before Lachlan died, dreamed about him, without even knowing it was his birthday. Leah mentioned the dream as she was waking up, and her quick-thinking mom grabbed her phone to video the sleepy-eyed, raspy-voiced little seven-year-old girl describing her dream. She concluded her story with amazement: "It felt like I actually got to saw him! And I totally forgot in my dream that I never met Lachlan."

Could a skeptic still doubt these connections? For sure. But so many people have unique stories of similar signs, that the number of occurrences alone is enough to make us pause and wonder if there are opportunities for intentional connection between earthly living and heavenly living souls. Studies on the phenomenon of after-death communications vary widely in reported prevalence, with some studies reporting up to 88 percent of grievers having experienced what they consider as some sort of sign from their loved one.[23]

This part of the experience of loss is not often spoken about, and when it is, it's often discussed with caution and in small circles of trusted people. This is a topic that easily sounds crazy to someone who has not had similar experiences of their own. When I've mentioned the idea to people who are skeptics, I get a side-eyed glance and a leery "good for you, I'm glad it gives you comfort." I was one of those skeptics for a long time. Now, in addition to my own personal experiences, I have been open to hearing the similar but unique stories of others.

A beloved cousin of David's recently lost her young husband. He thought $2 bills were neat, and since his death she finds them in random places on a regular basis—we joke that she could start a college fund for their little boy with the $2 bills sent from Daddy.

Another family told their story of a computer that had been turned off and tucked away for a long time. In the days after their son's death, although the computer had remained untouched, it started playing a song that was particularly meaningful for them.

Another instance occurred to a family grieving the loss of their little girl. As the family sat at the computer agonizing over the task of writing an obituary, the printer flipped on and printed out an image they had of the soundwaves of her laughter.

A nurse with whom I work lost her young adult son yet continued to hang her son's stocking at Christmastime. The other stockings stayed where they were put, but her son's stocking kept falling to the floor. At first she was bothered by this, but when she realized that this was exactly the kind of practical joke that her son would like to play, she laughed and received it as a sign of his presence. Once she recognized it as such, the stocking stayed put.

How does being open to these signs contribute to the healing in my grief, you ask? It gives me little tangible and notable moments that leave my heart cracked open and my being humbled to the idea that there is more to this universe than what I can see and understand. It brings a very personal and meaningful beacon of hope that there really is a continued life beyond death. Lastly, it is a place where I have to practice letting go of control. Often when I desperately want some sort of "sign," I rarely seem to find one. On the other hand, when my heart is open without grasping, the signs seem to come more readily.

In the end, maybe I will find out that these signs were all simply coincidences, but I will still be grateful for them. Finding connections and meaning in little things like this helps me keep my mind and heart focused on the eternal life that we are all created for. The signs help me build confidence in the hope that my son's spirit still lives and they remind me that my relationship with Lachlan can continue, even as we live in different planes of existence. I know that our relationships do not end with death, and because of this, as I part ways with my living children, I will often say to them, "I love you always and forever, here on earth and all the way to heaven." Our loved ones can continue to love us all the way *from* heaven too.

Download a free version of the accompaniment journal at www.aThousandPoundsBook.com

10

Wrestling with God

What characterizes the true people of God is the willingness to wrestle. That's really something because it indicates that you're here as a contender. You're not here to be happy. You're not here to be complacent. You're not here to be materially satisfied . . . but you're here to contend with the structure of reality, and that's what will satisfy you.

JORDAN PETERSON

If there's ever a time that an individual questions the meaning of existence and tries to figure out where they fit in the big picture of life, it will be in a time of big change. The birth of a child is a defining moment in our spirituality. A baby changes *everything*. They change our lives in every way. They change our priorities, the way we use our time and money, our relationships with the people around us, and our relationship with God. It is a time that we question what we believe so that we can decide what is important enough to teach our children.

It's a common understanding that the birth of a child changes everything about our lives. What many don't understand is that the death of a child changes our lives even more. The birth of a child fits in with the mostly-predictable order of life as we know it. We expect big changes, we prepare for them, and we look forward to them. The death of a child turns all of that upside down and plops us suddenly onto a momentous spiritual crossroads. *What do I believe? Why do I even believe that? Can I still believe that now? Will I walk forward with the faith that I've grown up with, or do I need to find a different path for my spirituality?*

Some people are firm enough in their faith that even this earthquake doesn't shake them. Some will need to stop and steady themselves for a while before moving on. And some will decide that they can't move forward on their current spiritual path and decide to take a different road. No matter what we believe, and no matter how strongly we believe it, intense grief will be a time that we hold our belief system under a microscope to re-examine it. Every psychological restlessness is ultimately a matter of spirituality. Saint Augustine said it like this, "You have made us for Yourself, O Lord, and our hearts are restless until they rest in You." My experience leads me to agree. The restlessness of my heart continued until I started to sort out how God fits into this picture of loss and grief.

I grew up in my faith, always believed what I was taught, and I religiously attended church every weekend, even through college when it's easy to drift away for a time. As a mother, I prayed often that God would take care of my babies and keep them safe. I had convinced myself that if I held up my end of the bargain, God would hold up His.

I didn't recognize it at the time, but my attitude was a bit of a "prosperity" gospel: believe in God, do the right thing, and the world will be your oyster. Lachlan's death shook my faith to its core. *How could an all-knowing, all-powerful, all-loving God "take" a baby from his mother!?* I felt deeply betrayed by God, and I was angry.

I continued to go through the motions of my faith externally—I didn't know what else to do, but internally I was hanging on by a thread. The only thing that kept me holding onto a faith in God was the promise of heaven. That was the *only* thing that made any of this okay—the promise that Lachlan was well, whole, loved, joyful, and home where he was meant to be. It was a promise that I would be reunited with him when my journey is complete, and we would one day be together forever. But that promise is God's—and I knew I couldn't cling to His promise of heaven without also holding onto Him.

I was in a bit of a conundrum. I felt deeply betrayed by God and was angry at Him—but at the same time, God was the only one that could make this hurt better. I was like an angry toddler who is mad at her mom but also needs to crawl into her mom's arms to throw her tantrum. I was hurt, I was mad, and I was broken, but there was nowhere else to go for comfort.

The *only* beacon of hope that I could find initially was that life didn't end with death. If this life on earth was all there was, then I would have had a hard time finding much that felt worth living for. If there is more beyond the grave, then I could walk through my days with hope of being together again. So I walked toward the only light I could find, and I leaned in. In every place where my spirituality, religion, and life experience didn't make sense or fit together with the enormity of my loss, I sought answers until my understanding expanded enough for me to see how those pieces of the puzzle could come together.

The atheist mama who shared her desire for the rituals of religion was also brave enough to state her observation that a belief in God didn't seem to spare Christians from feeling the agony of grief and uncertainty. She noted that those who believed in God still missed and longed for their child in the same ways that she did. She pointed out that Christians often leaned heavily on the hope of heaven, but that hope is in something invisible that doesn't entirely eliminate uncertainty about what happens after people die.

Faith in God does not excuse us from the painful grief experience, and there is nothing wrong or lacking in our faith because we grieve. We see the sorrow, the pierced heart, and the tears of Jesus' own mother as she witnessed His passion and death. This is a woman all generations call blessed because of her perfect faith and receptivity to God. She shows us clearly that intense grief does not indicate a lack of faith. C. S. Lewis, one of the great Christian writers, points out this nuance:

> And poor C. quotes to me, "Do not mourn like those that have no hope." It astonishes me, the way we are invited to apply to ourselves words so obviously addressed to our betters. What St. Paul says can comfort only those who love God better than the dead, and the dead better than themselves. If a mother is mourning not for what she has lost but for what her dead child has lost, it is a comfort to believe that the child has not lost the end for which it was created. And it is a comfort to believe that she herself, in losing her chief or only natural happiness has not lost a greater thing, that she may still hope to "glorify God and enjoy Him forever." A comfort to the God-aimed, eternal spirit

> within her. But not to her motherhood. The specifically maternal happiness must be written off. Never, in any place or time, will she have her son on her knees, or bathe him, or tell him a story, or plan for his future, or see her grandchild.[1]

This truth is both intensely painful and beautiful. The comforts offered by faith will only comfort the God-aimed spirit within us. That leaves everything temporal, and everything not aiming ultimately toward God, to mourn intensely. A mother finds a large part of her own identity, happiness, and purpose wrapped up in her child—those parts of her die when her child's heart stops beating. Hope in what is to come does not eliminate the pain of losing those parts of our motherhood.

If it is only the God-aimed spirit within that finds comfort in the hope of heaven, then by aiming to expand the parts of our spirits that are God-aimed, it would follow that we open the door to expand the portion of ourselves that can be comforted by what God has to offer. If we want to experience more comfort by God, then it helps to become more and more God-aimed. And so, we wrestle. We wrestle with ourselves and our God. We wrestle with every hurdle and obstacle, every doubt and uncertainty in order to prune the things from our spirits that are not ultimately God-aimed. And it is in this wrestling that we become someone new.

The story of Jacob in the Old Testament[2] teaches us an important lesson about wrestling with God. Jacob was a man who lived a life steeped in deceit. While he was on his way home to make amends with his brother, after being away for decades, he had an encounter with the divine. He wrestled all night with a divine entity (with a man, an angel, or God himself—we don't really know), and though he was wounded in this battle, he was not defeated. In the end, as the sun began to rise, God changed Jacob's name. In that battle with the divine, there was something about the core of who he was that was transformed. He would no longer be known as *Jacob*—a name that literally means "one who supplants and deceives," but as *Israel*, "one who has contended with God and with human beings and has prevailed."

This kind of tussling with the divine is not a half-hearted encounter. This is struggling. All. Night. Long. It is wrestling with the divine as long as there is darkness. And when the dawn breaks, we find that it has changed us in a fundamental way. Jacob, the deceiver, found a new identity. He was transformed to become Israel, the father of God's people, and the father of all those who wrestle with the divine.

When we wrestle with God, we must engage with Him. We bring Him every hurt, every question, every inconsistency, every anger, every sorrow—and we keep bringing them, over and over again. It is okay for us to have anger and doubts and questions for God. These are not indicators of a faith that is lacking, but an indicator of a *relationship*. The key is not to sit in a corner by ourselves, sulking and hiding from God—but to really *engage* in wrestling, bringing all our fury and confusion into the arena and using it to fuel our battle with the divine.

I wrestled in my darkness. In every question, every doubt, every perceived inconsistency, I sought until I found the answers that bandaged my wounds, wrapped me in a blanket of peace, and felt like Truth. When the answers I found failed to do that, I kept looking until they did. I read a lot of books, I asked questions to those who might be able to offer helpful perspective, and I prayed.

Little by little, I've journeyed from being ready to walk away from God, feeling forsaken, abandoned, and betrayed, to a place of deep love for my faith and my God. My faith has been transformed from one primarily of rules to one primarily of relationship. My heart has new understanding that our God is not one to protect us from all pain, but is one to be intimately present with us in our sorrows. I can see daylight again.

Like Jacob, I've come to the daylight as someone who is fundamentally changed and with a permanent limp. That limp is a dislocation of my pride. In every place where I was certain that I was right and God was wrong, I was humbled. I still have another good hip and plenty of pride to contend with, but the understanding of my place with God will forever be different.

When we sit with God, perspectives change, clouded vision clears, and our restless hearts eventually find stillness. I love the analogy about how we, as parents, often know our children better than they know themselves. We see what makes them tick. We see their struggles, their impulses, and their desires. We see how they live in their own little worlds and how that sometimes causes them to misinterpret a circumstance. And when we sit with them, letting them think it through, prompting them with questions, and offering new perspectives, we help them understand themselves and the world around them. The same goes for us when we spend time with God.

No matter where we stand in our belief of God, the death of a child will present the opportunities to wrestle fiercely with our beliefs. I have been transformed by engaging in the fight—where things didn't make sense, I kept seeking the answers until the sun came up and my heart once again found a place to be still. Peace and hope in the midst of grief and suffering are possible, but only if we're ready to do the tough work of wrestling with God. We are all starting from different places in our faith, but if we open our hearts and minds to Him and invite Him into our journey, He will show us the way to grieve with grace.

11

Finding Meaning

We need to find within us the courage to slowly stretch and strengthen our grief-bearing muscles so that one day, we are better able to cope with grief's weight and, perhaps, one day to help another.

JOANNE CACCIATORE[1]

The meaning we find after a significant loss is a process of discovery, a search for ways that allow our loved ones to be part of what is meaningful in our lives, even after they've died. There is often no obvious or inherent meaning in the loss of someone we love or when the life of a child is cut abruptly short. I could never find peace in the idea that Lachlan died to "fit into some grander purpose." His death was just a tragic event. That doesn't mean that there *can't* be inherent meaning in how and why a loved one died—there are examples where that seems to be the case—but I could never make that idea fit for me and for Lachlan.

As a human creature built to seek meaning in all the ordinary and extraordinary events of life, my instinct is to try to make sense of the insensible. At first this led my thoughts to things like: *God must be punishing me for something I didn't know I did. Maybe He's trying to teach me some life lesson. Perhaps God allowed my baby to die for the good that will eventually come out of it.* These thoughts were not helpful for me. They left me feeling ashamed, unloved, and unworthy.

People often attempt to comfort grievers with the platitude of "everything happens for a reason." Maybe. But if there is a reason for a tragedy, I'm not convinced that the reason exists before the event itself. Rather, it is more fitting in most cases that the reason comes after the fact by the meaning we choose to create. God did not orchestrate Lachlan's death to lay the foundation for the good things that have come since then. Wisdom 1:13 says, "God did not make death, nor does He rejoice in the destruction of the living." Rather, He meets us in our sorrow. If we invite Him into our story, He will help us create something beautiful from the ashes.

Lachlan did not die *so that* something else could be. He just died. There is no meaning in the whole world that could satisfy my pain and longing for my child who is no longer here. The reason and the meaning that come out of the tragedy are there because of how David and I have chosen to respond.

In our quest to find meaning, which is a powerful part of integration and healing, we proceed with the understanding that finding meaning will be only an appeasement in the pain—a consolation prize. But it is a consolation nonetheless. As an athlete with a fiercely competitive spirit, I hated consolation prizes. It still meant I lost. No matter how great the meaning that we create might be, none of it fully justifies the loss of my baby. I wouldn't wish this experience on myself or anyone ever, even for all the worldly good that can come through it.

There is disappointment in not being the one holding the grand prize trophy and having to accept a consolation prize instead. However, it is only in our losses that we are given the opportunity to become the best version of ourselves. The champion's heart and the hero's journey will meet crisis and despair, and then not settle for defeat. Rather, they rise after the fall and find a way to move toward a meaningful transformation. In losing what mattered most to us, our child, we met the real-life abyss of death and despair. The hero's journey shows us that the only way out of the pit of despair is through a change of heart and perspective, so I opened myself to look for those consolation prizes because the pit of despair is an ugly place to stay.

Well-known grief therapist, David Kessler, worked closely with Elisabeth Kübler-Ross, the mother of grief theory. Together they spent many years teaching the five stages (or pillars, as I prefer to think of them) of grief: denial, anger, bargaining, depression, and acceptance. In 2019, Kessler added a sixth stage, or pillar: finding meaning.[2]

Finding meaning is essential not only in grief, but in making all of life worth living. Since our time in grief is one of intense grappling with the significance of life and death, finding meaning in and through our loss can help us also find deep meaning and purpose in the rest of life. In *Man's Search for Meaning,* Viktor Frankl, a psychologist and concentration camp survivor, points out:

> Man's search for meaning is the primary motivation in his life and not a "secondary rationalization" of instinctual drives. This meaning is unique and specific in that it must and can be fulfilled by him alone; only then does it achieve a significance which will satisfy his own *will* to meaning. There are some authors who contend that meanings and values are "nothing but defense mechanisms, reaction formations and sublimations." But as for myself, I would not be willing to live merely for the sake of my "defense mechanisms," nor would I be ready to die merely for the sake of my "reaction formations." Man, however, is able to live and even die for the sake of his ideals and values![3]

Speaking from his experiences in the Auschwitz concentration camp, Frankl goes on to say, "Has all this suffering, this dying around us, a meaning? For if not, then ultimately there is no meaning to survival; for a life whose meaning depends upon such a happenstance—as whether one escapes or not—ultimately would not be worth living at all."[4]

We do not want a Band-Aid of meaning for our grief, but we do want our grief, and thus our life, to be deeply transformed by the meaning we find. Discovering ways to infuse meaning into our experiences of suffering changes them. Viktor Frankl witnessed this in a powerful way while he experienced torments beyond description and watched the responses of fellow prisoners. The environment of unspeakable suffering was essentially the same for all of them, but he was able to witness patterns of thought that separated those who were mentally, spiritually, and emotionally destroyed from those who found a way to rise above it with resilience and hope.

What Frankl discovered in the camp is that finding meaning in the midst of profound suffering is a primary source of resilience and hope. He explains: "We who lived in concentration camps can remember the men who walked through the huts comforting others and giving away their last piece of bread. They may have been few in number, but they offer sufficient proof that everything can be taken from a man but one thing: the last of the human freedoms—to choose one's attitude in any given set of circumstances, to choose one's own way." He goes on to reflect, "The way they bore their suffering was a genuine inner achievement. It is this spiritual freedom—which cannot be taken away—that makes life meaningful and purposeful."[5]

A bereaved parent cannot change that they will have to live the rest of their life without their child. That pain is unjust and lifelong. While we cannot change the past nor the current circumstances of being bereaved, we can shape and mold our future around the raw material that we are given. Psychologist Jordan Peterson, in his no-nonsense approach, said, "Pick up your goddamn cross and walk up the hill. You've got a heavy load of suffering to bear and a fair bit of it is going to be unjust. So what are you gonna to do about it? Accept it voluntarily and try to transform as a consequence."[6]

We get to decide how we want to live this life, and we can make it something beautiful—we can *become* something beautiful. It is not a betrayal to our loved one to choose to climb from the pit of despair and create meaning and purpose, light and hope in our lives. When we choose to stay in the abyss, we remember them, but we do not honor them. We express our love for them more abundantly when we choose the path of good, and true, and beautiful *because* of them.

With a desire to live with resilience and hope, we can find ways to build meaning and make something better because of our pain. We can work to reduce the suffering in the world where we can, and let ourselves be transformed into something that is better in some way. Our anguish brings us to the precipice where we are often called to community and to communion. It is especially in, and through, our wounds that an opportunity opens to bring something deeply valuable to the people around us. Our vulnerabilities, pain, and anguish are experiences that unite us deeply to the common experiences of humanity.

We might want to think that by diving into meaning, it will more quickly eliminate the pain that we feel. It won't. We cannot skip the hard parts of grief to get straight to the purpose, peace, and hope. But it is possible to seek meaning in and through the hard parts. For a long time, I felt like I was sinking deeper and deeper, despite every effort to find meaning and bring good out of my pain. Meaning is not a flotation device that keeps us from sinking, but it brings a reason to push off when we've hit rock bottom. While searching for meaning hasn't spared me from experiencing the hurt, I am convinced that the way we choose to carry our sorrow still matters. It matters to our own personal journey, and it matters for the people around us. Searching for whispers of meaning in our sorrow gives us a source of strength to bear our suffering with grace and enables us to find a will to make a life that feels worth living.

The search for meaning begins in finding ways to reflect the love that did not die. This is a very individual and subjective part of the grief journey. What we choose to do, and how we choose to honor our loved one is influenced by our own personality and by the practicalities of our life. How we seek to infuse meaning into our experience—whether in big or small ways, whether out loud for the world to hear or in an intimate and quiet way—in no way reflects the depth of our grief and our love. We don't have to do something giant because our love and our grief are giant. On the hardest days, when we're just trying to hold onto our will to live, we might simply fall back on the meaning that comes from knowing that we are the ones who can tell our children's stories, who can keep their memory alive, and who can continue to make meaning from the fact that they were here.

This is a deeply personal and intimate journey. Some people will have the time, resources, and ability to start large national organizations. Those are fantastic, and many influential outreaches have been launched to make meaning from pain and loss. Countless others find smaller, local ways to make an impact and honor their loved one. Most often grievers find contentment in the quiet and meaningful ways within their own homes and hearts to honor those they have lost.

In our search for meaning after Lachlan's death, David and I tried all kinds of ideas. We started with concrete little things. We did random acts of kindness and made little cards to tell the recipient that act of kindness was done in memory of our son. For example, I would buy coffee for the person in line behind me, drop off flowers at the doorstep of a stranger, or hand a Target gift card to a random person as they entered the store. Other ideas in our search to honor Lachlan and create meaning in our grief included building a memorial garden in our backyard with the help of our close friends and family; facilitating the creation of a bigger memorial garden in our neighborhood park; and purchasing bricks and nameplates at a number of public memorials.

As I searched desperately for resources to help me survive my grief, the seed for Lach's Legacy, our little nonprofit organization, was planted. I wanted to offer a hub where local grief resources would be easy to find. Appreciating the benefit I found in the companionship of other bereaved parents, especially those who walked a similar journey to mine, I envisioned a place where families who have experienced the unexpected loss of an infant could connect. The planning of a nonprofit was a place to put my grief energy. It took many conversations and phone calls as I learned how to start a nonprofit and what I wanted it to look like. The work was a way that I could be thinking about Lachlan, doing something *for him*, and also be inching forward into this new life I had to live. Using this avenue to create meaning and purpose was a healing part of my grief work. It continues to give me an outlet and a place to talk about Lachlan, while bringing something meaningful to the grief experiences of others.

I've seen other families create meaning in their grief with projects like building all-inclusive parks, adding sun-shades or special swings to a local park, changing career paths, taking an annual trip to a special place, creating artwork, or raising money for a meaningful cause. Some families build special traditions around the holidays. Others volunteer their time in ways that honor their loved one. There is no right or wrong way to create meaning in our grief, but there is comfort that comes in finding *something* to do in honor of the one we lost.

Sometimes, it's the small and ordinary things that are a more important avenue for building meaning. While our nonprofit has been a great source of healing and hope, the most valued meaning in my grief is in the subtler shifts within the core of who I am, my perspectives, and my values. These are more abstract forms of meaning and take time to begin to reveal and define themselves. Only the hindsight gained from more than a decade of grief allows me to see and embrace those internal changes as part of my meaning. These changes are common to the experience of post-traumatic growth. We become more aware of the gift of the present moment because of our experience of profound loss. We are more appreciative of the gifts people bring to our lives. We grow in our capacity for empathy as we become less fearful of difficult emotions. We are quicker to forgive. We are gentler in our judgments of others. Our faith is stronger. Our understanding of the temporal nature of our time on earth is deeper. If my time with Lachlan and my experience of losing him helps me love the people around me better and to cherish those relationships—even when they are imperfect and messy—then his life and his death were not in vain. These are internal changes that enrich my life and are a direct reflection of the lessons of love that came through Lachlan's life and death.

Success in the search for meaning requires a heart that is open to looking for meaningful moments. Some meaning might reveal itself very quickly, but it is also necessary to be patient because the fullness of the meaning can often take a long time and a process of trial and error. But, as Viktor Frankl says, "Once an individual's search for meaning is successful, it not only renders him happy but also gives him the capability to cope with suffering."[7]

Suffering is sometimes described as the tension between the amount of pain we are feeling and our perceived ability to cope with that level of pain. When we bring meaning into our experience, we reduce that gap and thereby soften the amount of suffering we feel in our pain.

Meaning does not take away our pain, but it does profoundly increase our capacity to cope. As we grow in confidence in our ability to cope with our pain, we can let the waves of grief come and go as they may. We will have peace and assurance that we will again be able to find our way through to the other side of that wave of sorrow.

12

Eternal Perspective

They say that time in heaven is compared to the blink of an eye for us here on earth. It comforts me to imagine my child running ahead of me through a beautiful field of wildflowers and butterflies; so happy and completely caught up in what she is doing that when she turns to look for me, I'll already be there.

UNKNOWN

My heart couldn't bear to leave Lachlan out of the lineup of the photos of our kids on the wall. While the pictures around Lachlan continue to reflect the growth of our living children, Lachlan's photo stays the same. His photo looks out of place in the lineup and it is a constant reminder that there is something different about our household. Yet, while the pictures on the wall are a daily reminder that someone is missing, they also are a reminder that heaven is our ultimate home and we are created for something beyond life on earth. When we imagine our family together, it has to be with heaven as the backdrop. The kids all know that Lachlan is in heaven, and that if we play our cards well, we will have the opportunity to join him in paradise. We dream together of what heaven might be like. Emmett grins and giggles at the thought of a new and improved body with the ability to teleport and walk through walls—like a superhero. Leo had a phase where he would ask in exasperation, "When can I die? It takes sooo long! I want to go to heaven!" While it was a little troubling to hear my preschooler whine about why he couldn't die already, I knew his comment was coming from a place of wanting to see this paradise we dream of and wanting to meet the brother he's never known.

Since Lachlan's death, I have a clearer understanding of the temporal nature of life on earth and a solidified hope in heaven. Growth in this eternal perspective has also given meaning to my loss. My heart now pines for something that is not here, every day, and in a very real and concrete way. That pining is a reminder that there is something more to long for. C. S. Lewis writes this in *Mere Christianity*:

> Creatures are not born with desires unless satisfaction for those desires exists. A baby feels hunger: well, there is such a thing as food. A duckling wants to swim: well, there is such a thing as water. Men feel sexual desire: well, there is such a thing as sex. *If I find in myself a desire which no experience in this world can satisfy, the most probable explanation is that I was made for another world* [emphasis added]. If none of my earthly pleasures satisfy it, that does not prove that the universe is a fraud. Probably earthly pleasures were never meant to satisfy it, but only to arouse it, to suggest the real thing. If that is so, I must take care, on the one hand, never to despise, or to be unthankful for, these earthly blessings, and on the other, never to mistake them for the something else of which they are only a kind of copy, or echo, or mirage. I must keep alive in myself the desire for my true country, which I shall not find till after death; I must never let it get snowed under or turned aside; I must make it the main object of life to press on to that country and to help others to do the same.[1]

Lachlan is no longer here, but my heart knows he continues to exist—exist in eternity, in a place outside of time and space. And if *eternity* is the future for all of us, then I must remember that the portion of my existence that is spent in the confines of time is quite minuscule—even if my life lasts a hundred years. Instead of despising the longing in my heart for what I don't have, I can be thankful for the longing. It turns my attention to the reality that we are made for more than what this world offers.

While we are here on earth our physical existence is bound to time and space, making it difficult to grasp how anything might exist outside of what we can see, and feel, and touch. The thought of living the rest of my life without the presence of my child is suffocating, but when I shift my attention to an eternal perspective, I can breathe again, knowing my separation from Lachlan will not last forever. "Indeed, before you the whole universe is like a grain from a balance, or a drop of morning dew come down upon the earth" (Wisdom 11:22). This separation from Lachlan, as big as it feels, is temporary—it is a grain—and not forever. Sixty years or so without Lachlan becomes just a moment when compared to eternity.

The relative nature of time is easier to understand if we look through the lens of a child. Take, for example, the days leading up to Christmas. Kids feel like each of those days is an eternity—waiting and longing for Christmas to finally come—while the adults are surprised how quickly the whole month flew by. Or, we could use an analogy of a less pleasant nature. When a child breaks a bone, in the eyes of that child, the time they have to spend in a cast feels like a lifetime. As an adult, we can recognize the discomforts of that circumstance, but we also understand that six weeks will actually be a very short window in the span of their lifetime. Time is relative to the personal perspectives that we hold, and with a shift in perspective we can shift how we view time.

Author and teacher Francis Chan gave a demonstration to help illustrate eternity. He brought on stage a length of rope that was meant to represent the timeline of our existence. The long, white rope stretched and coiled across the entire length of the stage, and the audience was encouraged to pretend the rope actually goes on forever. The first couple inches of that very long rope were colored red and represented our lifespan on earth. Chan said, "What blows me away is some of you—all you think about is this red part. That's all you think about! You're consumed with this." Gesturing to the rest of the white rope, he exclaimed, "Are you kidding me?! What about this?!"[2]

That's a beautiful illustration. If I choose to spend the "red part" of my existence with the hope and belief that there is much more to the rope, it changes the way I live. Through God's grace and mercy, eternity and all its promise can be mine. When my perspective grows to include eternity, something inside of me shifts. What I choose to do and how I choose to respond to the situations around me matters. Not just because it will have an impact on the way I feel during this "red part" of my existence, but because my faith teaches me that it also impacts how I will spend eternity.

Even as a concept in our head, the idea of eternity makes a difference in our ability to endure the grief we will experience in our time left on earth. But when that concept moves from our heads to our hearts, it deepens and solidifies that new perspective on time, on what we choose to think about, and on why we choose to live in the world the way we do.

It was the gift of a dream that moved the concept of eternity from my head and planted it firmly in my heart. For many years I longed and pleaded with God for a "visitation" dream that I had heard other bereaved people talk about, a dream where it truly felt like their deceased loved one was present. I prayed in every way I knew how for that kind of dream, yet night after night, I woke up empty-handed. I longed for this experience so fiercely that it made me doubt God's goodness—and my own worth—when a dream like that didn't come. After years of desperate prayer and constant disappointment, I was finally able to soften in the way I brought my request to God. I decided to trust that He knows how much I would love to have that experience and I then set that desire in His hands and walked away from it.

Almost a decade after Lachlan died, the dream came. It is an experience too big for words, and I held it quietly close to my heart for quite some time. I worried that if I tried to reduce the experience to what fits within the limitations of language, something would be lost. Words do feel inadequate as I describe this dream, but it has been an important part of my experience, so I am sharing it with you anyway.

The dream began with me trying to park my van in a wide grassy area of a park. I seemed to intuit that the area was connected to a local high school boy named Nehemiah who had been killed in a car accident two years previously. I had never met Nehemiah myself, but had several secondary connections to him. As I started to back my minivan into the parking spot, suddenly I saw Nehemiah through my rear-view mirror and he guided me into my parking place. He then playfully came around to the car door and greeted me with a warm hug as I got out. The hug felt comfortable, as if we had known each other well.

Looking around the park, I saw various groups of people. Some of the people appeared more colorful, radiating hues that were brighter and more saturated than everything else around them. I quickly understood that those who were brighter were from heaven and the others (who appeared much duller in comparison) were of earth. The park was a meeting place of sorts between heaven and earth. I stood in awe, slowly taking everything in. As I did, Nehemiah communicated to me without speaking that he would see if Lach could come.

I continued to turn around, slowly scanning my surroundings in wonder. As I turned to what was originally behind me, I saw a baby grand piano sitting just off in the distance. Lach was sitting on the bench reaching toward the keys of the piano. He was still ten months old, and wore the green and orange striped shirt that he wore both in our favorite picture of him and on the day he died. The muted colors of the shirt were now bright and almost glowing. Everything about Lachlan was radiant. The moment I spotted him, we made eye contact and Lach gave me a sweet and knowing little purse-lipped grin. I ran toward him and scooped him up, hugging him and kissing him. In that moment, everything in and around me felt right and whole.

As I held Lachlan, I felt *so much* love and peace and joy. *So much!* All at once, while I was standing at this edge of eternity, the grief that had always felt enormous and life-changing, dwindled into something that was barely perceptible. Compared to the joy I was feeling in that moment, my grief was like a teeny, tiny, and perfectly natural reaction to being separated from someone we love or something we are enjoying. The all-consuming and soul-crushing pain of losing a child became as insignificant as the whisper of sadness that we feel when any ordinary thing comes to its natural end, like at the end of an amazing movie or when a great roller coaster ride comes to completion. It was a sadness that would be barely perceptible if I hadn't been mindful to notice it.

As I was holding Lach and coming to understand my loss and grief with a new eternal perspective, I began to wake up. That time with him was only a brief moment—yet it was a moment that has left a permanent mark on my spirit. As I was waking up, I fully understood I would wake up to continue living a life separated from Lachlan. And the most surprising part was that, for the first time ever, *I was okay with this!* I had spent years of my life wanting nothing more than to have Lachlan back here, not being comfortable for one second that this was the life I had to live. With this new understanding of eternity, my separation from him suddenly became no big deal. For the first time I *felt* the reality of how small and insignificant our time of separation and grief is when it is compared to the overwhelming love, joy, and timelessness that is to come.

I woke up with tears in my eyes—but these were not tears of sadness, they were happy tears. They were tears of delight in my peek at a joy, a peace, and a love so abundant they can reduce a life-changing grief into something that is barely perceptible.

I don't dream often, and when I do, there is usually not much to make of it. This dream was so clear and vivid, unlike any dream I had ever had. It gave me new perspective to hold onto, as well as an infusion of hope and courage for the journey. The new perspective was applicable not just to the loss of Lachlan, but to the rest of my life's struggles too. If the crushing heaviness of losing a child is nothing but a sigh in comparison to eternity, how much smaller are all of the other struggles, discomforts, and disagreements that are part of the life on earth?

In the remainder of our time on earth, bereaved parents will never feel entirely whole or complete. A piece is always missing—and it's meant to be that way. It leaves us longing for the world beyond this one. We can view that persistent longing as a call to turn our attention toward God and His desire to give each of us an eternity that will satisfy every longing within us.

With a deeper appreciation for an eternal perspective, it made room for me to accept that this life will be imperfect. As C. S. Lewis explained, everything that gives us joy and satisfaction here is *a copy, a mirror, a mirage*. Imperfections leave room for our hearts to desire something better, something more. We can rest in the messy imperfection because, for now, it's *supposed* to be that way, and walk forward with a trust that the longings of our soul will one day be satisfied.

13

Discovering Our Strength

Sorrow, however, turns out to be not a state but a process.
It needs not a map but a history, and if I don't stop writing that history
at some quite arbitrary point, there's no reason why I should ever stop.
There is something new to be chronicled every day.

C. S. LEWIS[1]

Grief does not end. There is no point at which we feel like we have it all figured out, all processed, and we can check that box to move on to something else. Grief is always moving, changing, and morphing, bringing new presentations of sorrow to the forefront. It is like a spiral staircase, taking us around and around to processing the same concepts of life, death, meaning, and purpose at ever-deepening levels. Just when we thought we'd figured out all there is to one particular aspect, we find that when we've circled back around there's still more to learn.

This book is written with the hindsight of where I've been and how I've managed to traverse the chasms, fire pits, and dragons along the way. Written from this place and having processed much of the hard stuff, those battles can seem as if they weren't as hard as they felt in the moment. It is like the difference in perspective from the one who is dangling over the fire pit on a frayed rope bridge threatening to snap, and the one who has crossed that bridge and put her feet back onto solid ground on the other side.

Having my perspective, as someone who has crossed the bridge, in no way takes away the fear and anxiety of standing in the spot where your existence is hanging by the last frayed tassel. And it doesn't offer the comfort of a guarantee that you'll make it to the other side too. My way of meeting those obstacles might not work for you, and that's okay. Take what is valuable from my experiences and leave the rest, forging your own way through your own wilderness.

Recently, sitting next to a campfire with my boss-turned-friend, while our kids made s'mores, I mentioned that I was writing a book on my experience of learning to live again with peace and joy while carrying the weight of losing a child. He asked me to describe how my experience of happiness is different now than it used to be. In the moment I fumbled for a good answer, but the conversation prompted me to continue to reflect on that as I sought the right words to describe the change.

I once heard a snippet of a poem titled "On Joy and Sorrow" by Kahlil Gibran that says, "The deeper that sorrow carves into your being, the more joy you can contain. Is not the cup that holds your wine the very cup that was burned in the potter's oven? And is not the lute that soothes your spirit, the very wood that was hollowed with knives?"[2] Sorrow is the cup that holds joy. The deeper our experience of sorrow, the deeper our capacity for joy. This analogy rings true for me, but as I pondered how to describe my shift in perspective, I searched for something more. Gibran's poem leaves me with the impression that once the cup is carved, everything is always joyful and happy-go-lucky. It's not.

My brother once shared with me an image of the human person that came to him during a time of prayer. He saw the human person as a tiny planet covered in water. What is happening on the surface of the water is the emotional current of the moment. Sometimes, the water is still and calm, and we are peaceful in our present state. At other times the water is choppy, and our mood is a bit irritable. And sometimes there are big storms with giant waves that threaten our well-being. No matter what is happening on the surface of the water, we can dive into the deep and find a sanctuary of stillness. And even beyond those depths, there is a network of underwater caves. If we dare to go there, we'll find a window that peers into the center of that tiny planet. What we discover when we look into the core is a vast and infinite universe. There is something infinite contained *within* that finite body.

That imagery for the human person gave me a means to describe the shift that has happened since Lachlan died in how I experience happiness and peace. Before his death, I lived my life in the shallows, following the movement of the surface waters. Happiness was experienced when the waters were still and comfortable and the fishing was good. The tough moments were experienced when the external circumstances made the water less inviting. My peace was dependent on the conditions of the surface water. Lachlan's death thrust me out into the deep where the waves were much more ominous. It was scary and overwhelming at first, but there was also something for me to discover out in the deep. It was there that I learned I could go below the surface, and when I did I was not at the mercy of the surface water. In the deep I found a refuge of stillness that is always accessible.

As much as I'd love to stay in that deep stillness forever, I'm like an orca living in the deep waters but unable to stay under the surface forever. I need to live much of my life near the surface, where I experience the fullness of the emotional climate. However, I always know that the refuge of the deep is available to me if I make the effort to go there.

Even after working through much of our grief, my life will not be rainbows and sunshine every day. It is more like having an undercurrent of peace. There are plenty of storms and turbulence to be weathered. The difference is that now we have deeper waters in which to retreat. With that safety net of stillness in the deep, we can experience the hard things and know that we'll be okay. We can live largely outside of the thrashing that happens when we are confined to the surface. We can dive into a place of stillness and see the stormy waters from a different perspective.

In the nitty-gritty of the daily grind of grief, the healing journey doesn't feel like a beautiful transformation, or like growth, or like learning to be better. When we put all our efforts into "grieving well" or "doing something meaningful with our loss" or embracing the painful journey as a grand self-improvement project—in essence, aiming to force a transformation of our spirit—we move no closer to any of those things. If we turn our grief into a self-improvement project we will find nothing more than additional feelings of our own judgment, failure, disappointment, shame, and exhaustion from trying to be something that we aren't.

When we turn *toward our grief*—stop fighting it, stop judging it, stop expecting some magic to happen, stop trying to be something, and just *be*, just breathe, just accept *what* we are and *where* we are—we begin to know our worth and start to find meaning from the ground up. It is in the darkness, stillness, and surrender that we start to *become*. Grief is an opportunity for self-acceptance more than self-improvement. In the deepest parts of our being, we discover that we are enough and we are worthy of love, just as we are. Therein lies the transformation. It cannot be created, forced, or rushed, but grows organically from that still small place within.

Grief presents a powerful opportunity to dig deep and learn to understand ourselves. It is in learning to *be,* rather than striving to *do* something, that our hearts learn to rest in our own innate dignity and worth. When we nourish the roots of our being, digging through the dirt rather than reaching for the treetops, our spirits organically begin to grow and are transformed into something a little more wise, humble, and authentic than we used to be.

Most meaningful changes take place at a rate that is so slow they are nearly imperceptible. C. S. Lewis says it poetically: "Perhaps the changes were not really observable. There was no sudden, striking, and emotional transition. Like the warming of a room or the coming of daylight. When you first notice them they have already been going on for some time."[3]

And so we take courage in knowing that even though we will encounter many days that leave us uncertain about whether we can survive our grief, there is still a reasonable hope that we will find a life worth living. There are days when all we can do is remember to breathe—and so that's what we do. And then as often as we can, we bring our attention back to our desire and intention to rebuild a life that feels worth living. Even after the blackest and longest of nights, the daylight will surely come. And one day we will suddenly find we are living a life we love, even while we continue to carry a thousand pounds of grief.

Before We Part

To my friends in Christ

Despite covering so much material in these chapters, this story still leaves us wanting more. We touched on many of the temporal aspects of grief, but barely scratched the surface of how our loss impacts our relationship with the Lord. The death of someone close to us stirs up some of the biggest questions we will ever face about God and where we find Him in the midst of our suffering.

There is abundant overlap in the temporal aspects of grief and the concurrent wrestling with God that happens as we try to make sense of our suffering. Yet, there is enough distinction to be able to tell those parts of the story separately. My path to making peace with God felt too big to be fully contained within this story of finding a way to walk the earth without my child.

Like Jacob from the Old Testament, who is given a new name, *Israel*, to reflect the transformation that occurred within him as he wrestled with the divine, we too, become someone different as we wrestle with God in our grief. I invite you to join me as we peel back the next layer and explore the deeper roots of the spiritual journey that have unfolded for me because of the loss of Lachlan. It would be an honor to continue this grief walk hand-in-hand as we wrestle with God and grief in our own journey to *becoming Israel.*

www.LachsLegacy.org • Facebook: @Lach's Legacy

www.aThousandPoundsBook.com

You Have Been Cradled in Prayer

As you read *A Thousand Pounds*, you were held in prayer by a hermit in the Diocese of Rapid City. She embraces in prayer all those who read this book, immersing us in the 3 o'clock time of prayer (Midday Prayer), that hour when the Lord suffered and died on the cross, the hour of suffering in which his Blessed Mother shared so intimately. Sister's prayer intention for each reader is united to the Divine Mercy Prayer:

You expired, O Jesus,
but the source of life gushed forth for souls
and an ocean of mercy opened up for the whole world.
O Fount of Life, unfathomable Divine Mercy,
envelop the whole world and empty Yourself out upon us.
O Blood and Water, which gushed forth from the Heart of Jesus
as a fount of mercy for us, I trust in You.
Amen.

A hermit lives a life of silence and solitude, assiduous prayer and penance. Well-known figures who lived an eremitic life include Saint John the Baptist and Saint Anthony of the Desert. Her hermitage is "not a place where I get away," Sister explained, "it's where I meet the whole world in prayer and in Christ, because Christ prays for everyone." Her vocation, she said, "is almost like an infinite vocation—not limited to time or space; nobody is excluded. The whole world is in there from the beginning of creation until the end because God is there."

Sister is especially inspired to pray for the readers of this book, as it is a matter that is close to her heart. She too has family who lost their infant son, Peter, who died, like Lachlan, unexpectedly in his sleep at ten months of age. She warmly embraced readers, and became the prayer companion of each, with these words: "You can be sure that I will prayerfully hold all those who pick up this precious book that the healing Hand of God would rest on them to give them strength and great confidence in God's mysterious and loving ways."

For those who would like to make a personal prayer request, Sister may be reached via email at the Immaculate Heart Hermitage:
smcjacobsocarm@gmail.com

CREDITS

JOURNALING

1. van der Kolk, Bessel. *The Body Keeps the Score: Brain, Mind, and Body in the Healing of Trauma*. New York: Viking Penguin, 2015.
2. Scott, Elizabeth. "The Benefit of Journaling for Stress Management." Very Well Mind. 2020. https://www.verywellmind.com/the-benefits-of-journaling-for-stress-management-3144611; Smyth, Joshua, et al. "Effects of Writing about Stressful Experience on Symptom Reduction in Patients with Asthma or Rheumatoid Arthritis." *JAMA* 281, no. 14 (199): 1304-1309.

INTRODUCTION

1. Chesterton, G. K. *Orthodoxy*. San Francisco: Ignatius Press, 1908, 2018.

THE WEIGHT DROPS

1. Stickney, Doris. *Water Bugs and Dragonflies: Explaining Death to Children*. Cleveland: Pilgrim Press, 1997, 2004.

SAYING GOODBYE

1. Lupton, Rosamund. *Sister*. London: Piatkus Books, 2010.

THE WEIGHT STAYS PUT

1. Murakami, Haruki. *Kafka on the Shore*. New York: Vintage International, 2006.
2. Lewis, C. S. *A Grief Observed*. New York: Harper & Row, 1961.

INTENTION TO HEAL

1. Frankl, Viktor E. *Man's Search for Meaning*. Boston: Beacon Press, 1959, 1984, 1992, 2006.
2. Lewis, C. S. *A Grief Observed*. New York: Harper & Row, 1961.
3. Sittser, Jerry. *A Grace Disguised: Expanded Edition*. Grand Rapids, MI: Zondervan, 1995, 2004.

4. Frankl, Viktor E. *Man's Search for Meaning*. Boston: Beacon Press, 1959, 1984, 1992, 2006.

5. Lewis, C. S. "Answers to Questions on Christianity." *God In the Dock*. Grand Rapids: Wm. B. Eerdmans Publishing Co., 1970, p. 52.

6. Lewis, C. S. *A Grief Observed*. New York: Harper & Row, 1961.

STEPPING INTO THE ARENA

1. Brown, Brené. *Daring Greatly: How the Courage to be Vulnerable Transforms the Way We Live, Love, Parent, and Lead*. New York: Penguin Random House, 2012.

2. Cacciatore, Joanne. *Bearing the Unbearable: Love, Loss, and the Heartbreaking Path of Grief*. Somerville, MA: Wisdom Publications, 2017.

3. Williams, Margery. *The Velveteen Rabbit*. Ohio: Suzeteo Enterprises, 2017.

4. Wolfelt, Alan D. *Understanding Your Grief*. Fort Collins, CO: Companion Press, 2003.

5. Lewis, C. S. *A Grief Observed*. New York: Harper & Row, 1961.

6. Peterson, Jordan. *12 Rules for Life*. Toronto, Ontario: Random House Canada, 2018.

7. Stickney, Doris. *Water Bugs and Dragonflies: Explaining Death to Children*. Cleveland: Pilgrim Press, 1997, 2004.

THE WORK OF PRUNING

1. Rowling, J. K. *Harry Potter and the Goblet of Fire*. London: Bloomsbury, 2000.

2. Tahir, Sabaa. *An Ember in the Ashes*. London: Razorbill, Penguin Publishing Group, 2015.

3. Cacciatore, Joanne. *Bearing the Unbearable: Love, Loss, and the Heartbreaking Path of Grief*. Somerville, MA: Wisdom Publications, 2017.

4. Brown, Brené. "David Kessler and Brené Brown on Grief and Finding Meaning." Unlocking Us. Podcast audio. March 31, 2020. https://brenebrown.com/podcast/david-kessler-and-brene-on-grief-and-finding-meaning/

5. Wood, Geoffrey. *Leaper: The Misadventures of a Not-Necessarily-Super Hero*. Colorado Springs: WaterBrook, 2007.

6. Cacciatore, Joanne. *Bearing the Unbearable: Love, Loss, and the Heartbreaking Path of Grief*. Somerville, MA: Wisdom Publications, 2017.

7. Ellison, Ralph. *Invisible Man*. New York: Knopf Doubleday Publishing Group, 1995.

8. Philippe, Jacques. *Interior Freedom*. New York: Scepter Publishers, 2007.

BECOMING FRIENDS WITH THE ENEMY

1. Lopez, Barry. *Arctic Dreams: Imagination and Desire in a Northern Landscape*. New York: Vintage Books, Penguin Random House, 2001.

2. Max Roser, Hannah Ritchie, and Bernadeta Dadonaite. "Child and Infant Mortality." Our World in Data. 2013. https://ourworldindata.org/child-mortality.

3. Rowling, J. K. *Harry Potter and the Half Blood Prince*. London: Bloomsbury, 2005.

4. Piper, Don. *90 Minutes in Heaven: An Inspiring Story of Life Beyond Death*. Ada, Michigan: Revell, 2008.

5. Alexander, Eben. *Proof of Heaven: A Neurosurgeon's Journey into the Afterlife*. New York: Simon & Schuster Paperbacks, 2012.

6. Burpo, Todd. *Heaven Is for Real: A Little Boy's Astounding Story of His Trip to Heaven and Back*. Nashville: Thomas Nelson, 2010.

7. Magis Center. "NDE: The Definitive Guide to Near Death Experiences." Octo-

ber 10, 2018. https://blog.magiscenter.com/blog/nde

8. National Library of Medicine. "SIDS Sudden Infant and Early Childhood Death: The Past, the Present and the Future." Chapter 24. 2018. https://www.ncbi.nlm.nih.gov/books/NBK513401/

9. Rohr, Richard. *Preparing for Christmas: Daily Meditations for Advent.* Cincinnati: Franciscan Media: 2008.

10. van der Kolk, Bessel. *The Body Keeps the Score: Brain, Mind, and Body in the Healing of Trauma.* New York: Viking Penguin, 2015.

11. *ibid.*

12. *ibid.*

13. *ibid.*

14. Frankl, Viktor E. *Man's Search for Meaning.* Boston: Beacon Press, 1959, 1984, 1992, 2006.

15. Scripture quotation is taken from the *Holy Bible, New Living Translation,* copyright ©1996, 2004, 2015 by Tyndale House Foundation. Used by permission of Tyndale House Publishers, Carol Stream, Illinois 60188. All rights reserved.

16. Aquinas, Thomas. *Summa Theologiae* (Prima Secundae, #35 – 37).

17. Stromberg, Joseph. "The Microscopic Structures of Dried Human Tears." *Smithsonian Magazine.* November 2013. https://www.smithsonianmag.com/science-nature/the-microscopic-structures-of-dried-human-tears-180947766/

18. Blado, Rachel. "Secondary Losses: Losing a Child Changes You." October 3, 2022. https://onthewaytowhereyouregoing.com/secondary-loss-10-things-i-lost-when-i-lost-you/

19. Lewis, C. S. *A Grief Observed.* New York: Harper & Row, 1961.

20. *ibid.*

21. Nolan, Christopher. *Interstellar.* Paramount Pictures: 2014.

LESSONS TO LEARN

1. Tolkien, J. R. R. *The Return of the King.* London: HarperCollins*Publishers*, 1999, 2001, 2020.

2. Cacciatore, Joanne. *Bearing the Unbearable: Love, Loss, and the Heartbreaking Path of Grief.* Somerville, MA: Wisdom Publications, 2017.

3. Peterson, Jordan. *12 Rules for Life.* Toronto, Ontario: Random House Canada, 2018.

4. Aquinas, Thomas. *Summa Theologiae* (Prima Secundae, #35 – 37).

5. Genesis 2:2.

6. van der Kolk, Bessel. *The Body Keeps the Score: Brain, Mind, and Body in the Healing of Trauma.* New York: Viking Penguin, 2015.

7. Boland, Elaine M., et al. "Meta-Analysis of the Antidepressant Effects of Acute Sleep Deprivation." *Journal of Clinical Psychiatry* 78, no. 8 (2017): e1020-e1034.

8. Loder, Wayne. "Only 16 Percent of Bereaved Parents Divorce, New Survey Reveals." *Cision PR Web.* October 2006. https://www.prweb.com/releases/2006/10/prweb449794.htm.

9. Schwab, Reiko. "A Child's Death and Divorce: Dispelling the Myth." *Death Studies* 22, no. 5 (1998): 445-468.

10. Keith, Kent M. "The Silent Revolution: Dynamic Leadership in the Student Council." Terrace Press, 1968, 2003.

11. Frankl, Viktor E. *Man's Search for Meaning.* Boston: Beacon Press, 1959, 1984, 1992, 2006.

12. Tolkien, J. R. R. *The Fellowship of the Ring.* London: HarperCollins*Publishers*, 1999, 2001, 2020.

13. "Definition of paradox". Oxford University Press. Lexico.com. 1 August 2021. https://www.lexico.com/en/definition/paradox.

14. Brown, Joshua, and Joel Wong. "How Gratitude Changes You and Your Brain."

Greater Good. June 6, 2017. https://greatergood.berkeley.edu/article/item/how_gratitude_changes_you_and_your_brain.

15. H. H. "31 Benefits of Gratitude: The Ultimate Science-Backed Guide." Happier Human. 2020. https://www.happierhuman.com/benefits-of-gratitude/.

16. Brown, Brené. *The Gifts of Imperfection*. Minnesota: Hazelden. 2010.

17. Philippe, Jacques. *Interior Freedom*. New York: Scepter Publishers, 2007.

18. Brown, Brené. *Daring Greatly: How the Courage to be Vulnerable Transforms the Way We Live, Love, Parent, and Lead*. New York: Penguin Random House, 2012.

19. *ibid.*

20. Cacciatore, Joanne. *Bearing the Unbearable: Love, Loss, and the Heartbreaking Path of Grief*. Somerville, MA: Wisdom Publications, 2017.

21. *ibid.*

22. Norton, Michael I., and Francesca Gino. "Rituals Alleviate Grieving for Loved Ones, Lovers, and Lotteries." *Journal of Experimental Psychology* 143, no. 1 (2014): 266-272.

23. Streit-Horn, Jenny. "A Systematic Review of Research on After-Death Communication (ADC)." University of North Texas, ProQuest Dissertations Publishing, 2011.

WRESTLING WITH GOD

1. Lewis, C. S. *A Grief Observed*. New York: Harper & Row, 1961.
2. Genesis 32:23-32.

FINDING MEANING

1. Cacciatore, Joanne. *Bearing the Unbearable: Love, Loss, and the Heartbreaking Path of Grief*. Somerville, MA: Wisdom Publications, 2017.
2. Kessler, David. *Finding Meaning: The Sixth Stage of Grief*. New York: Scribner, 2020.
3. Frankl, Viktor E. *Man's Search for Meaning*. Boston, MA: Beacon Press, 1959, 1984, 1992, 2006.
4. *ibid.*
5. *ibid.*
6. "Joe Rogan Experience #1070 - Jordan Peterson" YouTube video. January 30, 2018. https://www.youtube.com/watch?v=6T7pUEZfgdI
7. Frankl, Viktor E. *Man's Search for Meaning*. Boston, MA: Beacon Press, 1959, 1984, 1992, 2006.

ETERNAL PERSPECTIVE

1. Lewis, C. S. *Mere Christianity*. New York: HarperCollins, 1952, 1980, 2001.
2. "The Rope Illustration" YouTube video (CEE2802). August 14, 2015. https://www.youtube.com/watch?v=cMbbVR88kdo

DISCOVERING OUR STRENGTH

1. Lewis, C. S. *A Grief Observed*. New York: Harper & Row, 1961.
2. Gibran, Kahlil. "On Joy and Sorrow." Public domain. https://poets.org/poem/joy-and-sorrow
3. Lewis, C. S. *A Grief Observed*. New York: Harper & Row, 1961.

ACKNOWLEDGMENTS

This book began long before I started writing it. It was seeded first by the community of bereaved parents who have been brave enough to share their experiences and their grief with me. Every story has helped me understand the universality of grief. And then as I started to write, journal, blog, and share thoughts about my grief there have been so many people who have offered warm encouragements, told me how they related to what I was saying, and said things like, "You should write a book!" *For all of you who are brave enough to share your stories and who have taken a moment to encourage me to write, thank you.*

This notion of writing a book was a big and abstract idea for many years. I liked the idea, but I couldn't quite sort out how to condense such a big story into a coherent narrative that would be worthwhile to readers. *Which parts of the story would I want to tell? Who would be my audience? What do I really want to communicate?* And with those big unanswered questions the idea of a book stayed in the abstract, until a conversation with my cousin, Krysti. She is known to have dreams that mean something. In the conversation that particular day, she said, "Oh yeah, I had a dream last night that you were writing your third book." I chuckled a little, thinking, *Three books? I can't even figure out how to put together one!* I took a chance and asked, "You didn't happen to catch a title and an outline on those, did you?" She said, "Not exactly, but one of them was called *A Thousand Pounds*." And that was the beginning. My formless ideas were crystallized by her answer. The moment I had a working title, an outline came with ease, and so I had a spine around which to start telling my story. *To Krysti, who has always supported my grief journey with so much love and empathy, and then took the time to tell me about her dream, thank you.*

I was about two-thirds through writing this book and just starting to explore what it looks like to find a literary agent and a publisher, when I was hit by a combination of overlapping ideas. In a powerful movement of the heart and an impulsive decision, I sent an email to Dr. Greg at the CatholicPsych Institute. I had a sudden idea for a second book and I sent a pitch to him to write it together. In hindsight, I was a little mortified that I had the nerve to do that. I really had no business even thinking that was a reasonable idea. *Who did I think I was anyway?!* Lo and behold, Dr. Greg replied warmly to my email, gently coaxing me to tell him more of my thoughts and ideas. After a few exchanges back and forth, I ended up sending him sample chapters of what I had written. His reply will always be ingrained in my memory: "This is intensely beautiful and painful. I'd love to collaborate with you on it... I'm actually about to launch a CatholicPsych Publishing Imprint. I'm looking for authors who want to partner with us. Providential?" *To Dr. Greg, for his approachability, his warmness, and his willingness to take a chance on me and my story, thank you.*

The CatholicPsych team connected me with an editor, Amy Welde. She took this big vulnerable story of mine, held it gently and warmly and, with heartfelt encouragement, helped me improve the form and definition of the manuscript. As we got to the part where I was talking about how dragonflies had become an important symbol that connect us to Lachlan, she shared with me that dragonflies are meaningful at her house, too. And then she mentioned, "Actually, the company that I work for is called Dragonfly Editorial." *What?! Are you kidding me? This editor was selected by a team who has no attachment to dragonflies—and they chose someone who works for Dragonfly Editorial to edit my book.* I felt deep affirmation again of God's hands in this project. *To Amy, who helped me mold this story into one that readers can appreciate and love, thank you. When this story came to her, it was just a tender shoot, but she bolstered my confidence that this was something worth putting into the world.*

Then, as the major edits were finished, with wobbly knees, it was time to start asking for others to read the story and provide their feedback. Each reader who warmly received the story and gave meaningful responses helped me get my sea legs underneath me so I can be standing firm as this book launches. *To David and my mom, to Kate, Lindsay, Dionne, Dr. Goldstein, Elaine, Lisa, Karri, and Jessy... thank you for your willingness and eagerness to participate, to read, and to share your thoughts on the book. My gratitude will always run deep.*

I thought we were nearly ready to send this book into the world, and then there was a long pause before moving forward with the final preparations. It was *so* hard to wait! By this time I had friends and family asking me on a regular basis, "When will your book be ready?" and I had no answer for them. I kept bringing this painful pause to prayer, and found my stillness in trusting that there was a higher purpose for the pause. And then, six months later, Veronica arrived on the scene. She was hired with a different job in mind, but came to the table with robust experience in publishing. She has been an extraordinary joy to work with as we've polished the last rough edges and put the final touches on turning this manuscript into a book. *To Veronica, who has brought challenge, critical thinking, and an eye for detail, as well as encouragement, excitement, and joy to the final phases of publishing, I am so grateful for you. You were definitely worth the wait!*

And then there's David, my dear husband who has been with me every step of the way, brainstorming to make sure I wasn't missing any important pieces of the story, painstakingly listening to me analyze every little triumph and tribulation along the way, and who has done loads and loads of laundry and baby-chasing while I've plucked away at the keyboard. You are the pillar that keeps us from toppling in every outreach endeavor I undertake. *To David, though you often prefer to operate behind the scenes, I see you and your sacrifice. Thank you, my love.*

And last but not least, to God, who coordinated the whole thing and made His thumbprints known along the way. Working with You on this project has grown my faith, trust, and wonder in enormous ways. May this story be one more way for You to comfort those who mourn. *To Father, Son, and Holy Spirit, and the communion of Saints who are cheering me on, thank you.*

About the Author

Brianne Edwards writes about the unexpected loss of her son and the depths of grief that followed as part of her mission to bring connection, comfort, and hope to other grieving families. She is a wife, mother of six, and founder of Lach's Legacy (*www.LachsLegacy.org*), a nonprofit created in memory of her son. She comes to the table with a Bachelor's in Psychology, a Master's degree as a Physician Assistant, and a Compassionate Bereavement Care Certification. Bri lives with her family in the beautiful Black Hills of South Dakota.

Made in the USA
Coppell, TX
12 July 2022

79901987R00128